Employment Policy

SPICERS EUROPEAN POLICY REPORTS

European Internal Market Policy
Kevin Featherstone

The Food Sector
Stephen Fallows

Youth Policy
Gordon Blakely

Transport Policy
Kerry Hamilton

Small and Medium Sized Enterprises
Kenneth Dyson

Regional Policy
Colin Mellors/Nigel Copperthwaite

Employment Policy

Compiled by
Margareta Holmstedt

Published by Routledge
in association with the University of Bradford and Spicers Centre
for Europe Ltd

First published 1991
by Routledge in association with the University of Bradford and Spicers Centre for Europe Ltd

Routledge
11 New Fetter Lane, London EC4P 4EE

Simultaneously published in the USA and Canada
by Routledge
a division of Routledge, Chapman and Hall, Inc.
29 West 35th Street, New York 10001

Printed in England by Clays Ltd, St Ives plc

British Library Cataloguing in Publication Data

Holmstedt, Margareta
Employment policy – (Spicers European policy reports)
1. European Community countries. Employment
I. Title II. Series
331.125094

ISBN 0-415-03830-8

Library of Congress Cataloging in Publication Data
has been applied for

CONTENTS

Contents

LIST OF FIGURES
(Figures appear on pp. 165-189)

List of Figures

FOREWORD

This volume is one of a series offering an informed guide to particular policies and programmes of the European Community. They are intended for the intelligent reader as well as for the specialist. They assume no prior knowledge of the European Community, but they each offer a comprehensive and up-to-date guide to what the Community is doing, or proposes to do, in important areas of economic, social and political life. The volumes should appeal especially to those involved in business and commerce, public administration, and education.

The volumes guide the reader through the maze of European Community legislation and policy proposals. Their main concern is with the official documents of the European Community institutions: helping the reader to understand Community policies and proposals. By doing so, each volume offers the reader a single reference source, collating all the essential information the reader needs to understand what is going on.

Each volume is structured so as to offer easy access to the specific information needed. A preliminary note explains what the European Community is and how it operates. Each volume focuses on a distinctive policy area, and **SECTION I** introduces the reader to European Community action in that sphere. It explains how Community policy has evolved, the problems currently being confronted, and what is proposed for the future. **SECTION II** highlights the key documents and proposals in the policy area, giving extensive summaries of each of them. Finally, **SECTION III** provides a comprehensive listing of all the relevant Community documents in this policy sphere, with full bibliographical details and a brief note as to their content.

As the reader progresses through each volume, he or

she will have been guided from the general to the very specific, and from little or no knowledge to an informed picture of developments in the policy sphere concerned. Moreover, the information has been structured so as to allow the more specialist reader to pursue particular inquiries yet further: the volumes guide the reader to the policy documents specific to his/her interest.

With the drive to complete the single internal European Community market by the end of 1992, more and more attention will be focused on Community policies and actions. By the end of this century, the European Community will be playing a more prominent part in the lives of its citizens and in a way which will have ramifications in other parts of the world also. The European Community is already an important actor on the world stage, and it will be even less possible to ignore it in the 1990s. This series of policy guides is designed to provide the information that is and will be needed to respond to this changing world. High-quality information is the key to effective action.

This series has been produced by the European Briefing Unit at the University of Bradford (UK) together with Spicers Centre for Europe Limited, a member of Spicer and Oppenheim International. The collaboration between these two bodies has brought together a team of specialist writers expert in the various policy spheres covered by the volumes. Each writer is actively engaged in the study and research of these policy areas, and each has long experience in communicating their skills to the lay audience. The series has been co-ordinated by Amanda Deaville (Spicers) and Kevin Featherstone (Bradford).

Both the European Briefing Unit (EBU) at the University of Bradford and Spicers Centre for Europe have an active interest in promoting knowledge and awareness of the European Community. The EBU is located in the Department of European Studies at the University of Bradford: the Department is the largest of its kind in the UK, and is actively involved in both teaching and research at all levels. The EBU was created in 1988 as a public resource, operating on a non-profit and open access basis. It acts as a neutral forum for the purpose of disseminating and advancing relevant knowledge about the Single European Market; new trading and business opportunities in Europe; the European Community's Structural Funds and technology programmes; the external trade, business and political relations of the EC; and the social, cultural and educational implications of European integration. The EBU exists to serve the needs of industry, commerce and public authorities as well as those of the University itself and other educational bodies. The EBU has established close collaborative links with a number of relevant bodies across different sectors so as to promote its activities.

Spicers Centre for Europe Ltd is a privately based organization serving the needs of its commercial clients. It offers expert EC advice and information to both private and public sector organizations and enterprises. It assists its clients in obtaining funding from EC sources, and it keeps them informed as to the changes in EC policy which might affect their interests. It advises organizations on how they might respond to the opportunities and challenges of the EC, by reviewing corporate strategies. It also offers a business information service based on its own and EC data bases, involving the Tenders Electronic Daily data base (TED) and the Business Co-operation Network data base (BC-NET). As a member of Spicer and Oppenheim International it is linked to an organization which has 250 offices in more than fifty countries throughout the world.

The collaboration between the EBU and Spicers is intended to produce a continuing series of publications to inform both specialist and lay audiences about the role and impact of the European Community. Readers of these volumes are invited to contact either body directly if they have any comments to make on the volumes, or if they would like to know more about the activities of either organization.

Both the EBU and Spicers would like to record their gratitude to Alan Jarvis (Routledge) for his support and patience in dealing with this publishing venture. Moreover, progress would have been more difficult had it not been for the efficient typing, by Christine Pratt of

Employment Policy

Spicers. More generally, thanks go to the full team of writers and assistants involved in this project for their willingness to see it succeed.

Kevin Featherstone
General Editor

Contact addresses:

The European Briefing Unit
University of Bradford
Bradford BD7 1DP
United Kingdom

Telephone: 0274-733466
Telex: 51309 UNIBFD G
Fax Number: 0274 305340

Spicers Centre for Europe
Second Floor
17 Marina Court
Hull
HU1 1TJ

Telephone: (0482) 589022
Telex: 592899 EUROPE G
Fax Number: (0482) 589008

THE EUROPEAN COMMUNITY: ITS ROLE, INSTITUTIONS, AND LEGISLATION

The European Community (EC) represents a unique development in the world: a new structure of relations between states. It has often been referred to as 'the Common Market' because it is a single trading entity: goods moving between the member countries are not subject to tariffs, while imports from the rest of the world enter under uniform conditions. But it is much more than that: it plays an important political and social role, in addition to its economic purposes. Moreover, the EC is set to develop much further in the 1990s.

In the 1958 Treaty of Rome, a commitment was made to seeking in the long-term 'an ever closer union among the peoples of Europe', an ambitious objective which it has found difficult to realize. However, the Single European Act which came into force in July 1987 provides for an expansion of the EC's political role and for the completion by the end of 1992 of a fully integrated, barrier-free internal market.

The 'European Community' actually stems from three Communities: the European Coal and Steel Community (ECSC) established in 1952; the European Economic Community (EEC) which came into being in 1958; and, the European Atomic Energy Community (Euratom) which also began in 1958.

The original Member States of each of these three Communities were Belgium, France, the Federal Republic of Germany, Italy, Luxembourg and the Netherlands. Successive enlargements of the Communities have increased their membership from six to twelve: Denmark, Ireland and the United Kingdom joined as of 1 January 1973; Greece on 1 January 1981; and Portugal and Spain on 1 January 1986. The population of the EC is now 320 million, greater than that of the USA (234 million), the Soviet Union (269 million), or Japan (119 million). Its Gross Domestic Product per head is significantly lower than that of either the USA or Japan. However, the Community today is the world's largest trading power, accounting for almost 20 per cent of world trade. Economically and politically, the EC dominates Western Europe, and it has established important relations with countries across the world.

Policy-making in the EC involves the Commission, the Council of Ministers, the European Parliament, and the Economic and Social Committee, with the adjudication of the Court of Justice and the Court of Auditors. In addition, the European Investment Bank (EIB) was established by the Treaty of Rome as the bank for financing capital investment promoting the balanced development of the Community.

Until 1967, the three original Communities had separate Councils of Ministers and executive Commissions (known as the 'High Authority' in the ECSC). By contrast, the European Parliament and the Court of Justice have been common to the ECSC, EEC and Euratom since 1958. From 1967 onwards there has been a single Commission and a single Council, simplifying the overall structure.

The three most important policy-making institutions of the EC today are the Council of Ministers, the Commission and the European Parliament. Since 1974, they have been joined by the 'European Council', a body given formal status by the Single European Act. The European Council is the term given to the summit meetings of the heads of government (and of state in the case of France) of the EC countries. It has no legislative power, rather its purpose is to place current issues in a more general perspective and to give impetus to those initiatives that it regards as priorities for action. Until 1985, it met three times a year, but this has since been cut back to twice a year. The Presidency of the European Council and of the Council of Ministers rotates between the member governments at six-monthly intervals. The European Council meetings are usually held in the country holding the presidency.

The Council of Ministers' headquarters is in Brussels, where the Commission is also based. The European Parliament, by contrast, currently holds its plenary sessions in Strasbourg, most of its committee meetings in Brussels, whilst its permanent staff are based in Luxembourg. This rather awkward compromise remains a source of controversy.

EC legislation is determined by the three main institutions - the Council of Ministers, the Commission, and the European Parliament - with the Economic and Social Committee offering its advisory opinion. The Commission acts as the initiator of legislation and as the executive authority responsible for implementing it. Legislation is finally enacted after it has been approved by the Council of Ministers, either acting unanimously or by a qualified majority. It has been estimated that, as a result of the Single European Act, two-thirds of the internal market proposals will be covered by majority voting. The Council's legislative role has been further amended by a new 'Co-operation Procedure' established by the Single European Act, which gives increased powers to the European Parliament. This provides, inter alia, for the Parliament to be able to reject the Council's initial response to a Commission proposal, and the Council can then only pass the proposal into law if it acts unanimously (Article 149: 2c of the EEC Treaty as amended). Prior to the Single European Act, the Parliament already had the final say over the annual EC budget, though its scope for manoeuvre on expenditure is set within limits.

Some description of each institution is necessary. The Council of Ministers is made up of representatives of the governments of the twelve Member States. Each government normally sends one of its ministers. Its membership thus varies with the subjects down for discussion. The Foreign Minister is regarded as his country's 'main' representative in the Council, but Ministers for Agriculture, Transport, Economic and Financial Affairs, Social Affairs, Industry, the Environment and so on also meet frequently for specialized Council meetings and sometimes sit alongside the Foreign Ministers. The Council is supported by a large number of working parties and by a Committee of Permanent Representatives (COREPER). COREPER is composed of the various national 'ambassadors' to the EC.

The Commission consists of seventeen members, appointed by agreement between the member governments. Throughout their four-year term of office, Commissioners are required to remain independent of national governments. An individual Commissioner cannot be sacked: the Parliament can pass a motion of censure compelling the Commission to resign en bloc.

The European Parliament is the world's first directly elected international assembly. It was first directly elected in 1979: it was previously composed of nominated national parliamentarians. The Parliament serves five-year terms and currently has 518 members (MEPs).

The Court of Justice, based in Luxembourg, acts as the supreme court of the EC. It should not be confused with the European Court of Human Rights in Strasbourg, which is not an EC body. The Court of Auditors began operating in 1977 and, as its name suggests, it audits the EC accounts. The Economic and Social Committee is an advisory body of 189 members, representing various sectors of economic and social life, offering opinions on EC policies and proposals.

EC Law

The nomenclature of EC legislation can be confusing. The essential point to bear in mind is that the Commission brings forward proposals for legislation, the outcome of which will be variously determined by the Council and the Parliament. 'Primary legislation' of the EC is embodied in the treaties; 'Secondary legislation' is derived from the treaties in the form of 'Regulations', 'Directives' etc. The EC represents a distinct legal system, and its strongest form of legislation is superior to national law.

When acting under the Treaty of Paris (ECSC), the Commission can take Decisions, make Recommendations or issue Opinions. Decisions are binding in their entirety; recommendations are binding as to the ends but not as to the means; Opinions are not binding. The Council acts in ECSC affairs mainly at the request of the Commission, either stating its opinion on particular issues or giving the assent without which, in certain matters, the Commission cannot proceed. The Commission's ECSC Decisions are mostly addressed to individual persons, firms or governments but they may also lay down general rules, since the Commission does also have general rulemaking powers.

Employment Policy

When acting under the Rome Treaties (EEC and Euratom), the Council and the Commission issue Regulations, Directives, Decisions, Recommendations and Opinions. Regulations are of general application: they are binding in their entirety and applicable in all Member States. Directives are binding on the Member States to which they are addressed as regards the results to be achieved, but leave the form and methods of achieving it to the discretion of the national authorities. Decisions may be addressed to a government, an enterprise or a private individual; they are binding in their entirety on those to whom they are addressed. Recommendations and opinions are not binding.

The discrepancy in terminology between the Paris Treaty and the two Rome Treaties is confusing. An ECSC 'Recommendation' is a binding enactment corresponding to the EEC and Euratom 'Directive', whereas an EEC 'Recommendation' is not binding and is not stronger than an 'opinion'. When examining the current progress of EC legislation in non-ECSC policy areas, the reader typically focuses on Commission proposals (e.g. for a Directive) to be agreed by the Council of Ministers (subject to the differential powers of the European Parliament).

It is clear from the above that the EC today is an important actor in international relations, enjoying both political and economic significance not only for its domestic citizens but also for those in other countries.

SECTION I
THE EMERGENCE OF EUROPEAN EMPLOYMENT AND SOCIAL POLICIES

(The figures referred to in this section are positioned between pp. 165 and 189)

INTRODUCTION

European Community policies on employment do not form a coherent or comprehensive programme, but are rather a patchwork of different policy areas where the EC reasons for acting and powers to act vary greatly.

This volume is intended to give a comprehensive overview of European Community legislation, action programmes, funding and research reports in the area of employment and social policy. Community activities in this area now cover a very large number of diverse subjects from health and safety and equality legislation to the funding of training projects. Some knowledge of Community activities in this field is essential for employers, training agencies, voluntary organizations, policy-makers, lobbyists, trade unionists, personnel managers and many others.

Several articles in the original European Economic Community Treaty refer to social and employment policy and authorize the Commission and Council to take an interest in this field. The rationale of Community legislation in the field of employment is two-fold. A very large proportion of the Community's efforts to harmonize provisions in Member States aim to produce 'a level playing field' for enterprise. Many types of provisions in the area of employment increase labour or production costs and are therefore a natural target for harmonization. An obvious example is health and safety legislation which impose obligations to install filters, extractor fans or personal protective equipment. The second reason for harmonization is to facilitate freedom of movement of labour which requires some regulation of the rights of migrant workers.

From the beginning there existed in addition a third motive for Community action in the social field which is not strictly generated by the customs union but by the wider political aims of the European Community. This is the need to create a Community which is relevant to the people of Europe as well as to entrepreneurs and businesses. This consideration has gained greater force with the implementation of the single market. It has been deemed by most member governments to be impossible to introduce measures which will increase competition and may at least in the short term cause new unemployment, without also taking some action to improve conditions for employees and citizens in general. This has led to a very substantial expansion of the potential scope of Community action in the social field. However, action in this sphere is hotly contested between member governments and between the two sides of industry.

A number of policy areas which all concern different aspects of employment are specifically mentioned in the EEC Treaty: freedom of movement, equal opportunities, health and safety, labour law and employment conditions. However, in only two of these areas are the Treaty provisions non-discretionary: free movement of labour and equal pay. In these areas Member States are required to act to eliminate discrimination and Community institutions are obliged to adopt legislation. Freedom of movement within the EC area is part of the original purpose of the Community. **Article 1** in the Treaty establishes the aim of the EC to be the setting up of a customs union which according to **Article 2** includes free movement of labour. The Treaty also stipulates that there shall be equal pay between men and women within the EC. From this provision in **Article 119** have followed legislation and action programmes on gender equality.

Other Treaty provisions on employment and social policy encourage rather then oblige Member States to take action. These include **Article 117** where the signatory states agreed on the need to promote improved working conditions and an improved standard of living, and **Article 118** which authorizes the Commission to promote co-operation between Member States in the areas of employment, labour law and working conditions, social security, various aspects of health and safety and industrial relations. In most of these areas the Community has legislated to set minimum standards and to ensure harmonization or at least co-ordination of the policies of Member States. In two areas, however, efforts to achieve harmonization or regulation have met with little success: social security and industrial relations. The EC has also become increasingly active in trying to promote both employment growth and measures to aid the unemployed. In this area the Community has acted not through legislation but through recommendations on co-ordinated action to member governments and by funding pilot projects on training and other types of support for the unemployed.

Finally more recent efforts to promote the integration of certain underprivileged groups, such as the disabled into the world of work, are part of EC employment policies. EC social policies have until very recently been almost entirely concentrated on policies relating to employment. In the few instances where such policies deal with groups outside the labour market or have objectives which are not related to employment, they have as far as possible been included in this directory, because they are often developments from employment-related policies and are difficult to separate from these without creating artificial boundaries which are more limiting than enlightening.

Originally the processes of regulation and harmonization of Member State policies in these different areas developed independently of each other. Not until 1974 was an action programme adopted by the Council of Ministers which pulled together all the different areas of action which could loosely be defined as relating to employment. Recently the single market programme has led to the development of the concept of the social dimension which includes not only employment-related policies but objectives relating to improved living conditions in general. The discussion about the social dimension has led to the adoption of the Social Charter, intended to be a bill of rights for European citizens in the social sphere. However, the Social Charter is no more than a series of recommendations on minimum standards. Most of these still relate to different aspects of employment. In the action programme adopted by the Commission on the different measures the Commission intends to propose to implement the Social Charter, almost all potential actions which the Commission intends to initiate fall within the distinct areas of freedom of movement, equal opportunities, health and safety, employment conditions (including remuneration), trade union rights, employee consultation and participation and employment promotion. The action programme is less coherent than the Charter. Very different levels of activities are proposed in different areas. With relation to health and safety, already a field covered by extensive legislation, the Commission is proposing a long list of subjects for future legislation. In other areas recommendations rather than legislation are proposed and, in the area of trade union rights and collective agreements, the Commission will take no action but leave the field to governments and their social partners without any enforceable minimum safeguards.

The lack of a coherence in the EC policies on employment and social policy is a consequence of the fact that EC institutions are not the government machinery of a nation state or even of a federal state, but still have very circumscribed powers, limited to framework legislation and funding of special demonstration and pilot projects. Community institutions do not have direct lines of command to national, regional or local administrations. This is still the monopoly of the national governments. The lack of coherence is also a product of the fact that individual member governments are the decision-makers in the Community and that until recently individual governments have had a veto over all policy initiatives. Agreement on Community action is easier to achieve in some policy areas than in others.

It is possible to categorize EC policies in the social sphere quite differently from the way it has been done in this book. The European Commission in its reports on the progress of the single market deals with the abolition of frontier controls under the heading 'the removal of physical barriers'; with freedom of movement for workers and non-workers under the heading 'the removal of technical barriers'; the structural funds and measures to combat unemployment appear in the section headed 'horizontal measures', subsection 'Social and Economic' cohesion; while all other aspects of employment policy are discussed in the same section under the heading 'the social dimension'. We feel that while this might make sense in the context of the implementation of the single market programme, the division set out in the Treaty is more practical for practitioners seeking information on EC policies in areas relevant to their work situation.

The division of policy areas in this volume is loosely based on the divisions adopted by the Treaty. It is also the division we have felt to be most useful for the practical users of the book. For example, we have assumed that people who want to know details of EC health and safety legislation would be helped by a chapter containing only policies which relate strictly to this subject without additional information on other types of employment conditions such as retirement or working hours.

There are a number of subjects within the social field which so far have been excluded from Community initiatives. The health services, housing (despite the ECSC funding of housing for miners and steel workers), compulsory and traditional secondary education - with the exception of language teaching - are large areas so far excluded from the EC areas of interest. Income tax and other employment taxes and social security with the exception of the social security rights of migrant workers are also areas where harmonization would contribute to the purpose of the Community, but where EC action is likely to remain politically impossible for some time to come.

Despite the political difficulties attached to harmonizing provisions in the area of labour law and industrial relations, the Commission has been very active in developing draft legislation in this field. A chapter on employee consultation and participation has therefore been included to discuss these different initiatives. However, in the early days of the Community the Member States stopped the Commission from developing any policies on co-ordination of social security except in relation to migrant workers. There is, therefore, no separate chapter on social security; social security rights of migrant workers are discussed in the chapter on freedom of movement.

There also is an introductory chapter which compares the situation in the member countries with respect to different aspects of employment and social policy.

EC actions catalogued here include legislative proposals, legislation in the form of Regulations and Directives, action programmes and other Recommendations adopted by the Commission and/or the Council, funding schemes and comparative research reports.

Employment Policy is intended to give a comprehensive overview of European Community legislation, action programmes, funding and research reports in the area of employment and social policy. Community activities in this area now cover a very large number of diverse subjects from health and safety and equality legislation to the funding of training projects. Some knowledge of Community activities in this field is essential for employers, training agencies, voluntary organizations, policy-makers, lobbyists, trade unionists, personnel managers and many others.

This book is aimed at policy-makers and researchers in the private, public and voluntary sectors who need quick access to EC legislation and other initiatives in the social and employment field. The first section consists of an account of the development of legislation including Commission proposals which have not yet been adopted. It starts with a chapter which looks at the demographic and employment situations in the Community member countries and provides a short comparative account of the education and training systems.

Section II contains summaries of the most important Regulations, Directives, draft Directives, Commission Proposals and Reports. Section III lists the majority of the remaining documents in each field of social and employment policy, including some of the most important European Parliament resolutions and committee reports and opinions of the Economic and Social Committee. Each item will include a very brief indication of the content where the title is not self explanatory.

In order to make this volume easily accessible, each chapter is intended to be self contained so that anyone wanting information on, for example, 'Freedom of Movement' would be able to read this chapter only without needing to refer to any other chapter. This inevitably leads to a certain amount of repetition of information.

A good strategy for tackling this book would be to read

the first two chapters on Employment and Social Policies in the Member States and Employment and Social Policies of the Community and leave the rest of the book to be consulted as required.

Any reader requiring access to the actual documents listed in this directory can refer to the nearest European Documentation Centre, to the relevant European Commission or European Parliament office in Member States or to the European Community's delegations outside the Community. The references to the Official Journal or Commission document number given under each entry in this directory will make it easy to find relevant documents.

EMPLOYMENT AND SOCIAL POLICIES IN THE MEMBER STATES

Before looking at European Community legislation in the field of employment it is useful to have an overview of the labour market and employment law in the different member countries. The labour market situation in the Member States influences national employment legislation and determines government employment policy. The member countries' different labour market experiences in the past, and expected trends for the future, have influenced existing Community policies and determined member governments' varying attitudes to current EC decision-making. Different national traditions in employment legislation and the different social security systems in Member States are also important influences on Community law and Community policies.

Employment and Unemployment

Employment and economic activity rates

Underneath cyclical variations in the unemployment rate there has been a long-term steady trend in all Community countries of a decrease in the proportion of men and an increase in the proportion of women between fifteen and sixty-four in economic activity (Figure 1). The reasons for increased female participation are well known. Women all over Europe normally now continue to work after they marry - indeed in many countries it would be hard to find any recently married woman who has withdrawn from economic activity following her wedding. Women now also return to the labour market after having brought up their children and increasingly the trend is for mothers to have a short child-care break at the birth of each child rather than to stay at home until the last child reaches school age.

The reasons for the falling economic activity rates for

men are less well known. More young people of both sexes stay on in full-time education after the school-leaving age. In some countries, notably Belgium, the Netherlands and the Nordic countries, between two-thirds and three-quarters of young people continue in full-time education until they are eighteen and many go on until they are in their early twenties (Figure 18). In addition the retirement age for men in many professions has been reduced. Opportunities for retiring early, either as a consequence of enterprises shedding labour or due to ill health, have increased in many countries. The proportion of the total EC population of working age who are economically active is now lower than in other developed countries like the United States, Japan and the EFTA countries.

Female activity rates are determined in part by attitudes to women and family life and it is therefore not surprising that the female activity rates vary much more between countries; from the high British and Scandinavian rates to the lower rates in Southern Europe and the Netherlands. In the Scandinavian countries the difference between the female and the male participation rates is now very small and still decreasing. The female participation rate is increasing everywhere and this trend is likely to continue as a consequence of falling birth rates all over Europe. Not surprisingly fewer women with three or more dependent children work outside the home. The proportion of women having more than two children is falling dramatically and, as a result, more women after child-care breaks will re-enter the labour market earlier than was the case one or two decades ago (Figure 2). The activity rates of people between the ages of twenty-five and forty-nine reveal first that the male labour force participation rate for the period after the end of tertiary education and the age when men start taking early retirement is nearly 100 per cent. Secondly, the female participation rate for this age group is higher in most countries than the overall female participation rate, although this is the period when women are likely to have the most intensive family commitments (Figure 3). Most countries in Western Europe now have no growth in their population (Figure 4). In Southern Europe and the

Netherlands the population is still growing but very slowly indeed and birth rates are still slowing down. The reduced birth rates are partly due to a decrease in the overall number of women who become mothers. However, the largest change is that families now are having fewer children. The proportion of families having a third child has dropped drastically in all European countries (Figures 5 and 6). The proportion of very large families has of course also dropped.

The reduced birth rate means a reduced workforce in the future with an increased shortage of labour and new opportunities for women, the handicapped and the retired to enter or re-enter the labour market.

Part-time work

The proportion of the workforce in each country which is engaged in part-time work varies much more than overall male and female activity rates (Figures 7 and 8). In all countries, however, part-time jobs are women's jobs. Only in Denmark does the proportion of men in the part-time sector exceed 5 per cent. The small groups of part-time men are likely to consist mostly of pensioners and students, who on the Continent tend to work while studying to a much greater extent than in the UK and Ireland.

Unemployment

The unemployment rates vary more than the activity rates between Community countries, ranging from 1.8 per cent in Luxembourg to 17 per cent in Spain (Figure 9). However, all countries, regardless of whether they have a high or low rate, experience the same or similar economic cycles, with unemployment rates rising and falling in broadly common patterns (Figure 10). There has been an almost continuous rise in unemployment across the Community since 1973 with the largest increases taking place between 1974 and 1977 and between 1981 and 1986. Recovery started in 1985 and has gathered speed in the last two years. However, the jobs lost in industry have not been regained. The majority of the new jobs are in the service sector.

Currently in all Community countries except the UK, the unemployment rate of women is greater than that of men (Figure 11). Germany and Denmark have, from time to time, had periods when the female unemployment rates have been the same or lower than that of men. Only in the UK, however, has this trend been consistent over two decades. Without careful study of the differences between the labour markets for women in European countries and the differences in practices in the registration of the unemployed it is not possible to explain with certainty why the UK should be different, but at least part of the explanation may lie in the high proportion of women in part-time work in the UK.

Two alarming features of the current level of unemployment in the Community is the high unemployment among young people under twenty-five (running at generally twice the level for people over twenty-five) (Figure 12), and the high proportion of the unemployed who have been out of work for a year or more (Figure 13). In both categories the majority of the unemployed are unskilled workers. Among the unemployed under twenty-five there is in most countries a larger percentage of females than males (Figure 14).

The self-employed and employment by sector

The largest sector of employment in all countries in Western Europe except Germany is services (Figure 15). Sixty per cent of all employees work in the services sector. This is a new development. Twenty years ago jobs in the service sector accounted for only 40 per cent of total employment. The most striking feature of sectoral employment is the very marked job segregation between men and women (Figure 16). In the more developed countries half or more of all male employees but about 80 per cent of all female employees are in the service sector. The proportion of women in industry ranges from less than 10 per cent in Luxembourg to a quarter in Germany, while the proportion of men in industry ranges from 34 per cent in

Ireland to 50 per cent in Germany. Only the new member countries still have a substantial proportion of the labour force employed in agriculture, ranging from one-quarter to one-fifth of the labour force. In all other European countries, including traditional food exporters like Denmark, agriculture now employs less than 10 per cent of the labour force.

The proportion of the economically active population who are self-employed also varies between countries, but differences may be explained more by variations in the number of farmers than by the entrepreneurial climate (Figure 17). European agriculture consists essentially of family enterprises: therefore countries with a comparatively high proportion of the population active in farming are also likely to have a relatively high proportion of people in self-employment. Differences in tax regulations between countries and other features which determine whether for example a plumber chooses to be employed or self-employed is also likely to contribute to differences in the self-employed ratio.

Education

Schools

A country's education system shapes the labour force. The Irish, English, Welsh and to some extent Scottish education systems differ from those on the Continent in several fundamental aspects. The most important is the early specialization in British and Irish schools. In all Continental countries children study a large number of subjects throughout the school system and the Baccalaureate or Abitur covers a wide range of subjects usually provided in two or three broad streams which are either language or science/maths based. In Britain and Ireland, from the age of fourteen children specialize in five to eight subjects and children in the upper secondary school usually study only three. The period spent in the upper secondary school (sixth form) is in addition shorter than in most types of education in the rest of Europe. British and Irish children also start school one year earlier than all other European children. The school-leaving age varies from fourteen in Portugal to sixteen in all other countries. The minimum legal age for employment is fourteen in Portugal; sixteen in France, Spain and the UK; and fifteen in all other Community countries. The right to conclude employment contracts without the permission of parents is in all countries gained at the age of eighteen.

Tertiary education

Increasingly the effective school-leaving age is eighteen in the more developed European countries (Figure 18). More and more young people now choose to stay on in education to gain occupational and vocational qualifications. School until the age of eighteen or nineteen is no longer limited to those who want to prepare for tertiary education. Some countries - notably Greece - have entrance exams for universities. In other European countries universities have traditionally been open to all young people who have taken their Baccalaureate or Abitur. Only engineering, medicine and some other subjects where teaching is dependent on limited laboratory places have restricted the entry and require high marks. However, increasingly Community member countries are introducing limitations on tertiary education entry to those with better results from secondary school. The UK and Ireland are the only EC countries where entry to university and polytechnic always has been limited to those with better grades in the secondary school exams.

Britain has the lowest proportion of tertiary sector students in Western Europe (Figure 19). However a comparison based on numbers only is misleading. First, some countries have longer undergraduate degree courses than the UK. A six-year degree course will of course register twice as many students as the UK three-year course with the same annual intake, yet produce the same number of students at the end. Secondly, the failure rate and the proportion of students who take longer than the standard time to finish their degree is much higher in all other European countries than in the UK. The UK has an exceptionally low failure rate of students in the tertiary sector and well over 90 per cent of students complete their course in the standard time. Until recently it was possible to find German university students who had been enrolled as undergraduates for twenty years or more.

Vocational and occupational training

Many observers fear that Europe is facing serious shortages of skills. The problem is two-fold. On the one hand Western Europe has a higher proportion of school leavers without any qualifications than the United States and Japan. Unskilled workers make up a very large proportion of the unemployed. On the other hand, many people have skills which are outdated. Even people with recent training find that their qualifications are inappropriate for the modern labour market. Industrial change produces large-scale training needs, both in terms of re-training workers whose skills are obsolete and in terms of changing existing training and education syllabuses to correspond to new requirements. This is an area where recently the European Community has become very active in an effort to promote an expansion of national training capacity (see chapter 'Measures to Combat Unemployment').

The systems for vocational and occupational training vary more between Member States than do the school and university systems. Applied training for specific occupations is given both as part of the upper secondary school curriculum (fifteen to eighteen year olds) and as post- secondary education. Post-secondary education is very varied even within Member States. The systems vary not just between different occupations and different local education authorities, but sometimes there are different ways of reaching the same qualification even within the same education authority.

Giving a detailed account of the different systems of vocational and occupational training is outside the scope of this book, but some general observations can be made. All over Europe the number of young people in apprenticeships has been substantially reduced. Instead the modern trend is towards occupational and vocational training in schools and colleges. The German model for training so often referred to in Britain is becoming rarer even in Germany. Occupational courses at Continental colleges usually contain a large element of general studies, maths and often a foreign language (usually English).

Social Security Systems

Most employees in Western Europe are protected by social security against loss of income due to sickness, maternity, accidents at work and old age. Their dependents and survivors are also protected when the insured employee suffers these risks and when he or she dies. The nine older members of the European Community all now spend about 20 per cent of their national income on social security (1) (Figure 20).

Different origins

The social security systems have converged from rather different origins. In Britain and Scandinavia the underlying principle of the development of the national insurance systems has been to provide a guaranteed minimum income for all citizens. In the other Continental countries social security has been seen as an insurance system to replace the earnings of employees during periods of sickness or unemployment. With some exceptions, such as young people or the handicapped who have no employment record and who consequently in some countries fall outside the social security system, most citizens in most countries are nowadays covered by social security provisions either as employees, voluntarily insured self-employed persons or dependants of insured persons.

The underlying ethos of some Continental social security systems has however led to problems for the long-term unemployed who may have no residual income support if they remain unemployed after the maximum permitted period for unemployment benefits - usually a year. France has just remedied this situation with a new system of benefits for the long-term unemployed introduced in the mid-1980s (2).

Most Continental countries, with the exception of the Nordic countries, also have social security systems where the actual insurance is provided by institutions which are either private or owned by trade unions or professional bodies. However, in most cases both the size of the contributions and the size of the benefits are regulated by the state and from the individual consumer's point of view these systems are not very different from the entirely state-run and tax-financed systems of Britain and Scandinavia.

What does vary between countries is the employer's contribution. This also varies within countries over time as governments use the employer's contribution as a tool in economic policy akin to taxation.

It should be noted that social security is different from 'social assistance', which is the discretionary final support system for people who either are not covered by the social security system or who have acute or additional need of support. In many European countries this system is administered by the local authorities. The different national systems vary greatly and this is one area which has not been covered by any European Community initiative until the inclusion into the Community's Social Charter of a commitment to adequate social protection for every citizen of the European Community (3).

Harmonization of social security

From the very beginning of the EC there was a discussion about the possibility of harmonizing the social security systems of the Member States.

In one respect this was essential to fulfil the basic objectives of the Community. In order to have freedom of movement of workers between Community countries it was necessary to ensure that migrant workers would have the same rights to social security as the native employees of the host countries. In this area the Council legislates mainly through Regulations. As will be discussed in the chapter on 'Freedom of Movement' a number of Regulations have been adopted and a large number of cases in the European Court of Justice have been brought by migrant workers claiming social security rights.

However, the discussion of harmonization went further than a system of reciprocal rights for migrant workers. From the beginning, trade unions and the Commission argued in favour of harmonization of benefits on the basis of the need to promote improved working conditions and an improved standard of living as laid down in **Article 117** of the EEC Treaty. For the Commission the motive was that the citizens of Europe should feel that their social levels are equivalent in order to be able to feel part of the same Community. Member governments and employers universally resisted this form of harmonization. Not surprisingly the Member States in the Council won this battle and effectively prevented the Commission from approaching the problem of social security harmonization until the early 1980s when proposals were made but not adopted by the Council on parental leave (see page 217). Not until the current discussion about the Social Charter, which does contain articles dealing with minimum social security standards, has this problem been approached seriously.

However, any real harmonization of social security benefits has become more problematic with the enlargement of the Community. After 1986, with a much greater span between the richest and the poorest members of the Community, it has become more difficult to harmonize both the types and size of benefits.

The employer's contribution

European employers have been concerned with the other side of social security: the cost of social security contributions. The level of employers' social security contributions has always varied a great deal between member countries. Traditionally these have been high in France and relatively low in the UK. Employers' contributions are of course a cost on production which, if very different, affect competitiveness. However, employers' contributions have also turned out to be difficult to harmonize and so far the activities of the Community in this field have been limited to continuous Commission monitoring of the comparative costs of social security.

Employment Legislation in the Member Countries

A modern industrial society seems to require government regulation of certain activities such as protection of the environment, protection of the health and safety of the workforce, producer liability for the goods manufactured and regulation of the location and shape of industrial buildings. In the employment field there are many areas where countries in Western Europe have developed similar legislation in response to similar problems (4).

However, there is an underlying difference in attitudes between EC countries to the role of the state in society which determines the scope and range of national employment law. In most Continental countries the state has from the eighteenth century had a greater role in regulating economic life than in the UK and Ireland. The obvious example of a 'statist' country is France but Italy, Germany and Belgium also share this tradition. In the UK, where the industrial revolution developed without either much state regulation or government encouragement, there are still some areas of employment which are not regulated by law, for example paid holidays and limitations on the weekly working hours. Ireland inevitably shares the British tradition. The two countries on the Continent with the least 'statist' tradition are Denmark and the Netherlands (5). These are also the countries tending to leave the regulation of some areas of employment to agreement between the two sides of industry. These differences colour the attitudes of member governments in discussions in the Council about Recommendations, Resolutions and Directives in the field of social and employment policy.

National employment legislation taken for granted by citizens and policy-makers alike will inevitably influence expectations at the European level. Anyone who wants to know in which areas there is likely to be pressure for new Community legislation in the future from trade unionists, employers, member governments, Community institutions and politicians needs to have some overview of the most important differences in provisions between different member countries.

The employment contract

In all Community countries - apart from the UK and Denmark - the freedom to conclude employment contracts is limited by constitutional provisions which prohibit discrimination on any grounds such as race, gender, religion, political or other opinion and social origin. European Community legislation on equal opportunities sets further limits on the freedom to conclude contracts with better provisions for men than women (or vice versa). The EEC Treaty and Community legislation on freedom of movement of Community citizens also stipulates equal treatment of EC nationals.

Employment contracts in Continental European countries are regulated in special employment legislation. In the UK and Ireland there is no general legislation on employment contracts. Instead, the interpretation of employment contracts is based on conclusions drawn from the application of ordinary contract law.

It is worth noting that most Continental countries have a wider definition of civil servant than the UK or the United States which means that special provisions for civil servants apply to much larger groups of public employees than in the UK and USA - such as teachers and railway staff.

Part-time and temporary work

This area of employment is nowadays, in EC jargon, labelled 'non-standard' or 'atypical' employment. In the majority of countries part-time work is governed by the same legislation as full-time permanent work with respect to basic terms and conditions of employment, redundancy and minimum-notice periods. All countries set a bottom limit of hours worked per week or over a longer period for the part-time employee to qualify for national insurance, but the UK is the only country where this limitation also excludes the employee from employment protection. In Ireland part-timers must work at least 120 hours per month to qualify for annual leave. In the Netherlands part-timers working less than one-third of standard hours are not covered by statutory minimum-wage provisions.

While part-time workers in all countries are covered by ordinary employment legislation, temporary contracts are by contrast in the majority of countries covered by special legislation which sets a time-limit on the duration of fixed-term contracts - usually to a maximum of two years. Countries without legislation on temporary work are the UK, Ireland and Denmark.

Employment agencies are banned in Greece, Italy and Spain and limited to certain areas of activity in Belgium, Germany and the Netherlands. Home-workers are covered by legislation on pay, working hours, safety and dismissal in France, Germany, Italy and Spain.

Pay

The main source of pay regulation in all member countries is collective agreements. State involvement in this area is low but occasionally governments intervene with incomes policies. Apart from equal pay for men and women, which is a legal requirement throughout the Community, a number of countries have a national statutory minimum wage - France, Luxembourg, the Netherlands, Portugal and Spain - which from time to time is adjusted more or less in line with inflation.

Working hours

The Social Charter of 1989 aims to limit the weekly standard working hours to forty. However in most member countries the weekly working hours for most workers have been reduced further either by law or through collective agreements (Figure 21). There is currently a trend towards regulating the number of standard working hours for a longer period than a week - most commonly a year. This means that overtime is not paid until employees have worked the annual number of hours - usually equivalent to a thirty-eight to forty hour week. Some countries have legislated to introduce this type of definition of standard working hours, some countries have instead legislated to permit the two sides of industry to agree such a system to replace the statutory weekly hours for an individual firm or a particular sector of industry. Belgium, Germany, France, Italy, the Netherlands and Spain have all introduced one or other type of legislation in this field.

All member countries, with the exception of Denmark, Italy and the UK, have laid down limits to the number of overtime hours which can be worked per day, week or year. Often collective agreements further reduce these limits.

The real hours worked are in all EC countries longer than the standard hours as determined in collective agreements or law. However, in most European countries the average number of extra hours worked per week are one or two hours. More workers in Portugal and the UK work considerably longer hours than their colleagues in the other EC countries. In fact in Portugal half and in the UK one quarter of all workers work on average forty-one to forty-five hours per week. In the UK a further one-third of the male employees in industry work forty-six or more hours on average per week. This is more than the upper legal limits on weekly overtime in some of the Member States (Figure 22).

The majority of countries apply limitations to night-work. Only Denmark, Luxembourg, Ireland and the UK have no laws concerning night-work. In Belgium and the Netherlands night-work is forbidden for both men and women but derogations may be and are granted for certain activities.

Other states prohibit night-work for women in industry. However, the European Commission is now aiming to outlaw this discriminatory practice. For further information on this aspect see the chapter on 'Equal Opportunities'.

Annual leave

Only Italy and the UK have no legislation laying down minimum provisions for paid holidays. Statutory minimum leave periods vary from three weeks to thirty days per year, but in the more developed countries longer holidays are commonly provided through collective agreements. The number of statutory holidays also vary greatly between member countries. All Europeans have time off at Christmas and New Year, but other holidays vary. The main difference is between protestant and catholic countries.

Employment protection

All Community countries have legislation which protects workers from arbitrary or unfair dismissal and ensures that employees get some weeks' or months' notice of dismissal or redundancy. The amount of time required varies with the length of time the employee has been working for the employer. Often better provisions than those provided by employment protection legislation have been achieved through collective agreements.

A number of countries - Belgium, Denmark, Luxembourg, France, Germany and Greece - have different levels of employment protection for blue- and white-collar workers. Full employment protection is usually only achieved after a probationary period during which time the employer can terminate employment without penalties (6).

Collective redundancies are subject to Community legislation which is dealt with in the 'Employment and Working Conditions' chapter.

All countries also have domestic legislation which covers areas not affected by Community Directives. These laws usually involve an obligation to consult with employee representatives, to inform the authorities of the impending redundancies and pay compensation.

Industrial Relations

With regard to collective bargaining, collective

agreements, trade union membership, worker participation and industrial action, legislation in Member States varies considerably from state to state. It is, however, possible to observe two main traditions. The continental European countries have a more comprehensive legal framework, while Ireland and the UK lack regulation in many areas of industrial relations. This has, on the one hand, left British unions free to call for re-negotiation of collective agreements at any time, but, on the other hand, deprived individual employees of legal protection of their right to join a union and unions of the right to organize when employers resist unionization. This is an area where the differences between national traditions in industrial relations are causing problems in the formulation of Europe-wide minimum standards.

In most European countries the right to join a trade union is protected in the Constitution. In addition trade unions often have the right, protected by law, to organize workers. The exception to this approach is the UK which does not recognize rights of association with regard to trade unions.

Collective agreements are in all EC countries the most important source for regulating working conditions, although most states also have certain legal minimum standards. In all countries, collective agreements are concluded between employers and their federations on one side, and trade unions and their federations on the other, although in Germany and France works councils may, under certain conditions, conclude agreements at the works level.

In Belgium, France, Luxembourg and Spain collective agreements apply to all workers in the industry covered by the agreement, regardless of whether they are members of the relevant union or not. In all EC countries except Ireland and the UK, collective agreements are legally binding with both sides of industry liable to damages if the agreement is broken prematurely.

In Denmark, Germany, Greece and the Netherlands the most important collective bargaining is carried out at the national level of the relevant industry. In the UK and Ireland negotiations at the level of the plant or company are more important.

All Member States apart from the Netherlands have systems for preventing and resolving industrial disputes through arbitration and mediation. Only in Denmark and Greece is this intervention in disputes compulsory.

The right to strike is guaranteed by the Constitutions of all member countries except Denmark, Ireland and the UK. In Denmark this right is instead provided through a national collective agreement from the 1930s. In addition most European countries in regulating industrial disputes prohibit the sacking of employees while they are involved in industrial action. In Ireland and the UK there exists no legal right to take industrial action. This is one of the areas covered by the European Community's Social Charter which is likely to cause the greatest controversy between the different traditions in Member States.

'Lock-outs' on the other hand are banned in Greece and Portugal and limited by law in France, Italy and Germany. In the other countries lock-outs are either legal or tolerated.

Employee participation

Eight Member States have legislated to make works councils mandatory - Belgium, France, Greece, Germany, Luxembourg, the Netherlands, Portugal and Spain. In Denmark a national collective agreement obliges firms with thirty-five or more employees to set up works councils. In Italy union organizations are traditionally set up by firms with fifteen or more employees.

Of the countries where works councils are regulated by law, Germany, Greece, Portugal and Spain have works councils which consist of employee representatives only. In Belgium, France and Luxembourg works councils also include management representatives, while in the Netherlands the worker-only works councils have some joint meetings with management. The size of company obliged to have works councils varies greatly between countries from five employees in Germany to 150 in Luxembourg. In France, Germany, Luxembourg and the Netherlands legislation also requires works councils at company level for large companies with a multitude of workplaces. Works councils normally have a right to information and consultation. In some areas the works councils may also have some limited co-decision rights. In Germany, works councils may conclude agreements in areas not covered by collective agreements and in Spain the councils have general negotiating rights.

In the UK and Ireland, shop stewards represent the workforce. However, the right to organize is, as previously mentioned, entirely founded on tradition and employers are free either to prohibit their employees from joining a union or to conclude agreements with the employees to this effect.

Industrial democracy is often understood to mean employee representation in the decision-making bodies of enterprises. Denmark, France, Germany and Luxembourg have mandatory systems of worker representation on company boards. Industrial democracy is also well developed in potential future Member States such as Sweden and Norway.

There are basically two different systems of employee representation in the company's highest decision-making body. In most countries the worker representatives, elected by the employees, form a minority of the members of the company board. In Germany companies have two boards: a management board and a supervisory board. Employee representatives sit on the supervisory board.

Industrial democracy is an area where the Community has tried to legislate for many years, but where it has been very difficult to achieve agreement between member governments. This is discussed further in the chapter on 'Consultation and Employee Participation'.

Notes

(1) John Holloway, Social Policy Harmonization in the European Community, Gower, 1981, p.63.

(2) See for example, International Social Security Review, 1/86 and 3/86.

(3) Article 13 of the Social Charter.

(4) A good overview of working conditions in European countries is found in the European Commission's summary report on the comparative study on rules governing working conditions in the Member States - COM(89) 360 final - Cat. No CB-CO-89-298 - ISBN 92-77-5 1892-8 - See Section II.

(5) A good account of the different traditions in Western Europe is given in K. Dyson, The State Tradition in Western Europe, Robertson, Oxford, 1980.

(6) A good source for comparative information about dismissal is a series of articles in the European Industrial Relations Review published between 1986 and 1987 under the collective title 'Termination of Contract'. These articles have been collected in a booklet with the same title published by the EIRR in 1989, see bibliography.

EMPLOYMENT AND SOCIAL POLICIES OF THE COMMUNITY

A commitment to social progress has played a prominent part in national politics in most countries in Western Europe since the First World War, and more intensely since the Second World War. Issues such as the introduction of comprehensive social security schemes and protection of employees in terms of health and safety, job security, working hours and paid leave have been a much more important part of government programmes in Europe compared to those of the USA and Japan. Another feature of Western Europe is the protection of individual employees' rights to organize and take action and the regulation of industrial relations, whether in law or by custom. In addition politics in Western Europe has a corporatist dimension with the two sides of industry having a more or less formalized consultative role in national policy-making. Although there are differences in levels of development between countries and in the individual measures which make up the social and employment policy of different countries as well as differences in emphasis between political ideologies and parties, social policy in the widest sense is very much a hallmark of politics in Western Europe, regardless of country or government. Social policy is indeed a European invention.

It is therefore not surprising that the European Economic Community was from the beginning given, however tentatively, a social dimension. The wider political and federalist objectives of the founding fathers meant not only that the process of economic integration was given a social dimension, but also that the purpose of economic integration was social progress. The preamble to the Treaty of Rome demonstrates this commitment by declaring one of the objectives of the signatories to be **'to ensure the economic and social progress of their countries by common action to eliminate the barriers which divide Europe'.**

ECSC

This was equally true for the Coal and Steel Community (ECSC) which had extensive powers to fund and promote improvements both in the working conditions and in the housing and other living conditions of steel workers. Training programmes have been another important part of the ECSC social programme as was support for workers made redundant as a consequence of restructuring of the coal and steel industry.

Social Policy in the EEC Treaty

The EEC Treaty contains a number of articles which authorize Community institutions to take action in various areas of social policy. In a few areas of social policy the Treaty also lays down rules for the conduct of the Member States.

Some of the areas in the sphere of social and employment policy where the Community is empowered to act are a direct corollary to the customs union. This is most obviously the case with freedom of movement for workers and the right of Community citizens to set up in business in other member countries. As economic integration makes it easier for enterprises to locate anywhere in the Community, there is the risk that they will set up or move to Member States where legal conditions in areas such as the working environment and health and safety are most lenient, unless national legislation is harmonized or at least co-ordinated. Equally, employers who do not move are keen not to be burdened with greater costs than employers in other countries. One of the most important clauses in the Treaty, which springs from the motive to level the playing field for enterprises in the Community, is **Article 119** on equal pay for men and women. The inclusion of this clause was argued by the French government which feared competition from countries with cheap female labour. Health and safety provisions are another area where employers incur costs as a result of legislation.

However, competition was never the only reason for EC

action in the area of employment and social policy. The Member States also agreed in the Treaty on **'the need to promote improved working conditions and an improved standard of living for workers, so as to make possible their harmonization while the improvement is being maintained'** (**Article 117**). This provision not only enabled Member States and the Commission to act in this area, but it also laid down the principle that harmonization must not mean the adoption of the lowest common denominator.

The Article continued: **'They** [the Member States] **believe that such a development will ensue not only from the functioning of the common market, which will favour the harmonization of social systems, but also from the procedures provided for in this Treaty and from the approximation of provisions laid down by law, regulation or administrative action'**. In **Article 118** the Member States empowered the Commission to take action to promote close co-operation in the fields of employment, labour law and working conditions, vocational training, prevention of occupational accidents and diseases, occupational hygiene and industrial relations.

Binding and non-binding Treaty provisions

Some Treaty provisions are binding on Member States, some merely enable institutions and Members States to take action. Freedom of movement provisions and the clause on equal pay are in the former category, other social provisions belong in the latter. There are in addition a number of non-binding social provisions in the Treaty relating to the common agricultural policy and the common transport policy.

This division between binding and non-binding provisions has had a very practical impact on the influence of the European Parliament on budget allocations in different areas. The minor Treaty reforms in 1972 gave Parliament greater opportunities to affect changes to the budget in areas not covered by binding provisions.

Another important provision in the social field, included from the beginning, concerned the setting up of the **European Social Fund** (ESF) to provide funding for retraining or settlement allowances for workers threatened by loss of employment **(Articles 123 to 128). Article 128** also refers to the possibility of developing **'general principles for implementing a common vocational training policy capable of contributing to the harmonious development both of the national economies and the common market'.**

Articles 48 to **51** provide for freedom of movement for workers by the end of the initial twelve-year transitional period. **Article 7** prohibits discrimination on grounds of nationality **'within the scope of application of this Treaty'**, i.e. in those areas covered by the Treaty. Together these provisions give Community citizens the right to accept offers of employment in other member countries, to move freely within the territory of Member States for the purpose of taking up employment, to stay in a Member State for the purpose of employment and to remain in a Member States after having been employed there. **Article 49** requires the Council to legislate to create equal conditions for EC migrant workers with citizens of the host country. **Article 50** obliges Member States to encourage the exchange of young workers. **Article 51** concerns social security for migrant workers. The right of establishment in self-employment is a necessary complement to the right to take up employment in other Member States. However, the right to set up as a self-employed professional or to set up in business has turned out to be more difficult to achieve than equal rights for employees.

Another corollary to the freedom of movement is the right to provide services by a business in one state for a customer in another member country. The freedom to provide services is dealt with in **Articles 59** to **66** and freedom to move capital - another essential for persons who wish to set up in business in another country - is covered by **Articles 67** to **73**.

Progress in the 1960s

Until 1972 few initiatives were taken in the field of social policy. Legislative efforts concentrated on achieving freedom of movement of workers. Although complete freedom of movement cannot be said to have been achieved today, most of the important regulations providing free entry, the right to reside and work in other Member States and the necessary provisions to give migrant workers equal treatment in social security with workers in the host country had been achieved before the end of the 1960s.

Progress during the 1970s

Apart from opening up freedom of movement for persons and making a start on harmonization of health and safety provisions, social policy formed a very minor part of the European Community's activities until the 1970s. In the boom years of the 1960s it was assumed that general growth and increasing prosperity would gradually eliminate or at least alleviate existing inequalities between different regions and different social groups.

As recession struck in the early 1970s it became evident that the common market had not alleviated regional disparities. Unemployment rose dramatically between 1973 and 1976 and was very unevenly distributed between regions. Underdeveloped regions suffered greatly, regions with declining heavy, traditional industry even more.

Two of the new members who joined the Community in 1973 contributed new regional problems. Ireland had a lower GDP per capita than Italy, a larger proportion of the labour force employed in agriculture than any other member country and a comparatively small and underdeveloped industry. The recession hit the UK's traditional heavy industry areas, the cradles of the industrial revolution, worse than most other EC regions with traditional industry. Unemployment in the UK rose above the EC average and the proportion of people living in poverty in Britain started to increase. Common measures to help sectors and regions with restructuring problems were necessary. The most important measure was the setting up of the European Regional Development Fund (ERDF) in 1975 and the drawing up of a Social Action Programme for the Community in 1974. In addition the Social Fund which had been rather limited in scope was reformed for the first time in 1971 to facilitate changes required as a result of Community policies and to support structural change in underdeveloped or declining regions. Later the Regulations were further amended to allow support for projects for special groups such as migrant workers (1974), young unemployed people (1975), women (1978) and, most recently, handicapped people.

The 1974 Social Action Programme

The Social Action Programme adopted by the Council on 21 January 1974 was very comprehensive and became the foundation for all action in the social sphere for two decades. Many of the new proposals for legislation and action in this area which now are launched as part of the single market programme are found in the 1974 Action Programme.

The Paris Summit in October 1972 provided the impetus for the development of the Social Action Programme. The Heads of State declared that economic expansion is not an end in itself but should result in an improvement in the quality of life as well as of the standard of living and emphasized that they attached as much importance to vigorous action in the social field as to the achievement of Economic and Monetary Union. The resolution adopted at the Summit (1) invited the Commission to draw up a social action programme providing for concrete measures and corresponding budget resources. The programme covers issues such as measures to promote employment growth, the improvement of living and working conditions, worker participation and the beginning of the process, which later came to be called 'the social dialogue'. The programme contains one of the earliest clauses on the need to reconcile family responsibilities with work and first established the need for action programmes for the handicapped, for migrants and on poverty. The Social Action Programme led to the establishment of the European Foundation for the Improvement of Living and Working Conditions, the European Institute for Vocational Training and the European Trade Union Institute.

Employment Policy

Apart from urging consultation between Member States and better co-operation between national employment services, the 1974 programme surprisingly does not contain any proposals for action against unemployment. However, as unemployment rose from 2.6 million registered unemployed in 1973 to 5.2 million in 1976, a series of Council resolutions and action programmes to combat unemployment were adopted during the 1970s to co-ordinate national efforts.

The process of legislation on social policy ground to a halt in the beginning of the 1980s. The deepening economic crisis led to government cut-backs in social spending and a general reluctance to take on new commitments of any kind. As all legislation had to achieve unanimity in the Council, individual member governments, notably but not only the UK government, were able to block Draft Directives. A large backlog of Commission proposals, often amended several times but failing to be agreed by the Council, built up.

The single market programme

The single market programme has brought new momentum to the development of the Community's social policy. This was heralded by the Council of Social Affairs Ministers in the spring of 1984 which stated that **'the Community will not be able to strengthen its economic cohesion in the face of international competition if it does not strengthen its social cohesion at the same time. Social policy must therefore be developed at Community level on the same basis as economic, monetary and industrial policies'** (2). The internal market programme must not been seen to benefit enterprise only but also employees and ordinary citizens. Achieving support for the single market programme from both sides of industry and all major political parties requires parallel efforts in the social field.

The single market programme includes measures to complete the traditional areas of Community legislation. First of all the programme includes a commitment to achieve full freedom of movement of persons. Secondly, the programme also commits Member States to encourage improvements in social policy, **'especially in the working environment, as regards the health and safety for workers' (Article 118A).** These two areas of concrete action - freedom of movement and the working environment - were inserted into the Treaty by the adoption of the Single European Act.

Thirdly, a new **Article 130A** with a general commitment to action in the social area was added by the Single European Act: **'In order to promote its overall harmonious development, the Community shall develop and pursue its actions leading to the strengthening of its economic and social cohesion. In particular the Community shall aim at reducing disparities between the various regions and the backwardness of the least-favoured regions'.** In consequence **Article 130D** requires a revision of the Regulations of the Structural Funds. 'Social cohesion' is a code-word for action in a number areas with the purpose of eliminating disadvantage. The most important is the elimination of the handicaps affecting underdeveloped and declining regions. To this end the spending programmes of the Structural Funds and the Social Fund for underdeveloped and declining regions have been increased and will be doubled between 1987 and 1993.

Freedom of movement, health and safety and reform of the Structural Funds were included in the Single Act, but there are other forms of action which are regarded as part of the single market programme in a wider sense, and constitute a new move forward in the social area. The most important of these are the various programmes to combat unemployment.

Employment

The creation of free movement of goods and capital within the internal market is in itself expected to create new employment. The Commission's research programme on the cost of non-Europe (3) estimates an increase in jobs of between 1.8 million and 5 million depending on the accompanying economic policy. However, restructuring resulting from increased competition is also likely to cause unemployment in certain sectors and regions.

The activities of the Social and Regional Funds have in terms of spending played a very limited role in comparison with national measures to promote regional development and improved training programmes. However the new programme for the Structural Funds, which doubles their resources and concentrates their action in the poor new member countries in the European Community - Greece, Portugal, Spain - and on the only underdeveloped north European country - Ireland - together with two most underdeveloped regions in the wealthier parts of Europe - Mezzogiorno and Northern Ireland, begins to amount to a real programme of redistribution of resources from wealthy to poor regions. The amount of EC spending, allocated for the poor Mediterranean members, will amount to nearly ECU 14 billion annually by 1993. This sum does not include the cheap loans for large infrastructure programmes and for the development of small and medium sized businesses by the European Investment Bank.

The Council has also adopted a number of action programmes of a microeconomic nature to promote employment growth. However a Commission proposal for a co-operative growth strategy trying to achieve Europe-wide co-ordination of economic policies, launched in 1986 has still not been adopted by the Council.

The Commission adopted a Communication on the social dimension of the internal market in September 1988 which in addition to the policies included in the Single Act also included a commitment to policies to raise training levels, and the creation of new jobs by promoting new business initiatives combined with measures to help the long-term unemployed into jobs. The Commission concludes: **'If satisfactory solutions cannot be found despite the efforts made, available social security measures must be stepped up, for instance an ideal measure would be to provide a guaranteed minimum income'.**

A People's Europe

Another programme which emphasized the need for social progress was the report on a 'People's Europe'. The

Fontainebleau European Council - or Heads of Government meeting - in June 1984 undertook to give the Community a new dimension which would bring it closer to its citizens. To this end it appointed an ad hoc Committee to investigate what measures could be adopted to strengthen and promote its identity (4). The Adonnino Committee, made up of representatives of the Heads of State or Government, produced two reports after six months. The Committee identified the elimination of the last obstacles to freedom of movement as a priority to make citizens in the Member States feel European and the first report concentrated on this subject (5). The second report was a plan to give the Community a new political, cultural and social dimension by implementing new citizen's rights, increased opportunities to travel in other Community countries for young people, and Community-level action for health protection and the promotion of culture (6). The European Council in Milan in June 1985 approved the report (7).

The Social Charter

The most recent social policy instrument adopted in connection with the 1992 programme is the **Social Charter.** This idea was launched by the Belgian government when holding the presidency of the Council in 1987 (8). The idea was supported by the Economic and Social Committee (9). The Social Charter was originally intended to be a 'Bill of Citizens' Rights' in the social area. The final result is more a collection of targets for Community action and minimum standards for Member States. The Social Charter was adopted by the Council in December 1989 (10). It is not legally binding on Member States but forms the platform for a future series of legislative initiatives by the Commission. The final Charter was somewhat watered down in comparison with the original Commission proposal and Parliament's demands. Probably the most controversial chapter of the Charter deals with trade unions' rights and the right to take industrial action. There are also important chapters on employment rights and minimum employment standards. The Charter includes a commitment to further progress in the areas of equal opportunities and freedom of movement. Action for old people is included almost for the first time in Community policy-making. The three most novel pledges in the Charter are the movement towards a right to minimum pay - watered down by the Council in the final version of the Charter - a right to social protection for those without other means and a right of all workers to an employment contract. The Charter is partly based on the twenty-year old Social Charter adopted by the Council of Europe in 1961 (11). The content of the Social Charter is discussed in detail under each subject heading in Section I.

The Commission Action Programme on the Social Charter

The Commission issued its action programme in November 1989. This programme provides the framework for Community action in the social and employment field for the next decade. The programme contains a large number of new measures which the Commission intends to develop in the near future to give the Social Charter teeth.

The Commission is proposing a number of practical actions to make the European labour market function more smoothly, including the integration of the different information systems on employment such as MISEP and SYSDEM. In the area of employment conditions the Commission is proposing Directives on employment contracts and a revision of existing European legislation on collective redundancies and the adaptation of working time. It intends to open the discussion on equitable wages by publishing an opinion on this subject. In the area of social protection the Commission intends to issue recommendations on minimum standards for national social security systems in providing minimum social assistance for those without other income. The Commission announces that it will not propose any initiatives under the controversial chapter on freedom of association and collective bargaining. However, under the Social Charter chapter on employee consultation and participation, the Commission intends to take a new initiative to get European legislation on industrial democracy in multinational companies adopted - the so called Vredeling Draft Directive. The Commission also intends to propose legislation on profit sharing. Legislation to achieve equal opportunities in employment for men and women has largely been completed. In this area the Commission intends to concentrate on action to make it easier for parents and other carers to combine work and family responsibilities. This includes a future Directive on the protection of pregnant women at work, recommendations on child care and on job security for pregnant women. The Social Charter contains a far-reaching commitment to lifelong training for employees. The Commission intends to propose a legal instrument to implement this commitment. It also proposes to improve EC programmes on training and exchanges. The chapter on health and safety contains the largest number of future legislative proposals and an intention to propose the establishment of a safety, hygiene and health agency. Finally the Commission intends to propose a Directive on the protection of young people at work, an action programme for the elderly and a Directive on mobility for the disabled. The detailed provisions of this action programme are discussed in the chapters on the different subject areas in Section I.

Social Dialogue

Consultation with the social partners as part of the EC decision-making structure goes back to the European Coal and Steel Community which was given a committee for consultation with the two sides of industry in the coal and steel industry. In the EC the Economic and Social Committee has to be consulted by the Commission and the Council on all issues related to employment and social affairs. The legal basis for ECOSOC is found in **Articles 193 to 198** of the Treaty.

Over time several other consultative networks have been created. There are nine sectoral joint committees where the two sides of industry comment on development within the relevant industries. The old ECSC consultative committee is now one of these. In addition the

Consultative Committee of the European Social Fund is a tripartite committee with the two sides of industry as well as national governments represented.

There are also employer and trade union representatives on various Commission advisory committees in the social and employment area. At the beginning of the 1970s a Standing Committee on Employment was created consisting of representatives of the two sides of industry and of the Council and the Commission. So far the Committee has concentrated mainly on measures to combat unemployment. It is now the only forum where the social partners meet with the Community's policy and decision-makers.

The Social Dialogue nearly ground to a halt during the early 1980s and was revived as part of the single market initiative. A more detailed discussion of the social dialogue is found in the chapter on 'Employee Consultation'.

Institutions

Employment and social policies are handled within the Commission by Directorate General V - Employment and Social Affairs. Training programmes are the responsibility of the newly formed 'Human Resources Taskforce', which is discussed in more detail in the chapter on 'Measures to Combat Unemployment'. DG V is organized in four directorates:

A. Employment, which includes sections dealing with: employment and labour-market policy; social aspects of industrial policies, new technologies and industrial relations; ECSC readaptation and social aspects of iron and steel policies; employment and equality for women;

B. Living and working conditions and welfare with sections on Social Security and social action programmes, poverty and welfare measures for families and the elderly; freedom of movement, migration policy and social security for migrant workers; measures for the disabled;

C. European Social Fund where subsections deal with groups of member countries apart from a co-ordination, planning and administration section;

D. Public health; industrial medicine and hygiene; toxicology and safety at work; mines and other extractive work.

In the European Parliament Commission proposals and members' initiatives in the employment and social sphere are referred to the Committee on Social Affairs, Employment and the Working Environment. Equal Opportunities issues are the domain of the Committee on Women's Rights (see the chapter on 'Equal Opportunities'). Proposals for Directives are also discussed by the Parliament's Committee on Legal Affairs and Citizen's Rights.

When Commission proposals in the social field arrive at the Council of Ministers, they are usually sent to the sub-committee on social affairs, which consists of national civil servants, often on secondment from their national ministry of social welfare and attached to their respective Permanent Representative, i.e. their nation's ambassador to the European Community.

The Single European Act

A precondition for progress in the social area, as well as the legislative action necessary to achieve the internal market, was reform of the EC decision-making process. The adoption of the Single European Act meant the introduction of majority voting in the Council in all areas specifically included in the Act as part of the programme to achieve the internal market. This reform abolished the opportunity for one or two governments to block decisions.

The Single European Act also gave a greater role to the European Parliament in the legislative process. The European Parliament has not achieved powers to amend proposed Regulations and Directives outright. The Single Act provides for a complicated procedure where the

Parliament with the agreement of the Commission can stop the Council from adopting certain provisions. This is of limited use where governments are reluctant to adopt any legislation at all, but may be an important instrument to force member governments to agree to individual Parliament amendments in a legislative package which a majority of governments are anxious to approve. It is also increasingly difficult for the Council to disregard decisions adopted with a large majority by directly elected parliamentarians representing a wide political spectrum from left to right. In terms of democratic legitimacy it is an advantage for the European Parliament that no one party group has a majority in the Parliament. Few decisions are taken without the agreement of both the Socialist and the Christian Democrat groups, and a number of decisions are supported by all five major party groups from the Communists to the Conservatives, representing the vast majority of the electorate in the Community.

Parliament has played a very active role in the field of social policy. In the European Community, where so many decisions deal with highly technical details of agricultural or trade policy, the social area is attractive to parliamentarians, because it contains easy to understand policy initiatives, which affect voters directly. Parliament has taken a number of initiatives by reporting on topical social problems and demanding Community legislation, some of which have resulted in Commission initiatives.

Community legal instruments

Legislation on freedom of movement is in part done by **Regulation**, which is European legislation directly applicable in Member States without further national legislation (see opening section of this volume). This is because freedom of movement is one of the original objectives of the Community. Full freedom of movement can only be achieved if discrimination against migrants is removed in all member countries.

In other policy areas most European legislation takes the form of **Directives** which require Member States to adopt national laws implementing the aims of the Directive through national legislation. Member States have to implement legislation to achieve the objectives of Directives within a timetable attached to the Directive. This varies from one year to sometimes a decade. The European Court of Justice has established that national governments and public authorities are bound by the provisions in the Directives, even if appropriate national legislation has not been adopted.

As Directives are implemented through national legislation it is often for practical purposes sufficient to know the national legal instruments. However, many cases before the European Court of Justice have involved the issue of whether the national legislation implementing a Directive is different from the latter. Sometimes it is therefore important to also know the European legal provisions in detail.

There are also Council **Decisions** which do not have the force of law but which still are important. A number of **action programmes** have been adopted over the last two decades to combat poverty, unemployment, promote growth, positive action for women and equal opportunities in education for boys and girls. These action programmes are really a series of recommendations to member governments. However, the Council decision-makers are of course the same governments, so action programmes are by definition backed by all or a majority of members - depending on what procedure has been used. Usually an action programme also requires the Commission to oversee the implementation. Very often action programmes include a requirement for governments to report progress to the Commission after a certain time. The duty to report exercises mild pressure on the national administration to achieve some progress in some of the areas covered by the action plan. Less comprehensive calls to action are usually called **Recommendations.** Council **Decisions** usually concern actions at the European level, such as the Decision to develop a future action programme.

Recommendations issued by the **Commission** without the support by the Council have much less influence than Council Recommendations. The Commission usually issues such Recommendations on policies which would not be accepted by the Council. Often Commission Recommendations aim to alert Member States of the existence of a particular problem and request that Member States do not take action to increase divergence in areas where harmonization or co-ordination cannot be achieved.

Action Programmes

Apart from legislation EC institutions have in the area of social and employment policy very limited powers. The Community tries to influence Member States' policies through action programmes which are part exhortation, part promotion of certain actions through grant funding. The Member governments meeting in the Council adopt resolutions which requests Member States, i.e. the same governments, to take action of various types. The other main policy instrument is Community part-finance of measures undertaken in the Member States by local or regional governments, private enterprise or voluntary organizations. In addition the Commission undertakes research and surveys either on its own initiative or at the request of the Council. Often action programmes also contain a requirement of Member States to report on progress to the Commission.

Most action programmes have to be agreed by the Council and are launched in the form of a Council **Resolution** or **Decision**. These Resolutions often share a common structure:

- The first part contains a list of all previous Council Decisions, Resolutions and Directives and Commission initiatives. There is also usually a reference to the Opinions of the Parliament and ECOSOC, including relevant Official Journal references to the original Commission proposal. There are often also references to the general principles or problems which constitute the reasons for launching the programme. Most clauses in this section start with the word 'whereas'. These paragraphs are not numbered. All other text in the Resolutions/Decisions have the form of numbered Articles.

- The second part contains the general guidelines of the programme, the objectives for the action to be taken.
- The third part of the programme contains the different measures which Member States are required or encouraged to implement;
- The fourth part consists of the action to be taken by Community institutions - usually the Commission. This section will often also include some notice of the budget allocation made for the programme.

EC policy in the social area has from the beginning been very much a matter of pump-priming, encouraging pilot projects and innovation. An important part of most EC action is the promotion of an exchange of national experiences and ideas through the Community funding exchanges of experts and practitioners and European conferences. Attached to the larger action programmes is often a transnational publication or newsletter to disseminate information about national policies and projects. An important part of most action programmes is an obligation on Member States to produce a progress report to the Commission on developments at the national level in the relevant policy area. These reports are then summarized and published by the Commission. The Commission also undertakes or commissions comparative studies.

In the late 1970s and 1980s the Commission funded a large number of small projects run by regional and local authorities, private companies and voluntary organizations under different policy initiatives. The trend for the 1990s is a move towards larger and more comprehensive projects which cover a larger geographical area and involves all the actors within the area from local authorities to the social partners. The Commission is also keen to develop more effective evaluation and monitoring of projects.

Privatization of EC research and administration

The Commission has increasingly commissioned other

bodies, both public and private to take over for a fee both the administration of action programmes in the Member States and the central function at the European level. In the social sphere these outside administrators are often called 'animateurs'. A large amount of the extensive research activities carried out by the Commission is done by outsiders, often academics working on commission. Sometimes comparative reports and research projects are carried out by **networks** of researchers, with one representative in each country. Both animateur and research contracts are offered to tender through the Official Journal.

The Role of the European Court of Justice

As in other areas of Community legislation there has been a number of infringement cases where the Commission has taken individual Member States to Court for failure to implement Directives in full by the allotted deadline. In the area of social policy there have also been a few cases where Member States have take the Commission to Court for exceeding its powers.

However, the Court's preliminary rulings are in many ways more interesting. There have been a large number of cases within two of the subject areas within the social and employment sphere. The first are cases concerning the right of entry, residence and equal treatment for EC internal migrants. The second is the complex area of equal opportunities. In both these areas Court rulings make up an important source of interpretation of the legal texts which has extended the validity of the Directives. Here the Court's pronouncements on the concept of indirect discrimination have been particularly useful. Some of these cases have also had a wider importance in defining the relationship between the Community and its citizens and the applicability of Community law.

Subsidiarity

In the choice between national and European legislation

or action the basic principle guiding decision-makers should, according to both federalist and functionalist theories, be **subsidiarity**, i.e. decisions and administration should take place at the lowest level where it can be performed effectively. This means that decisions at the European level should be complementary to national or local measures. Issues should only be handled at the European level where local, regional or national government cannot achieve results. This is most obviously the case in areas where conditions need to be the same or similar across the whole of Europe. Economic integration in combination with both producer and consumer interests require harmonization or co-ordination in many areas which may not be obvious at the first glance. However, EC institutions are often working with issues where harmonization is not a major concern. An obvious example is the promotion of vocational training and of employment growth and the anti-poverty programme.

In reality the process by which an issue becomes a European concern is often less based on theory than on accident. Reasons for Europeanizing issues are found at all levels of the Community's decision-making machinery. The European Community sometimes needs to be seen to 'do something' about topical problems even when action at the European level is not the most effective or logical. Commission departments may have ambitions to become involved in new interesting issues, even if they are not necessarily natural subjects for decisions at the European level. Members of the European Parliament have the greatest incentive of all to elevate issues to the European level. Detailed Regulations harmonizing lawnmower noise or fixing the intervention price for wheat do not make good press releases. Parliamentarians raise issues which are unlikely to become subjects of European Community decisions, but which are of interest and immediate concern to voters. Recent examples are the adoption by the Parliament of a draft patients' charter (12) and a report by the Committee of Women's Rights with detailed prescriptions for health services for women (13).

It is now difficult to find any policy area where the European Community does not have some involvement however unlikely the Europeanization of the issues might seem. In many cases the European activities are complementary to national government policies. This is particularly the case where the Community is trying to encourage Member States to more efforts or promotes new thinking by funding pilot schemes, as for example in the area of vocational training or measures to combat unemployment.

The European Community competence is growing organically, producing patterns of responsibility which are not necessarily logical but seem to work for the moment. If the Community in the future is enlarged to include the EFTA states, Eastern European states and more Mediterranean states, the EC policy profile may have to change fundamentally to avoid the institutions grinding to a halt, while at the same time more policies may become necessary subjects of harmonization in a more diverse Community. In recent statements on political union the need to develop a more logical and coherent theory of subsidiarity has been given considerable airing.

Notes

(1) Summit meeting, Paris, October 1972.

(2) Official Journal of the European Communities, No C175, 4/7/84.

(3) Cecchini, P., 1992 The European Challenge: The Benefits of a Single Market, Aldershot, Wildwood House Ltd, 1988. ISBN 0-7045-0613-0, p.98.

(4) Council meeting, Fontainebleau, June 1984.

(5) Bulletin of the EC 3-1985, points 2 to 18, Supplement 7/85.

(6) Bulletin of the EC 6-1985, points 141 to 148, Supplement 7/85.

(7) Summit meeting, Milan, June 1985.

(8) Meeting of Social Affairs Council, May 1987.

(9) Economic and Social Committee: Opinion on the social aspects of the internal market (European social area), CES(87) 1069, 19/11/87.

(10) Reprinted in Social Europe, vol. 1/1990. See also ISEC/B25/89, 11 October 1989.

(11) The Council of Europe was formed in 1949 and included from the beginning the UK, Norway, Denmark, Sweden and the other neutral European states. The membership now includes all states in Western Europe with the exception of Finland. The Council of Europe is the parent organization of the European Convention on Human Rights and the European Court and Commission of Human Rights.

(12) Proposed by the now Commissioner Christiane Schrivener when she was an MEP in 1984. Official Journal of the European Communities, C46, 20/2/84.

(13) Report drawn up on behalf of the Committee on Women's Rights on women and health, European Communities European Parliament Reports, PE DOC A 2-78/88, 17/5/88.

EMPLOYEE CONSULTATION AND PARTICIPATION

The industrial relations systems in most European countries include an obligation on enterprises to regularly inform and consult their workforce concerning major changes in company policy and in particular about redundancies and changes in the ownership of the enterprise. In some countries employee participation has developed further and now includes the involvement of employee representatives in decision-making.

Industrial relations is an area where the Commission has been active in introducing a number of proposals but singularly unsuccessful in achieving their adoption by the Council. The single market programme is now providing a new impetus to efforts to achieve agreement on a number of individual proposals.

It could be argued that industrial democracy, because it involves additional costs for the employer - at least in terms of lost working hours for workers representatives and management, should be subject to harmonization in order to remove competitive disadvantages for employers in countries with a tradition of worker participation. However, the Commission's main motive for action in this area has always been the need for the Community to introduce the best employment practices in any one country in the whole of the Community and to bring benefits to and improve standards for working people.

This view has been endorsed by the Council in declarations of intent from the Social Action Programme adopted in 1974 to the Social Charter of 1989. In the Social Action Programme the member governments express the political will to adopt the measures necessary to achieve a number of social objectives including **'progressively to involve workers or their representatives in the life of undertakings in the Community'.** The Social Action Programme also contained a commitment to increased involvement of management and labour in the economic and social decisions of the Community.

The Commission started first in the limited area of the right of employees to be informed and consulted in connection with transfers and take-overs, redundancies and bankruptcy - a logical step, as some transnational concentrations of enterprises could be considered to be a consequence of the process of economic integration.

Worker Participation

Worker participation is a politically charged area and this explains the Commission's lack of success. As is seen in the chapter on 'Employment and Social Policy in the Member States', conditions vary greatly between member countries. Some countries have no legal provisions and few traditions of employee involvement and in countries which have industrial democracy the systems used vary greatly.

Essentially there are two major differences between member countries in the area of employee involvement. First, there is a difference between those countries which have legislated on industrial democracy, such as Denmark, France and Germany, and those which have left this area entirely to be agreed by the two sides of industry, such as the UK. Secondly, there are two main systems of industrial democracy. In one system, essentially epitomized by French company law but shared by most of the other Community countries, there is a one tier company board usually with some form of separation between executive and non-executive directors. The executive directors are in charge of the day-to-day management of the company while the non-executive directors fulfil a supervisory role. The employee representatives on the company board are non-executive directors. The German and Dutch systems have two tiers with an executive board and a supervisory board. The employee representatives serve on the supervisory board.

The Commission produced a first consultative document on employee participation in the early 1970s (1). This was translated into the draft 5th Company Law Directive in 1972 (2). An amended proposal was submitted by the

Commission in 1983 taking account of the European Parliament's and the Economic and Social Committee's Opinions on the original proposal (3). In December 1989 the Council at expert level adopted a position paper on this draft Directive representing the majority view of the national experts in the Council's sub-committee. There are now rumours that the Commission may withdraw the proposal altogether.

Employee participation has also been included in the proposals for a European Company Statute. The Commission submitted a proposal for a Regulation in 1975 (4), though the first draft was produced as early as 1970 (5) and a new proposal in 1989 (6). It is now argued by the Commission that the European Company Statute is part of the single market package and therefore should be adopted by the Council with a majority vote.

Another proposal which has so far failed to be adopted concerned the rights of employees in undertakings with complex structures, in particular multi-national companies, to be informed and consulted on major company policy initiatives. The first proposal was submitted by the then Commissioner for Social Affairs, Mr Vredeling in 1980 (7). An amended proposal was presented in 1983 incorporating some of the changes adopted by the European Parliament (8).

It is clear that the first legal instrument on employee participation to be adopted will be the European Company Statute and that no further progress will be made on other Directives until this has happened. The Statute is optional rather than mandatory and may be adopted by a majority vote in the Council. The latest draft Statute which permits choice between a number of different models of worker participation represents the latest Commission news on the subject. However, recently some have proposed that the provisions on employee participation in the Company Statute should be split off into a separate Directive, which would make it possible to adopt the Statute in the first instance without any provisions on employee participation. This proposal is resisted by a number of governments who fear further delays in achieving progress on employee participation at the EC level.

Since 1985 a series of Commission initiatives have also

aimed to create a dialogue at the European level between the organizations representing employers and labour. A permanent forum for consultation with both sides of industry on EC policy proposals exists in the Economic and Social Committee.

The 5th Company Law Directive

On the basis of Article 54(3) of the Treaty a number of Directives seeking to co-ordinate company law between member countries have been adopted covering the following topics:

1st Directive	Disclosure of information
2nd Directive	Company capital
3rd Directive	Internal mergers
4th Directive	Annual accounts
6th Directive	Company prospectuses
7th Directive	Group accounts
8th Directive	Auditors' qualifications (9)
11th Directive	Disclosure requirements of branches
12th Directive	Single-member private limited companies

There is a further list of draft Directives submitted by the Commission but not yet adopted by the Council:

5th Directive	Company structure and administration

9th Directive	Conduct of groups of companies (not yet formally submitted)
10th Directive	Cross-border mergers
13th Directive	Takeover bids (10)

Most of these Directives and draft Directives deal with the public obligations of companies to keep accounts, to publish prospectuses and to disclose information. These are not discussed here. The 5th Directive deals with the internal structure and decision-making of companies including employee participation for companies with 1,000 or more employees.

The first proposal in 1972 sought to impose the German company model with one management board and one supervisory board. The amended proposal requires Member States, where company law currently stipulates one-tier companies, to introduce legislation on a two-tier system. However, Member States may permit companies to have a choice between a two-tier structure and a one-tier structure. The structure of the one-tier company board as laid down in the Directive makes the one-tier system resemble the two-tier system. **Article 21A** stipulates that **'the company shall be managed by the executive members of an administrative organ under the supervision of the non-executive members of that organ. The number of executive members shall be divisible by three and greater than the number of executive members'**. The draft Directive also stipulates that the executive members shall be appointed by the non-executive members. In this way the company's decision-making body or bodies are divided into an executive and a supervisory function regardless of whether these members sit together on one board or are divided between two boards.

Up to two-thirds of the non-executive members may be appointed by the shareholders at the general meeting and a minimum of one-third up to a maximum of half are to be appointed by the company's employees. Where employees appoint half of the members, voting procedures -

presumably through the Chair's casting vote - shall ensure that decisions may ultimately be taken by the members appointed by the shareholders. Member States are offered the possibility of limiting employee representation to one-third of the non-executive members by way of derogation of the relevant articles in the Directive (11).

Member States may also opt to provide for employee participation through a separate body of employee representatives rather than employee board members or to leave the details of employee representation to be agreed between the company and the unions or between employers' organizations and unions. In the case of works councils these would have the same rights to full consultation and information as non-executive board members.

Employee participation in small and medium sized companies is not covered by the draft Directive, which only deals with companies with 1,000 or more employees. According to the Commission, by 1982 agreement between member governments was more or less achieved on the issue of company structure, but no agreement has been reached on the issue of industrial democracy.

The European Company Statute

A European Company Statute is intended to provide a statutory framework for companies set up at the European rather than national level. The idea of a European Company Statute goes back to the 1960s but has acquired greater urgency with the arrival of the single market. The Cecchini report on the cost of non-Europe estimates that **'Costliest of these barriers for transborder co-operative start-ups and managements appear to be the near-absence of relevant European Company and tax law'** (12). The lack of progress in co-ordinating national company law has given further impetus to the Commission's efforts to create the legal framework which would 'permit the formation of European companies capable of facing up to their American or Japanese rivals'.

From the beginning the Commission has seen employee representation as an integral part of a European company law. In 1988 the Commission argued that **'worker**

participation is essential not just as a matter of social rights, but as an instrument for promoting the smooth running and success of the enterprise through promoting stable relationships between managers and employees in the workplace' (13).

The system of worker participation included in the original version of the statute was again modelled on German practice. The European Parliament proposed that the supervisory board should instead consist of one-third shareholders' representatives, one-third of workers' representatives and one-third of members co-opted by these two groups and representing the general interest. This idea was incorporated in the Commission's amended proposal but was strongly resisted by the employers' organizations.

In the 1988 memorandum the Commission instead proposes a more flexible approach based on the latest version of the draft 5th Company Law Directive. Three optional models are proposed:

1. Employee representation of not less than one-third and not more than half of the members on the company's supervisory board;

2. Employee participation through a separate body from the company board, i.e. a works council;

3. Systems of participation which are set up through collective agreements.

The Commission further offers Member States the option to limit the choice of structure of companies setting up within their territory to just one of the models above. There would then be no need for governments to fear that companies would try to set up as European companies in order to avoid their obligations to provide employee participation under existing national legislation.

The Vredeling Draft Directive

The core of this proposal is that all large companies with complex structures in the form of one or more subsidiaries should be required to consult and inform employee representatives in all subsidiaries before the adoption of any decision which significantly affects the employees' interests. The information should give a clear picture of the activities of the dominant undertaking and its subsidiaries taken as a whole. Member States are required to ensure that companies fulfil their obligations to all subsidiaries under the Directive and to impose appropriate penalties on undertakings which fail to comply.

The draft was subject to a number of amendments adopted by the European Parliament. Originally the Commission proposed that such information should be given every six months. The Parliament wanted this changed to once per year. The definition of the companies affected by the proposal was also changed from subsidiaries with 100 or more employees to companies which employ at least 1,000 workers in all its undertakings within the EC.

In its amended proposal the Commission has incorporated the main comments by the European Parliament. There are also more detailed definitions about the right of companies to withhold secret information and a new option for Member States to exempt undertakings whose main objectives are political, religious, humanitarian, charitable, educational, scientific, artistic or related to public information or expression of opinion.

Employee Participation in the Social Charter

The European Community's Social Charter should not be confused with the Social Charter adopted by the Council of Europe in 1961. This Charter also includes an article on the freedom of workers and employers to form local, national or international organizations for the protection of their economic and social interests and to join those organizations. Another article deals with the right to bargain collectively and to take collective action including the right to strike (14).

The European Community's Social Charter contains a chapter on 'Freedom of Association', which includes not only the right of workers and employers to join professional organizations and trade unions, but also the right to collective bargaining and to collective action including the right to strike. These articles appear to be modelled on the provisions in the Social Charter of the Council of Europe, but are more detailed and include a paragraph which looks forward to the possibility of collective agreements adopted by the two sides of industry at European level, particularly at inter-occupational and sectoral level (15).

The Social Charter also includes a chapter on **'Information, Consultation and Participation for Workers'**, which has no equivalent in the Council of Europe Charter (16). The Charter stipulates that information, consultation and participation for workers must be developed taking account of existing national practices. Article 18 states that such measures must be implemented in due time and particularly in the case of technological change which has major implications for the workforce, in connection with restructuring and redundancy and when trans-frontier workers are affected by employment policies pursued by their employer.

In the Social Charter action programme the Commission states that it will not initiate any legislation or any other action to provide minimum standards in the field of freedom of association and collective bargaining as the Commission considers the realization of these rights to rest with the Member States 'in accordance with their national traditions and policies'. Instead the Commission develops plans for the future of the social dialogue under this heading - see the section on the social dialogue. However, the Commission plans 'a communication' on the development of collective bargaining and collective agreements at the European level with special reference to the resolution of disputes.

Under the heading 'Information, Consultation and Participation', the Commission explores the possibilities for developing instruments laying down general principles concerning information, consultation and participation for employees. In the Commission's view the single market is likely to lead to restructuring of industry and it is important that such changes take place 'in a context which is socially acceptable'. Generalized minimum standards for

consultation would be one way of achieving this objective.
The Commission proposes the following basic principles:

- the establishment of equivalent systems of workers' representation in all European-scale enterprises - as opposed to the world-wide multinational companies targeted by the Vredeling Directive;
- general and periodic information to employees about the development of the enterprise;
- information to the workforce before decisions are taken;
- an obligation for dominant associated undertakings to provide information.

The Commission is also announcing its intention to produce a proposal on equity-sharing and financial participation by workers. Here the Commission is acting on a request by the European Parliament (17). The Commission is proposing to overcome the differences in national traditions in this area by giving Member States a choice of legislating to set up equity sharing systems or leaving this to negotiations between the social partners. Workers can get a share in the equity of their workplace enterprise through:

- a share in the profits capital growth or capital of firms;
- a redistribution to the salaried workers under forms to be negotiated, of a share of the enterprise's results.

The Commission points out that it would be easier to set up equity-sharing schemes if national fiscal procedures could be co-ordinated.

ECOSOC and the Social Dialogue

Consultation with the unions and employers' organizations prior to decisions on employment issues started in the European Coal and Steel Community which was given a permanent committee for consultation with the social partners in the coal and steel industry. Built into the decision-making structure of the EEC is the Economic and Social Committee which has to be consulted by the Commission and the Council on all issues involving employment, economic and social policy. The Commission and Council are in addition free to consult ESCSOC on any issue not specifically covered by the Treaty but deemed appropriate.

The Economic and Social Committee has currently 189 members representing not only the two sides of industry but also a number of other economic interests labelled various activities or the third interest, including representatives of agriculture, the liberal professions, transport and 'representatives of the general public' - i.e. the consumer interest. The members of the committee are nominated by national governments and appointed by the Council. Member States have to nominate twice as many persons as there are seats. The Council consults with the Commission and relevant interest groups established at the European level. The places are distributed between Member States in proportion to size of population.

The Economic and Social Committee is a purely consultative body. In 1972 it was in addition given the right of initiative, so that the Committee now may discuss topical issues without waiting for a proposal from the Commission or Council.

The ECOSOC pronouncements on legislative proposals and the own-initiative reports are called 'Opinions' and are published in the C-series of the Official Journal. ECOSOC has its own secretariat. This issues press releases which are normally not obtainable through the Commission's offices or through European Documentation Centres.

The ECOSOC claims some success in influencing Council decisions in about half of all opinions it has adopted. As most opinions include a number of different points and the ECOSOC counts as a success any opinion where one point has been taken on board by the Council, it must be said that the influence of the Committee so far has been relatively limited.

Belgium, France and the Netherlands (18) have similar permanent constitutional bodies to represent the two sides of industry in talks with their governments about economic and social policy, but most countries in Western Europe have some sort of system for consultation with unions and employers. In those countries which have no permanent machinery for consultation, ad hoc consultation over particular problems takes place from time to time. The machinery for consultations and the issues discussed vary over time and with the political complexion of governments.

Another consultative network has gradually developed in the form of a number of joint sectoral committees. The role of the Advisory Committees is to act as a sounding board for the Commission. Most of these Committees include representatives of the two sides of industry and other interested parties:

1. Advisory Committee on Vocational Training;
2. Advisory Committee on Freedom of Movement for Workers;
3. Advisory Committee on Social Security for Migrant Workers;
4. Advisory Committee on Safety, Hygiene and Health Protection at Work;
5. Advisory Committees for the liberal professions to facilitate implementation of the Directives on the right of establishment and freedom of services;
6. Advisory Committee on Equal Opportunities for Women and Men;
7. ECSC Consultative Committee.

The sectoral joint committees provide a forum for the two sides of industry to comment on developments in the relevant industries. There are currently eight of these committees:

1. Two Mixed Committees on the Harmonization of Working Conditions, one for the coal industry and the other for the steel industry;
2. Sea fishing;
3. Footwear;
4. Inland waterways;
5. Railways;
6. Road transport;
7. Maritime transport;
8. Social problems of agricultural workers.

The old ECSC consultative committee is now one of these. In addition there are informal groups with participation from both sides of industry for certain sectors where agreement between employers and trade unions about setting up committees has not yet been reached.

At the beginning of the 1970s a tripartite Standing Committee on Employment was created in response to demands by the European Confederation of Free and Christian Trade Unions which were supported by UNICE. This Committee consists of representatives of the two sides of industry and the Council and the Commission. The Commission chairs the Committee. The purpose of the Committee is to provide a forum for discussion with the view to achieve basic co-ordination between national and EC employment policies. So far the Committee has discussed measures to combat unemployment policies, training policies, youth unemployment, the reorganization and flexibility of working time, the social consequences of introducing new technology. The Committee's resolutions and reports are published in the C-series of the Official Journal. Although the Committee is now the only forum where the social partners meet with the Community's policy and decision-makers the effectiveness of the Committee has been criticized by the European Trade Union Confederation.

There are also representatives from the two sides of industry on some of the special advisory committees set up to advise the Commission on issues such as vocational training, freedom of movement and social security for migrant workers.

Neither ECOSOC nor the more specialist advisory or sectoral bodies was suitable for consultation on social and employment policy as a whole, nor do they provide a forum where the social partners can meet with governments. For a few years in the 1970s such a forum was provided by the tripartite conferences on employment which included the national Ministers of Labour and Commission representatives and representatives of the two sides of industry. These conferences held annually between 1974 and 1978 mainly focused on employment and growth problems. However, the conferences did not produce concrete results and the European Trade Union Confederation at the end of the 1978 conference threatened to withdraw unless initiatives were taken to give the conferences a chance to produce positive results. The Commission produced proposals to this effect in 1980, but no conferences have been organized since then.

The Social Dialogue nearly ground to a halt during the early 1980s and was revived as part of the single market initiatives. In 1985 the Commission President Jacques Delors set up a forum for dialogue between the social partners at the European level. The first meeting took place in November 1985 at Val Duchesse outside Brussels. The talks are guided by **Article 118A** included in the Treaty by the Single Act. **'The Commission shall endeavour to develop the dialogue between management and labour at European level which could if the two sides consider it desirable, lead to relations based on agreement'.**

The Val Duchesse dialogue has produced three joint opinions agreed by ETUC on the one side and UNICE and CEEP on the other. The first opinion adopted in 1986 was a comment on the Commission's proposed strategy for growth (19). The second opinion dealt with the Community's annual economic report in 1987 (20). The third opinion concerns the introduction of new technology. Current discussions include the divisive issue of adaptability and flexibility. The purpose of the social dialogue is to reach agreement between the two sides of industry at the European level, which could then be presented to and discussed with the two sides of industry at the national level. The procedure for this process is currently under discussion. The hope of the Commission is that the dialogue eventually will lead to formal agreements creating an industrial relations framework for the whole of Europe. The first target is the standardization of the basic legal concepts attached to collective agreements. The Commission is also increasingly seeking to have priorities for future EC action in the whole employment field set by the social partners.

The Commission is examining ways of improving information in the social sphere for certain target groups; directors of small and medium sized businesses, those responsible for staff and industrial relations in forms and regional trade union leaders. The Commission states in the Social Charter action programme: 'It is desirable to improve the present day perception of the problems dealt with at Community level affecting the lives of firms and workers at local and regional level, which are often far removed from Community concerns and initiatives'.

Social partners organized at European level

Trade unions had been organized at the European level before the creation of both the EEC and the ECSC. The European Confederation of Free and Christian Trade Unions was set up in 1947 as a joint organization for Socialist and Christian Democrat trade unions but excluding Communist unions. ECFCTU includes trade unions from the whole of Western Europe rather than just the European Community. The European Trade Union Confederation was set up in 1973, both these organizations share headquarters in Brussels with the free trade union international ICFTU.

In 1977 a trade union research institute was set up, the European Trade Union Institute. ETUI publishes important comparative reports on employment conditions and trade union issues in Western Europe. Employers' associations are organized in two European organizations: the Union of Industrial and Employers Confederations of Europe, UNICE, established in 1958 and the European Centre of Public Enterprise, CEEP. Employers' sectoral organizations cover all major industries. Trade unions are also organized in sectoral organizations with a presence in Brussels. There are, for example, union confederations which organize chemical workers, airline pilots, agricultural workers, construction workers, actors and public servants. (See Appendix 2 for list of addresses).

Notes

(1) Official Journal of the European Communities, No C13, 12/2/74. Official Journal of the European Communication Information and Notices, No C131, 13/12/72.

Employment Policy

(2) Official Journal of the European Communities, No C7, 28/1/72.

(3) Official Journal of the European Communities, No C240, 9/9/83.

(4) Official Journal of the European Communities, No C93 and C124 of 1974.

(5) 4th General Report on the Activities of the Community 1970, p.102.

(6) Official Journal of the European Communities, No C263, 16/10/89.

(7) Official Journal of the European Communities, No C297, 15/11/80.

(8) Official Journal of the European Communities, No C217 12/8/83.

(9) 1st Directive: Disclosure of information (68/151/EEC) 9/3/68 - Official Journal of the European Communities, No L65, 14/3/68.

2nd Directive: Company capital (77/91/EEC) 13/12/76 - Official Journal of the European Communities, No L26, 31/1/77.

3rd Directive: Internal mergers (78/855/EEC) 9/10/78 - Official Journal of the European Communities, No L295, 20/10/78.

4th Directive: Annual accounts (78/660/EEC) 25/7/78 - Official Journal of the European Communities, No L222, 14/8/78.

6th Directive: Company prospectuses (82/891/EEC) 17/12/82 - Official Journal of the European Communities, No L378, 31/12/82.

7th Directive: Group accounts (83/349/EEC) 13/6/83 - Official Journal of the European Communities, No L193, 18/7/83.

8th Directive: Auditor's qualifications (84/253/EEC) 10/4/84 - Official Journal of the European Communities, No L126, 12/5/84.
11th Directive: Disclosure requirements of branches (89/666/EEC) 21/12/89 - Official Journal of the European Communities, No L395, 30/12/89.
12th Directive: Single member private limited companies (89/667/EEC) 22/12/89 - Official Journal of the European Communities, No L395, 30/12/89.

(10) 5th Directive: Company structure and administration. Official Journal of the European Communities, No C240, 9/9/83.
9th Directive: Not yet formally submitted.
10th Directive: Cross-border mergers. Official Journal of the European Communities, No C23, 25/1/85.
13th Directive: Takeover bids (10). Official Journal of the European Communities, No C64, 14/3/89.

(11) Article 4(1), Article 4b(1) and Article 4c(1) for two-tier companies and Article 21b and Article 21d for one-tier companies.

(12) P. Cecchini, 1992 The European Challenge, p.87.

(13) COM(88)320 final, section VIb, Office of Official Publications, 15/7/88.

(14) The Council of Europe Social Charter, Articles 5 and 6.

(15) Ibid., Articles 11 to 14.

(16) Ibid., Articles 17 and 18.

(17) EP Resolution on employee participation in asset

formation - Official Journal of the European Communities, No C307, 2/12/88.

(18) For information on these bodies see G. Smith (1976), 'The representation of group interests' in Politics in Western Europe, Heinemann, London (latest edition 1990).

(19) Official Journal of the European Communities, No 328, 29/12/86.

(20) Official Journal of the European Communities Information and Notices, No C356, 31/12/87.

EQUAL OPPORTUNITIES

The most comprehensive EC legislation in the field of employment has been developed in the area of equal opportunities. Since the mid-1970s almost all aspects of gender equality in employment, education and training have been subject to European Community legislation. As a consequence of EC legislation all EC Member States have since the late 1970s had legislation granting women equal pay for work of equal value and outlawing all gender discrimination in employment and education. Since then, EC work in this field has had two strands: extending the provisions into social security and making the legislation a reality through a number of smaller complementary directives and decisions; and by promoting positive action and access to training.

The commitment to equality between the sexes goes back to 1958 and the Treaty of Rome. The legal base for the European Community's activities in the field of equal opportunities is **Article 119** in the Treaty.

'Each Member State shall during the first stage (1) ensure and subsequently maintain the application of the principle that men and women should receive equal pay for equal work'.

The first international conventions on equal pay were the ILO Convention No 100 relating to equal remuneration for men and women workers for work of equal value signed by governments in 1951 and the ILO Convention No 111 on discrimination in employment and promotion of 1958. Most countries in Western Europe ratified this convention but ILO Conventions, unlike European Community legislation, are not enforceable.

The Treaty of Rome, however, is primary legislation directly enforceable in the Member States, but little effort was made either at the European or at the national levels to enforce the principle of equal pay until the early 1970s. This is not surprising. Both Italy and the Federal Republic of Germany have a commitment to equal pay for men and women included in their Constitutions adopted in 1946 and 1949 respectively (2) without these provisions being enforced until the mid-1970s.

A conference of Member States on the implementation of equal pay was held in December 1961 (3) which adopted a resolution but no action followed. All Member States had sectors of the labour market where pay scales were different for male and female workers doing the same jobs. However, demands for legislation on the right of women to equal pay started in most European countries in the 1950s or early 1960s. Britain was the first country in Western Europe to outlaw pay discrimination on grounds of gender in 1970. France legislated in 1972 and Ireland in 1974.

In the early 1970s the European Commission started to work on a series of Directives on equal pay and other equal opportunities provisions in employment and education. The first declaration of intent was made in the Social Action Programme adopted by the Council in 1974 (4). The Council Directive on the application of the principle of equal pay for men and women was adopted by the Council in 1975 (5). Member States undertook to implement national legislation guaranteeing equal pay for work of equal value to men and women within two years.

The Equal Pay Directive introduced the principle of equal pay for work of **equal value** into EC legislation. ILO Convention No 100 also covered work of equal pay for equal value, but **Article 119** of the Treaty of Rome speaks only of equal pay for equal work.

The Equal Pay Directive was quickly followed by the Directive on the implementation of the principle of equal treatment of men and women in the labour market, adopted by the Council in February 1976, and by the first Directive on the progressive implementation of the principle of equal treatment for men and women in matters of social security, adopted in December 1978, which obliged governments to bring into force the necessary laws, regulations and administrative processes by 1984 (6).

Community Action Programmes

There have been two Community Action Programmes on equal opportunities covering the periods 1982 to 1985 (7) and 1986 to 1990 (8). A new action programme is currently being drafted in the Directorate on Social Affairs.

Under the First Action Programme the Commission produced a draft Directive on parental leave (9) submitted in 1983, which has not yet been adopted by the Council. This draft proposes a right to parental leave for either parent to follow the statutory maternity leave.

In 1982 the Commission submitted a draft Directive on part-time work (10) which at first glance seems gender-neutral. This draft proposes to end wide-spread discrimination of part-time employees in comparison with full-time employees by stipulating that part-timers should have, pro rata, the same rights as full-timers to pay, bonuses, paid leave, sick-pay, occupational pensions, training and promotion. As between 90 and 95 per cent of all part-time employees are women and 28 per cent of all working women in the Community work part-time this proposed Directive is of great importance for achieving equal opportunities for women at work (Figures 7 and 8). This Directive was vetoed by the British government.

The Second Action Programme (1986-1990) included a large number of actions to be taken by the Member States and by Community institutions under the headings:

- Improved application of existing provisions
- Education and training
- Employment
- New technologies
- Social protection
- Sharing family and occupational responsibilities
- Increasing awareness
- Improvement of Community concertation

Under the Second Action Programme the Commission has submitted one draft Directive (11) on the burden of proof in sex discrimination cases in 1988 respectively. The draft Directive on sexual harassment seeks to define sexual harassment and to create an obligation on employers to deal constructively with complaints from women employees. This Directive has not yet been discussed in the Council.

The Burden of Proof Directive splits the burden of proof in sex discrimination cases between the complainant employee and defendant employer. After a prima facie case of unequal treatment has been established it would fall on the employer to show that the reason for this treatment was not the complainant's gender. This draft Directive was discussed by the Council, amended and considerably watered down and then vetoed by the British government in December 1988. Following a **European Parliament Resolution in 1986 on violence against women** (12), which called on national governments to achieve a legal definition of **sexual harassment** and to campaign against it, the Commission set up a research network on sexual harassment. The network found sexual harassment to be a serious problem for many working women across Europe and produced a draft Directive, which was, however, never adopted by the Commission. In the Spring of 1990 the Council adopted a Resolution (13) which: called for action from the Member States; required the Commission to draw up a proposal for a code of conduct; and defined the concept of sexual harassment.

Under the heading 'sharing family and occupational responsibilities', the Commission started to work on a proposal for a Directive setting minimum standards for child-care provisions in Member States, and on a proposal for minimum provisions of maternity leave following a report on provisions in Member States (14). In the face of Member States resistance the Commission instead decided to produce a Code of Conduct (15).

The European Parliament has taken a keen interest in this issue. In a resolution adopted in 1988 the European Parliament (16) urged the Commission to draw up a Directive designed to bring all national regulations and provisions regarding pregnancy, childbirth and parenthood into line **'as far as possible with the regulations and provisions in force in the most advanced Member State'**. The Parliament criticized the Commission's plan to draw up a code of conduct for social protection during motherhood and called for a Directive on this subject.

Finally the Parliament called on the Commission to draw up a Charter on the rights of women in childbirth.

The Second Action Programme includes a very large number of recommendations on actions to be taken by the Member States. As with the First Action Programme, Member States are required to report to the Commission on the progress made in implementing the recommendations. The deadline for these national reports was 1 January 1990. The Commission will publish an assessment of the implementation of the programme by 31 December 1990.

A number of action programmes with more specific targets than the two general programmes discussed above have also been adopted by the Council, with objectives such as combating unemployment among women (17) and equal opportunities for boys and girls in education (18).

The Social Charter

The Social Charter includes a short section on the 'right of men and women to equal treatment' which contains a commitment to develop equal opportunities further. It then proposes 'intensified' action in the following areas:

- remuneration;
- access to employment;
- social protection;
- education and vocational career development.

These are all subjects already covered by Community legislation, action programmes or Recommendations. The commitment to **new** action appears as a reaffirmation and expansion of the objective established already in the 1974 Social Action Programme to develop amenities enabling employees to reconcile their occupational and family obligations more easily.

In the action programme on the implementation of the Social Charter, the Commission sees its task as **'ensuring that formal equality can become genuine equality'**. The Commission stresses that discussions about the three proposed Directives on parental leave, burden of proof and retirement age must be resumed. The action programme lists three new areas where the Commission will develop proposals:

- a Directive on the protection of the health and safety of pregnant women at work;
- a Recommendation concerning child-care;
- a Recommendation concerning a code of good conduct on the protection of pregnancy and maternity, with protection against dismissal, a right of return to employment after maternity leave and protection of accrued rights.

The Commission explains that Member States must carry the primary responsibility for action in the area of child-care, parental leave, etc. For this reason the Commission is intending to propose Council Recommendations rather than Directives. However, the minimum rules covered by the Recommendations would, according to the Commission, 'have to be implemented within a certain time limit'.

Positive action

Positive action is mentioned for the first time in the First Equal Opportunities Action Programme. Two years later the Council adopted a Recommendation with detailed provisions on positive action to be taken by the Member States. The aim of positive action policies is **'to eliminate or counteract prejudicial effects on women in employment...which arise from existing attitudes, behaviour and structures based on the idea of a traditional division of roles in society between men and women'** and to encourage the participation of women in occupations where they are at present under-represented, in the new technologies and at higher levels of responsibility.

In 1988 the Commission published a guide for employers on how to set up and manage a positive action programme (19).

European Court of Justice Rulings

No one tried to invoke **Article 119** to achieve equal pay until 1969, when SABENA air hostess Gabrielle Defrenne, in two separate actions against SABENA, claimed that she had been paid less and had been forced to retire earlier than male cabin staff. In addition she claimed that the pension scheme for aircrews were less favourable for female staff than for men. The Belgian Conseil d'Etat, finding that Dufrenne had no case in Belgian law concerning the discriminatory pension scheme, asked for a preliminary ruling from the European Court of Justice. In the first Defrenne case the Court ruled (20) that statutory social security schemes fall outside the scope of **Article 119**. In the second case concerning equal pay referred by the Belgian Labour Appeal Court, the Court of Justice ruled (21) inter alia **'The principle that men and women should receive equal pay, which is laid down by Article 119, may be relied on before the national courts. These courts have a duty to ensure the protection of the rights which that provision vests in individuals, in particular in the case of those forms of discrimination which have their origin in legislative provisions or collective labour agreements, as well as where men and women receive unequal pay for equal work which is carried out in the same establishment or service, whether private or public'**. The Court also went on to say **'The application of Article 119 was to have been fully secured by the original Member States as from 1 January 1962, the beginning of the second stage of the transitional period, and by the new Member States as from 1 January 1973, the date of entry into force of the Accession Treaty'**.

The Court's ruling that **Article 119** is directly applicable to private sector employers was surprising. Previously it had been assumed that the Treaty only imposed directly enforceable duties on states.

The Court drew a distinction 'between direct and overt discrimination, which may be identified solely with the aid of the criteria based on equal work and equal pay and, indirect and disguised discrimination, which can only be identified by reference to more explicit implementing provisions of a Community or national character'. Direct discrimination **'has its origin in legislative provisions or in collective labour agreements and which may be detected on the basis of a purely legal analysis of the situation. This applies even more in cases where men and women receive unequal pay for equal work carried out in the same establishment or service, whether public or private'.**

Since the Defrenne case there has been a number of equal opportunities cases referred to the Court of Justice for preliminary rulings, where the Court has made important interpretations of the applicability of the **Article 119** and the Directives. Some of these cases have not only been important in the jurisprudence of equal opportunities but have also settled issues concerning the direct applicability of the Treaty on citizens in Member States.

The case of **Macarthys v. Smith** established that the principle of equal pay is valid not only when a women receives less pay than a **contemporary** colleague but also when she is paid less than her male **predecessor** (22). In the case of **Warringham and Humphreys v. Lloyds Bank** the European Court of Justice extended the meaning of the word 'pay' to include employer contributions to a pension scheme (23). In the case of **Jenkins v. Kingsgate** (24) the Court ruled that a difference in hourly pay-rates between full-time workers and part-time workers does not in itself amount to direct discrimination under **Article 119**, but an employer has to justify the different pay rates on objective grounds. The case of **Garland v. British Rail Engineering Ltd** (25) concerned British Rail giving **travel concessions** to families of retired male employees but not to families of retired women employees. The Court ruled that this constituted discrimination within the meaning of **Article 119**. In the **Bilka** case (26) the Court ruled that **occupational pension schemes** are a benefit related to pay and that excluding part-timers who are mainly female from a firm's pension scheme amounts to discrimination unless it can be attributed to objectively justified factors not related to gender. In the case of **Murphy and others v. Bord Telecom Eireann** (27) concerning a claim for work of equal value, it was established that the fact that women's jobs in a job evaluation were found to be **more** valuable than the jobs of the men with whom the women claimed equal pay could not stop the women's claim for equal pay. Although the Irish equal opportunities legislation by the Irish Court was found not to cover this possibility, the European Court ruled that **Article 119** was directly applicable. A Danish collective agreement was found to be in violation of the equal pay provisions in the **Danfoss** case. The collective agreement provided for a fixed minimum pay rate but left employers free to make additional pay increases to individual workers based on capacity or responsibility. The firm Danfoss was found to have paid more bonuses to male staff than to female staff and was therefore taken to Court by the Union (28).

There has also been a number of cases concerning discrimination in social security. In the case of **Drake v. Chief Adjudication Officer** (29), the Court found that paying an **invalid care allowance** to men and unmarried women only but not to married women when they care full-time for handicapped member of the family is discrimination. In the case of **Marshall v. South-West Hampshire Area Health Authority** (30), the Court ruled that although the first Social Security Directive explicitly excludes retirement pensions from its application, forcing women to retire earlier than men is a violation of the Equal Treatment Directive. However, in the absence of national legislation to implement this particular provision, the Directive, unlike the Treaty, only has direct effect on public employers. In this case the British government quickly amended national pension legislation to permit women to stay on in employment until the male retirement age, should they so wish. This ruling is particularly important for all women with a broken pension record, who by staying on in work for another five years until the male retirement age can increase their final pension.

In the British social security system, married women who had to give up work due to long-term illness would only qualify for **invalidity pension** if they could prove that the illness also prevented them from carrying out normal household duties. The Court declared this provision to be in breach of the social security Directive in the **Clarke v. Chief Adjudication Officer** case (31). Exclusion of married women, who leave work to look after ill or disabled relatives, from the disability care allowance which is paid to men and unmarried women in a similar situation was declared illegal in the **Drake** case.

The case of the **Dutch Trade Union Movement v. the Dutch Government** (32) concerned discriminatory rules on **unemployment and supplementary benefits.** The Court ruled that until such time as the national government adopts the necessary implementing measures, women are entitled under the First Social Security Directive to have the same rules applied to them as men, **'since where the Directive has not been implemented, those rules remain the only valid point of reference'.** In this case the Advocate General expressly stated that equal treatment may be achieved by levelling down rather than levelling up.

The case of **Teuling v. Bedrijfsvereniging** (33) resolved the question as to whether it is lawful under **Article 4(1)** of the Social Security Directive to include a supplement for dependent spouses in invalidity and unemployment benefits, although significantly more married men than married women receive this supplement. The Court ruled that Community law does not prevent a Member State which wishes to control its social security expenditure from taking into account that the needs of claimants with dependent spouses, i.e. supplements for defendants, are permissible. Indirectly this ruling also confirms that 'levelling down' is permissible.

Institutions

The European Commission's work on equal opportunities and women's rights is managed by the small **Bureau of Equal Opportunities for Men and Women in Employment** which is part of Directorate General V - Social Affairs. The Bureau consults with the Advisory Committee on Women's Rights which consists of the chairs of the equal opportunities bodies in the Member States. Each country has two representatives. This Committee usually meets four times a year and comments on national developments in the field of equal opportunities, and on all Commission proposals in the field. There is also a **Women's Information Service,** which is part of **Directorate General X - Information, Communication and Culture.** This service publishes a bi-monthly free news bulletin, started in 1977 in response to requests from women's organizations at a colloquium in Brussels a year earlier. The bulletin Women of Europe covers the development of social policy and equal opportunities both at the EC and national level. It also carries information on future conferences and contact addresses of equal opportunities bodies, women's organizations and researchers. Women of Europe is mailed free to anyone requesting to be added to the mailing list (see Bibliography for further details)

European elections since 1979 have produced a larger proportion of women members than any of the national parliaments, with the exception of the Danish Parliament (34). After the first direct elections, the newly elected women members insisted that a Parliamentary Standing Committee on Women's Rights/Affairs should be set up. Originally Parliament only agreed to a temporary committee to be set up for the purpose of making a special report on the situation of women in Europe. Dame Shelagh Roberts was appointed rapporteur. The comprehensive report was published in 1983.

After the 1984 elections the Committee was made permanent. All Commission proposals with implications for equal opportunities and for women are discussed by this Committee before reaching the Parliament's plenary session.

Race and ethnic origin

The Community equal opportunities policies concern only gender and do not cover discrimination on the grounds of race, ethnic origin, religion, disability, etc. The prohibition against discrimination in the Treaty - **Article 7** - outlaws discrimination against a Community citizen in other Member States. It does not seem to be concerned with discrimination between EC citizens within their own countries, and does certainly not give non-EC citizens any rights. However, in recent years the rise of the new Right in France and their election to the European Parliament has triggered a concern to protect both EC ethnic minorities such as Jews and gypsies and non-EC migrants. The European Parliament has adopted a couple of resolutions concerning the needs of non-EC immigrants and also a resolution on racism and xenophobia. The Council has also adopted a resolution condemning racism and xenophobia. Some of the EC funding programmes, such as the anti-poverty programme, specifically target migrant communities. However, the Social Charter makes no mention of non-EC migrants or other ethnic minorities and there seems to be no intention to start work on equal opportunities legislation for black and ethnic minorities.

Notes

(1) The first stage - the first part of the transition period of setting up the EEC. The first stage was finished on 31/12/61.

(2) Italy: Article 37; Germany Article 3(2) and (3).

(3) 30 December 1961.

(4) Official Journal of the European Communities, No C13, 12/2/74.

(5) 75/117/EEC, Official Journal of the European Communities, No L45, 19/2/75.

(6) 76/207/EEC, Official Journal of the European Communities, Nos L39 of 14/2/76 and 79/7/EEC, L6 10/1/79.

(7) Official Journal of the European Communities, No C186, 21/7/82.

(8) Official Journal of the European Communities, No C203, 12/8/86. The action programme is presented in detail in Women of Europe - Supplement No 23.

(9) COM(83) 631 final.

(10) Official Journal of the European Communities, No C18, 22/1/83.

(11) COM(88) 269 final, Office of the Official Publications of the EC, 24/5/88.

(12) Official Journal of the European Communities, No C176, 14/7/86.

(13) 23 May 1990.

(14) Report on the protection of working women during pregnancy and motherhood in the Member States by Dagmar Coester-Waltjen - V-1829/84.

(15) V/323/86.

(16) Adopted 8/7/88 - European Communities European Parliament Reports, PE DOC A 2-38/88 - Official Journal of the European Communities, No C235, 12/9/88.

(17) Reprinted in Social Europe, Vol 1/1990.

(18) Official Journal of the European Communities, No C166, 5/7/85.

(19) Commission Documents COM(88) 370 final, 30/6/88.

(20) Case 80/70, First Defrenne case, 23 May 1971. ECR (1971) p.445.

(21) Case 43/75, Second Defrenne case, 8 April 1976. ECR (1976) p.454.

(22) Case 129/79, Macarthys Limited v. Smith, ECR (1980) p.1275.

(23) Case 69/80, Warringham and Humphreys v. Lloyds Bank, ECR (1981) p.767.

(24) Case 96/80, Jenkins v. Kingsgate, ECR (1981) p.911.

Employment Policy

(25) Case 12/81, Garland v. British Rail Engineering, ECR (1982) p.359.

(26) Case 170/84, Bilka Kaufhaus GmbH v. Karin Weber von Hartz. Judgment 13/5/86. ECR (1986) p.1607.

(27) Case 157/86, Murphy and others v. Bord Telecom Eireann. Judgment 4/2/88. Official Journal of the European Communities, No C63, 8/3/88.

(28) Case 109/88, Danfoss A/C v. Handels og Kontorfunktionaerernes Forbund. Judgment 17/10/89. Official Journal of the European Communities, No C289, 17/11/89.

(29) Case 150/85, Drake v. Chief Adjudication Officer. Judgment 24/6/86. ECR (1986) p.2002.

(30) Case 76/207, Marshall v. South-West Hampshire Area Health Authority. A good summary of this case is found in the ECR B No 308, 8/7/86.

(31) Case 384/85, Borrie-Clarke v. Chief Adjudication Officer. Judgment 24/6/87. Official Journal of the European Communities, No C188, 17/7/87.

(32) Case 71/85, Federatie Nederlandse Vakbevegingen (FNV) v. The Netherlands. Judgment 4/12/86. ECR (1986) p.3870.

(33) Case 30/85, Teuling v. Bedrijfsvereniging voor Chemische Industrie. Judgment 11/6/87. ECR (1987) p.2516.

(34) The proportion of women in the European Parliament after each election: 1979 - 16 per cent; 1984 - 17 per cent; 1989 - 19 per cent.

FREEDOM OF MOVEMENT

Freedom of movement concerns both freedom for EC nationals to travel freely within the Community's territory and freedom to move, live and work in another EC country. Freedom of movement of labour was an integral part of the Common Market; one of the core objectives of the European Community along with the freedom of movement of goods and of capital.

The concept has changed over the thirty years of the EC's existence, from an emphasis on employers' rights to recruit labour from the Member States in an era of labour shortage, to a right for individuals to move in search of work in an era of unemployment.

Further facilitation of free movement of persons is now part of the 'People's Europe' programme which seeks to make the Community mean something to the ordinary citizen. Actual movements of EC citizens have also changed fundamentally over the last thirty years. In the 1950s and 1960s mass migration from the south of Europe to the north and from rural to urban areas. The recession of the 1970s and increasing prosperity in the Mediterranean countries and Portugal have stopped this internal movement in Western Europe.

The European Single Market includes the completion of the citizen's right to move freely within the Community. The intention is to create a single Community labour market. This may lead to a new increase in the number of Europeans who seek employment or self-employment outside their native country, but this will not be mass-migration of unskilled labour from south to north, but skilled people moving in all directions. The new migrants may also stay for shorter periods than the migrants of the 1960s who often stayed for life whatever their intentions may have been when they arrived.

Freedom of Movement in the Treaties

Free movement is extensively regulated in the EEC Treaty. **Article 3(c)** of the Treaty states that one of the European Community's aims is to abolish obstacles to the free movement of persons. **Article 7** prohibits discrimination on grounds of nationality between EC citizens. **Article 48** establishes the right for individuals to take up employment or to work as self-employed workers in any EC country without discrimination. This right is limited only on grounds of public policy, public security and public health. **Article 49** requires the Council to adopt Directives to abolish restrictive employment practices in Member States which limit the right of foreign EC nationals. **Article 50** requires the Council to legislate to give migrant EC workers social security rights in the host country.

Article 52 gives EC nationals the right of establishment. An EC national can either set up an undertaking in any other EC country or set up as a self-employed professional. The activity can either be a principal activity or a secondary activity such as setting up an agency, branch or subsidiary. **Article 59** lays down the freedom to provide services across national boundaries, for example by travelling to a client in another country or by having a client visiting the country where the service provider is established. **Article 51** requires Member States to encourage the exchange of young workers.

Obstacles in a number of different areas had to be removed to make moving to another country in search of work a realistic option. First, the requirement of a work permit to take up employment was abolished and right of residence for EC nationals employed in another EC country established. Secondly, workers need the right to bring their families and dependants. Thirdly, detailed legislation was required to give migrant workers full social security protection. Migrant workers' children were given the right to go to school in the host country. Finally, for freedom of movement to be a reality for skilled workers and professionals their qualifications had to be made acceptable to other countries. Of less importance, but problematic enough in individual cases, are rules about double taxation and the right to move household belongings to the new country of employment.

Visa requirements for nationals of West European countries travelling to other countries in the region were abolished before the setting up of the EC. EC citizens have the right to enter other EC countries on presentation of a passport or an identity card. Work permits were abolished for EC citizens seeking employment in other EC countries during the 1960s. Full freedom of movement for EC nationals, including the abolition of internal border controls, is now part both of the internal market programme and the programme for 'A People's Europe'.

However, the freedom to move and remain for longer than three months in another country has until now been limited to people who are economically active - either in employment or in self-employment. The EEC Treaty only covers freedom of movement for the purpose of employment and self-employment. The arguments for free movement of labour were at the inception of the Community very much the same as the arguments about the relative economic advantage of free movement of goods. Labour should be free to move and employers free to recruit from areas with surplus labour i.e. unemployment and low pay, to areas with labour shortages and higher wages. Apart from the migrant worker's dependents, movement of people for other purposes than employment was originally not considered.

In addition, although the right of residence and relatively comprehensive social security rights were established either in the Treaties or through Regulation early on, a number of obstacles to real freedom of movement remained. The most important of these was the lack of harmonization of qualifications. The right to take up employment or self-employment in another EC country has been subject to the migrant's qualifications being recognized by the Member States and, despite many years of efforts to harmonize qualifications between Member States, very limited success had been achieved until the single market programme was launched in 1985. There was also a number of minor bureaucratic obstacles encountered by people moving to another EC country.

The internal market programme includes proposals to make freedom of movement a reality for EC nationals who are not economically active. A new draft Directive covering residence rights for students, pensioners and other 'non-active' Community citizens has now been submitted. Another important part of the single market programme is the mutual recognition of qualifications to open the European labour market to professionals and other skilled workers. There are also moves to simplify the bureaucracy involved in obtaining residence permits.

Freedom of movement has always been limited to citizens of Community countries only. Non-EC citizens who have rights of residence in one EC country have no right to enter other EC countries. There are no single market proposals in this area, but, as a consequence of the proposals to abolish border controls, the Ministers of the Interior in the Member States have opened negotiations outside the European Community decision-making machinery to achieve harmonization on migration regulations for non-EC citizens between Member States.

Right of Entry

Community nationals have the right to enter any EC country on presentation of their identity card or passport. No other document is required. They have the right to remain for three months for whatever purpose.

The first small step towards relaxing internal border controls for EC nationals was the decision to permit the use of national identity cards as travel documents within the European Community. It might seem surprising that a common passport union has been placed relatively low on the agenda of European integration as the Nordic countries in their much looser and more informal integration process had created a common passport union as early as 1954, long before they established a Nordic Council of Ministers. The Benelux countries did likewise in 1960. The possibility of establishing a passport union was first approached by the Council in 1974 (1), when it requested a study on this issue. In 1975 the Council agreed to the introduction of a standard passport (2). The formal decision was not taken until June 1981, when Member States undertook to start issuing this passport from 1 January 1985. However, Britain and the Netherlands did not do so until 1989. These passports are still national passports issued by national authorities, but in a common European format and colour. In 1984 the Council also adopted a Resolution recommending that border posts should have special checkpoints or channels for EC nationals and that the frontier formalities should be limited to spot checks. These decisions were part of the recommendations made in the Adonnino reports on 'A People's Europe (3).

The failure to progress towards passport union led five countries; France, Germany and the Benelux countries; to try to abolish internal frontier controls on their own. These countries agreed on a Convention in 1985 - the so-called Schengen Convention - which adopted the principle of visual checks at road frontiers between the five countries. Since then the Schengen countries have been working on a second Convention to achieve the abolition of internal frontiers controls. However in the Autumn of 1989, when the second Convention was ready to be signed, the talks broke down due to an unexpected complication: mass migration from the German Democratic Republic to the Federal Republic of Germany. According to the Federal Republic's constitution, citizens of the GDR automatically acquire full citizenship rights in the Federal Republic. The other signatory parties did not want to grant automatic freedom of movement to these new arrivals and, potentially, to the total GDR population of 17 million. The Federal Republic was on the other hand not prepared to impose restrictions on people who since the birth of the Republic have been regarded as full citizens - no different from Germans from any other part of Germany. Another factor in the delay in implementing the Schengen Convention was alarm among parliamentarians, particularly in the Netherlands - the only country where the original Schengen agreement was debated in Parliament - about restrictions in the rights of asylum seekers and other travellers from non-EC countries. The second Schengen Convention was signed on 19 June 1990.

Here lies the main problem for abolition of internal frontier controls: agreement must be reached about immigration regulations - including the treatment of asylum seekers - at the joint external EC borders. The European

Council has called for a Decision before the end of 1990 on two Conventions on these topics, which by April 1990 had not yet been submitted as proposals by the Commission (4).

Simplification of travel procedures has led to the introduction of a 'green disc' for cars in a number of Member States. There is also a proposal for a Community medical card to facilitate the formalities now surrounding the right to get emergency medical care for travellers in EC countries. A Directive of 1980 (5) introduced a Community model driver's licence. EC countries now accept each other's drivers' licences but immigrants have to exchange their licence for one issued by the host country after one year of residence. The Commission has proposed a standardization of driving tests to avoid this obligation (6).

Rights of Residence

The EC citizen's right to remain in another EC country for more than three months is still limited. EC citizens have the right to reside in another member country for longer periods only if they are pursuing or intending to pursue an occupational activity.

The first Directives and Regulations adopted in the 1960s regulated the conditions and the procedure under which EC nationals could enter another Community country to take up employment (7). Article 48 stipulates that Member States cannot refuse entry to an EC national who comes to take up employment or in search of employment except with reference to public order, public safety and health. Member States were prohibited from requiring EC citizens to apply for work permits before taking up employment in Regulation (EEC) No 1612/68 (8) and in Council Directive 68/360/EEC on abolition of restrictions on movement and residence in the Community for workers and their families (9). This Regulation also outlawed other restrictions on recruitment of foreign EC nationals for employment and stipulated that employment conditions with regard to qualifications, pay, dismissal and trade union membership have to be the same for foreign EC workers as for nationals.

Employment Policy

An EC immigrant with a job has the right to a renewable five-year residence permit. The permit is issued when the worker provides a 'declaration from the employer or a certificate of employment' (10). A migrant worker without a job has the right to remain for three months while looking for work (11). A worker has also got the right to remain after he or she has become unemployed or retired from employment in the host country (12).

The EC national has also got the right to bring his/her spouse, his or his wife's dependent children and his and his wife's dependent parents and any other dependant in the direct descendant or ascendant line. This right is equally valid for spouses and children who are not nationals of a Member State. Both spouse and children have the right to seek employment without the need to acquire work permits.

To bring a spouse the migrant needs to be employed. Another Court case has established that part-time employment qualifies a person to bring a spouse - provided that the employment is genuine and not taken up only for the purpose of acquiring residence rights for spouse of dependants (13). Children are counted as dependants up to the age of 18, now the age of legal majority right across the Community. Spouses and children of migrant workers have the right to take up employment and children have the same right to education as native children. These provisions, however, do not eliminate the need for EC nationals to register according to the rules of the host country. The bureaucracy surrounding the move to another Community country can still be daunting.

Although EC students have the right to study in another Community country and a right of residence for the period they are enrolled at a school, college or university, this period of residence does not qualify them for future citizenship - unlike any period of residence granted for the purpose of employment.

The Adonnino Report on 'A People's Europe' proposed full freedom of movement for all EC citizens. The European Council meeting in Brussels in March 1985 approved the proposals in the Report. The European Council in the Hague in June 1986 called on the Council of Ministers to give special attention to implementing the proposals in 'A People's Europe'. The European Council meeting in London in December the same year and in Hanover in 1988 repeated this request.

In 1979 the Commission presented its first proposals on extending the right of residence in any Community country to EC nationals over 18 who have not yet got that right in existing EC law. This proposal was then amended a number of times in the 1980s (14). However, it has turned out to be impossible to reach unanimity in the Council of Ministers on any of these proposals. The Council meeting on the internal market in April 1989 came to the conclusion that failing new initiatives further discussions were doomed to failure.

The main problem has been some governments' fear of large numbers of pensioners from southern Europe choosing to live in those European countries which have better health and welfare services. Recently some Mediterranean countries have also voiced alarm at the possibility of people from Northern Europe retiring to the Mediterranean and eventually becoming a burden on the local medical and social services.

The Commission withdrew its 1979 proposal and instead submitted three different draft Directives (15), each concerned with one of the three groups currently not having automatic right of residence: students, pensioners and 'other non-active persons'. The previous Commission proposals required unanimity in the Council to be adopted. The new proposals fell under the Single European Act procedure (16) which gives the European Parliament a greater role and permitted the final adoption of the Directives by a majority vote on 28 June 1990.

The basic principle of all three Directives is that Member States are permitted to subject the right of residence for these groups to the condition that beneficiaries are members of a sickness insurance scheme in their country of origin or subscribe to a private insurance scheme. Migrants must also show that they have the financial means to support themselves at a higher level than the social assistance payments in the host country. It should be noted that invalidity benefits, sickpay and pensions, but not unemployment benefits, already are portable from one member country to another under Community law.

Public Health and Public Safety

The only grounds on which entry and residence can be refused a Community citizen are public policy, public health and public security (**Article 48**). The public health restriction operates only at the time of entry. A worker cannot be expelled from the host country on the grounds of disease. Refusal of entry or residence or expulsion on grounds of public policy can only be based on the behaviour of an individual. It cannot be based on economic reasons. Conviction for a criminal offence may not automatically lead to expulsion. However, a person's past convictions can be cause for refusal of entry or expulsion if they reveal personal behaviour constituting a potential threat to public policy or security.

European Clearing House for Vacancies

Regulation No 1612/68 established an obligation for the Member States to exchange information on vacancies and applications which have not been filled at the national level. In 1972 an information exchange for job vacancies was set up - the European system for the international clearing of vacancies and applications for employment, SEDOC (17). However, SEDOC, created for a situation of labour shortage, is not meeting current needs. The Commission has therefore declared the intention to reform SEDOC.

Mutual Recognition of Qualifications

The largest proportion of migration of labour from one Community country to another has been made by unskilled and semi-skilled people. For professionals the only way to practise in another country has often been to qualify in that country. The Commission started work on proposals to harmonize specific qualifications in the mid- to late 1960s. To get agreement between even the original six member countries turned out to be difficult. The Commission's efforts resulted in a series of Directives adopted in the 1970s, mainly in the area of medical and related qualifications. These Directives concerned doctors (1975), nurses in general care (1977), dentists (1978), veterinary surgeons (1978), midwives (1980), architects (1985), pharmacists (1985) and doctors in general practice (1986) (18). The difficulties involved in harmonization of qualifications are illustrated by the fact that the first proposal to harmonize architects' qualifications was submitted in 1968. The first proposal concerning engineering qualifications was submitted at the same time and has not yet been adopted.

In the field of self-employment a number of Directives has been adopted covering occupations such as hairdressers (1982) and insurance agents and brokers (1977) (19). To exercise an occupation in another country it is sufficient for an EC national to prove that he or she has practised this occupation in the country of origin for the periods laid down in the Directives. There are also Directives covering the right to establish in the wholesale trade, intermediaries in commerce, industry and craft occupations, retail trade and personal service, food industry, wholesale coal trade, toxic products and itinerant activities.

The list of professions and occupations where agreement about harmonization has been achieved is the rather limited result of two and a half decades of work by the Commission in this area. A new approach was clearly required to achieve the results required by the single market programme. The Commission is now using the same method as in the field of technical standards: mutual recognition of existing national qualifications rather than harmonization. The first Directive to be adopted under the new system dealt with recognized professions requiring at least three years' post-secondary studies (20). Member States are obliged to accept these qualifications but may under certain circumstances either require an examination/test or a period of practice in the host country (see also Section II). This Directive covers only professions which require official recognition in Member States, such as lawyers, accountants, architects, medical doctors. The Directive amends the Directives previously adopted on specific professions. A supplementary Directive was adopted at the same time extending the system of mutual recognition to qualifications in the recognized professions obtained by EC nationals in non-EC countries (21). It should be noted that recognition is not extended to non-EC nationals with these qualifications.

Without waiting for the Directive to come into force in January 1991, the Commission has started talks with the authorities in the Member States responsible for implementing the new system, so as to co-ordinate their interpretation of the Directive when drafting national transposition measures (22).

The Commission is now working on a second Directive on professions and occupations which require less than three years' studies (23).

In 1985 the Council requested that the Commission should develop a 'correlation of vocational training qualifications' for a certain number of professional activities (24). To implement this decision the European Centre for Development of Vocational Training, CEDEFOP, is currently involved in carrying out the listing and comparison of the national structures of qualifications in specific occupational areas such as electrical engineering. The result of work on five professions was published in 1989 (25). This is not legislation and does not provide new rights for migrant workers in these fields, but is a preparation for mutual recognition of qualifications. A glance at these comparisons reveals the great variety of secondary and post-secondary education and training systems in Member States and the difficulties facing EC legislators. The intention of the Commission is that in the future any worker who has achieved a recognized national qualification will be issued with a European vocational training card valid across the Community.

Employment in Public Service Exemption

The right to take up employment in another member country is limited by **Article 48(4)** of the Treaty, which reserves access to employment in public services to nationals. The Court of Justice has ruled that this reservation should be given a limited interpretation. Only posts which involve the exercise of powers conferred by public law should be reserved for nationals (26). Following the jurisprudence of the Court, the Commission has stated that the exemptions in **Article 48(4)** definitely apply to the armed forces, police, courts, tax authorities, the diplomatic services, and State Ministers. The exemption also applies to regional government and central banks. The Commission is choosing to approach this area of liberalization cautiously, in stages. The Commission has selected four sectors of the public service for an initial liberalization effort:

- bodies charged with managing a commercial service, public transport and the provision of gas and electricity;
- public health;
- teaching in public sector education;
- research in public establishments, with the exception of defence research.

The Commission is starting by preparing a report on how this type of bodies operates and on the legislation, regulations and statutes which regulate them.

Social Security Rights for Migrants

The Treaties give migrating EC nationals the same right to social security benefits as the nationals of the host country. **Article 51** also gives EC nationals working in another country the right to aggregate periods spent working in different countries for the purpose of qualifying for a pension and other benefits which require a record of having been insured over time.

The main law in this area is the much amended Regulation (EEC) No 1408/71. This Regulation does not seek to harmonize social security systems - a task achievable if at all only in the very long term. It regulates the transfer from one social security system to another. The basic principles are as follows:

1. Migrant workers are normally covered by the social security system in the country where they work, both

with regard to contributions and benefits on the same conditions as natives of the host country.

2. Qualifying periods for pensions, invalidity benefits and unemployment benefits earned in one country are portable to other EC countries according to the rules about aggregation. This means that where a benefit is conditional on a certain period of insurance having been completed, for example unemployment benefits, a period worked in one country is added to the qualifying period in the current host country if the worker becomes unemployed.

The detailed rules of how to calculate a pension earned through employment in two or more EC countries are extremely complicated. The basic principle is that the insurance institution in each country calculates the pension earned by the worker as a proportion of the full pension the migrant worker would have earned if he had a full employment record in that country. A person who has worked for ten years in a particular country would be entitled to one-third of the full pension earned during thirty years of working life. This pension is then added to any pension rights earned in other countries.

Sickpay is portable and will be paid even, for example, if the worker returns to his country of origin to be nursed by his family. Benefits in kind, such as medical treatment, are provided in the country of residence.

Unemployment benefits are normally not portable, but an unemployed person may continue to draw benefit if he is authorized by the host country's social security authorities to seek employment in another country.

Migrant workers also have a general right to the same treatment as nationals to other types of benefits such as social assistance and cheap travel for pensioners and large families.

The Social Charter

The Social Charter contains a reiteration of the basic principles of freedom of movement within the Community and to equal treatment of Community citizens who work in another EC country. The only new item in this section follows directly from the fact that the single market is being opened for services. Clause 6 states that contracting and sub-contracting of services, which leads to workers from one state performing temporary jobs in another state, cannot be an obstacle to the principles of equal treatment with workers of the host country, especially in relation to pay and social benefits. This provision is intended to prevent a particular type of social dumping where a contractor with labour from a low-wage country bids for contracts in high-wage countries.

In the action programme for the implementation of the Social Charter, the Commission flags up three remaining areas of reform:

- co-ordination of supplementary social security schemes which are currently not portable from one country to another;
- improving mobility in frontier regions;
- protection of workers of employers involved in contracts for services in other Member States.

The Commission also intends to amend an existing Regulation and two existing Directives on the right of residence:

- Revision of Commission Regulation No 1251/70 of 29 June 1970 on the right of workers to remain on the territory of a Member State after having been employed in that state.

- Revision of Regulation No 1612/68 on the free movement of workers and their families.

- Revision of Directive No 68/360/EEC on the abolition of restrictions on movement and residence within the EC for workers and their families (27).

The Commission intends to extend the right to equal treatment in social security matters to persons who are currently not covered: public servants, students and non-active persons.

In order to protect workers of employers who provide contracted or sub-contracted services in another member country the Commission states its intention to propose appropriate Community instruments to ensure the application of the following principles on such contracts:

- application of national legislation on public order;
- respect for generally binding collective agreements.

The Commission also intends to strengthen the provisions against social dumping in the Works Directive (28) and the Supplies Directive on public procurement (29) and to introduce a 'transparency clause' into the Works Directive whereby the contracting authority may provide tenderers with the necessary information concerning working conditions in the area concerned. The Commission is also considering the possibility of introducing a social clause in public contracts.

Right to Education and Training

Both the migrant EC national and his or her children have the right to education and training on the same conditions as the nationals of the host country.

A Directive has also been adopted requiring Member States to provide education in the home language and culture within the ordinary school system for migrant workers' children (30). Some countries such as Denmark, Germany and the Netherlands have provided such training for migrants' children both from other Community countries and from third countries for decades. However, the Commission has had some difficulties in achieving general acceptance of such programmes.

EC students have for some time had the right to enter schools, colleges and universities in other member countries on the same conditions as native students. They cannot be charged higher fees or be required to have better entry qualifications than the host country's nationals. In the UK where very substantial fees are charged for further and higher education, these fees are paid by the local authority in which the student is resident. The prohibition on charging EC students higher fees than British students has, after a case in the Court of Justice (31), meant that students from other EC countries wanting to study in the UK have their fees paid by the British government.

Taxation

Co-ordination of taxation of migrants to avoid double taxation is not covered by EC Regulations but by the general network of bilateral double taxation treaties which has been created since the Second World War. The Commission submitted a proposal for a Council Directive concerning the harmonization of income taxation provisions for workers moving within the EC area.

Two Regulations from 1984 provide freedom from VAT and other taxation for the import of personal property when an EC national moves household from one country to another (32).

Political rights

The migrant worker's rights do not extend to the right to vote in general elections in the host country. **Article 123** which requires a uniform electoral system to be introduced for elections to the European Parliament also requires voting rights to be given to all EC nationals wherever they may reside in the Community. However, it has been politically difficult to achieve agreement about implementation of **Article 123**. The main difficulty in providing voting rights in the country of residence for migrant workers has been the reluctance of Luxembourg, where one-third of the total labour force consists of workers from other EC countries, to accept that these workers should have voting rights in Luxembourg. However Ireland gives voting rights in European elections to all EC nationals resident in Ireland. France therefore grants Irish citizens in France reciprocal rights in European elections. Irish people resident in the UK have had full political rights since the creation of the Republic. Some countries such as Italy and Greece grant their emigrants the right to vote in general and European elections. Other countries remove voting rights from emigrants after a certain period of absence. The Commission is favouring the introduction of the right to vote in local elections to all EC nationals resident in another EC country (33).

Three countries already grant immigrants voting rights in local elections: Denmark after three years, Ireland after six months and the Netherlands after five years of residence. In Germany voting rights for migrants in local elections have been discussed for some time.

Exchange Programmes

There are a number of Community programmes to encourage and fund exchange programmes to give Community nationals the opportunity to experience life in other countries. Most of these are directed to enable young Europeans to travel, study and work in other countries. The Adonnino Report states: **'Action at Community level to encourage exchanges of young people between different Member States helps to promote the identity of Europe for young Europeans'**. Some of these programmes go back quite a long time.

The oldest programme finances exchange of young workers. The first programme was adopted in 1964. The current third programme was adopted in 1984 and has just been extended to 1991. In this programme participation is extended to young unemployed people (34). The ERASMUS programme finances university students who want to take part of their degree in another Member State. The COMETT programme, which aims to encourage the development of application of new technology through joint development of training programmes which bring universities and private enterprise together, has encouragement of exchanges as a large component. The LINGUA programme which starts in 1990 funds educational exchanges and other measures of which the purpose is to promote the learning of European languages. An action programme called Youth for Europe for general youth exchanges was adopted in 1988. These programmes are dealt with in detail in another volume in this series, Youth Policy (35).

A number of programmes which have another primary objective also contain an element of assistance towards exchanges. This is true for IRIS, a programme to develop the access of women to vocational training and EURYDICE, a programme for exchange of information on national education systems between education officials. Even the European anti-poverty programme which funds pilot programmes of Community action for certain underprivileged groups involves the staff of the pilot projects in exchange visits with one another. The times are long gone when only diplomats and exporters were involved with Europe in their daily work. There is now a very large body of EC nationals in all walks of life who have a European dimension to their job, from teachers and social workers to local government officers and officers in voluntary organizations.

Migration within the Community

Despite the fact that the most important steps towards freedom of movement had been taken up by late 1960s, the number of EC citizens who have made use of this freedom has been limited. The most important obstacles to freedom of movement which cannot be eliminated through legislation are the barriers posed by the different languages and cultures in member countries.

As a result, the proportion of European citizens who live and work in another EC country is relatively small. It is estimated that approximately 2 million EC citizens live in countries other than their country of origin. In fact, in all EC countries, except Belgium, Luxembourg and France, homes of the majority of EC institutions, and Ireland with its open borders to the UK, the number of migrant workers who originate from non-EC countries exceeds the number of EC citizens (Figure 23). In addition it should be noted the a large proportion of those now counted as internal Community migrants arrived in their host countries as non-EC migrants before Greece, Portugal and Spain joined the European Community in 1981 and 1986 respectively.

Further, freedom of movement from the new member countries (Greece, Portugal and Spain), traditional suppliers of migrant workers for the rest of Western Europe, has been limited by the imposition of long transition periods before full freedom of movement is granted to migrants from these countries. The transition period for Greece has now run out but free movement for citizens of Spain and Portugal will not be achieved until 1993.

However, the ending of the limitation on emigration to other EC countries by Portuguese and Spanish citizens is unlikely to lead to large movements of people. The era of large-scale movement of unskilled labour from Southern to Northern Europe is over. Greece, Portugal and Spain now have a small immigration surplus (Figure 24). Only Ireland still exports people, most of whom come to the UK.

The increased opportunities of free movement created by the single market is very unlikely to produce movements of unskilled labour. Instead it is expected to lead to increased movement of skilled people and specialists, many of whom may be seeking relatively short periods of work experience in other countries. The shortage of skilled workers caused by the reduction in the birth rate in Western Europe may in the future be filled by workers from Eastern Europe.

Non-EC Citizens

Although the Articles on freedom of movement in the EEC Treaty use the word 'persons' and not the word 'citizens' or 'nationals', the right to move freely within the European Community does not extend to non-EC citizens with residence in EC countries. A Turkish citizen resident in the UK for example usually still needs a visa to visit the Netherlands or France. EC Member States have very different rules for entry of third-country aliens. They also have very different rules for the acquisition of citizenship by immigrants.

Traditionally European countries have given preferential treatment to inhabitants of their former colonies and attracted large numbers of non-Community workers from the 1950s to the early 1970s. Indeed many economists claim that the economic boom in Western Europe in the post-war era would not have been possible without this import of labour (36).

Immigration of non-EC nationals has been strictly controlled by all countries in Western Europe since the Second World War. Immigrants require visas, residence permits and work permits. During the boom years of the 1960s there were, despite these controls, large movements of people from Yugoslavia, Turkey and the Arab Mediterranean states to Germany, the Benelux and the Nordic countries and of people from former colonies to France and the UK. The recession of the 1970s meant an end to large-scale primary immigration. Most of the immigrants coming to Western Europe since then have either been seeking asylum, or are families of already arrived immigrants.

Western Europe now has a large number of inhabitants who were born in non-EC countries or whose parents were and who are still not citizens of the host country either by preference or because they do not qualify (37). For this group of European inhabitants the future free European labour market is likely to remain closed. At the moment non-EC nationals residing within the EC also frequently meet problems at border controls when taking holidays or travelling on business to another Community country.

As mentioned above, the removal of border controls envisaged in the single market programme has led to member countries trying to harmonize their entry regulations for third-country aliens. Since 1987 the Ministers of the Interior of all Member States have met in the Trevi Group trying to achieve harmonization of immigration regulations for the whole EC area. These talks are thought to have closely followed the Schengen talks. The main feature of the package considered by both groups has been the introduction of a uniform 'Euro-visa' for non-EC nationals. However, although the criteria for granting visas would be harmonized, residence and work permits are likely to remain valid only in the country granting the permit.

The criteria for acceptance of asylum seekers also need to be harmonized or at least co-ordinated. The proposals in the Schengen Convention seem potentially harsher than existing provisions in many EC countries. The Schengen Convention introduced a liability for substantial fines on carriers of passengers to the Schengen countries, such as ferry companies, shipping lines and airlines, if they carry people to a country who are not entitled to enter. Legislation on 'carriers' liability' has now been introduced by a number of European countries. Carriers' liability obviously introduces serious obstacles to persons wanting to escape repression and seeking asylum in a non-European country. The Trevi group is expected to embrace the principle of 'carriers' liability'. Another feature of both the Schengen agreement and the Trevi talks is the setting up of data exchanges. Countries would exchange information about applicants for visas, work and resident permits and asylum. An applicant refused by one member country may be automatically rejected if he or she applies to another country.

Another problem for people moving in from outside the Community is the status of the residence permits of their spouse and dependents. In most cases the right to residence for the family of a migrant worker is entirely tied to status of the breadwinners and primary immigrants. If the migrant worker loses his right to stay, the family is expelled as well. This is the case even if the husband is expelled because he is convicted for violence against his wife or children - the family has to leave with the husband or ex-husband. The European Parliament has discussed this problem and demanded independent rights of residence for the spouses of migrant workers (38).

Notes

(1) 1974 Summit.

(2) 1975 Council on December 1975.

(3) March 1985. See also 'A People's Europe', Communication from the Commission to the European Parliament, COM(88)331 final, 7/7/88.

(4) See Commission Communication on the abolition of controls of persons at intra-Community borders, COM(88) 640 final, 7/8/88.

(5) 80/1263/EEC, Official Journal of the European Communities, No L375, 13/12/80.

(6) COM(88) 640 final. See note 4.

(7) 64/221/EEC, Official Journal of the European Communities, No L56, 4/4/64.
68/360/EEC, Official Journal of the European Communities, No L257, 19/10/68.
1612/68/EEC, Official Journal of the European Communities, No L257, 19/10/68.

(8) Official Journal of the European Communities, No L257, 19/10/68.

(9) Official Journal of the European Communities, No L257, 19/10/68.

(10) Official Journal of the European Communities, No L257, 19/10/78.

(11) The right to remain for three months to find employment is found in a declaration of the Council attached to the minutes of the Council meeting on 15 October 1968.

(12) Regulation (EEC) 1251/70, Official Journal of the European Communities, No L142, 30/6/70.

(13) Council Directive of 15 October 1968 on the abolition of restrictions on movement and residence within the Community for workers of Member States and their families, 68/360/EEC, Official Journal of the European Communities, No L257, 19/10/68. Regulation of the Council of 15 October 1968 on freedom of movement for workers within the Community, 1612/68, Official Journal of the European Communities, No L257, 19/10/68.

(14) COM(79) 215 final, Official Journal of the European Communities, No C207, 1979. Amended by COM(80) 356 final, Official Journal of the European Communities,

No C188, 1980. COM(80) 649 final, Official Journal of the European Communities, No C292, 1980. COM(85) 292 final, Official Journal of the European Communities, No C171, 1985.

(15) COM(89) 275 final, Office of Official Publications, 26/6/89.

(16) EEC Treaty Article 100.

(17) Commission Decision of 8 December 1972 and Regulation 1612/68, Official Journal of the European Communities, No L257, 19/10/68.

(18) 75/362/EEC, Official Journal of the European Communities, No L167, 30/6/75; 77/452/EEC, Official Journal of the European Communities, No L176, 15/7/77; 78/686/EEC, Official Journal of the European Communities, No L233, 24/8/78; 78/1026/EEC, Official Journal of the European Communities, No L362, 23/12/78; 80/154/EEC, Official Journal of the European Communities, No L33, 11/2/80; 85/384/EEC, Official Journal of the European Communities, No L223, 21/8/85; 85/433/EEC, Official Journal of the European Communities, No L253, 24/9/85; 86/457/EEC, Official Journal of the European Communities, No L267, 19/9/86.

(19) 82/489/EEC, Official Journal of the European Communities, No L218, 27/7/82; 77/92/EEC, Official Journal of the European Communities, No L26, 31/1/77.

(20) 89/48/EEC, Official Journal of the European Communities, No L19, 24/1/89.

(21) 89/49/EEC, Official Journal of the European Communities, No L19, 24/1/89.

(22) Fifth Report of the Commission concerning the implementation of the Internal Market - COM(90) 90 final.

(23) See Official Journal of the European Communities, No C263, 16/10/89.

(24) Council Decision 85/368/EEC, Official Journal of the European Communities, No L199, 31/7/85.

(25) See Official Journal of the European Communities, Nos C166 3/7/89, C168 3/7/89, C209 14/8/89, C292 20/11/89, C321 22/12/89.

(26) See the following cases:

Case 152/73, G. M. Sotgiu v. Deutsche Bundespost. Judgment 12/2/74. ECR 153.

Case 149/79, Commission v. Belgium. Judgments 17/12/80 and 26/5/82. ECR, p.1845.

Case 21/74, Reyners v. Belgian State. Judgment 21/12/73. ECR (1974), p.631.

Case 307/84, Commission v. France. Judgment 3/6/86. ECR (1986), p.1725.

Case 66/85, Lawrie-Blum v. Land Baden-Württemberg. Judgment 3/7/86. ECR (1986), p.2121.

Case 225/85, Commission v. Italy. Judgment 16/6/87, Official Journal of the European Communities, No C181, 9/7/87.

(27) Official Journal of the European Communities, No C100, 21/4/89.

(28) 71/305/EEC, Official Journal of the European Communities, No L185, 16/8/71 (as amended by Directive No 89/440/EEC, Official Journal of the European Communities, L210, 21/7/89).

(29) 77/62/EEC, Official Journal of the European Communities, No L13, 15/1/77 (as amended by Directive No 88/295/EEC, Official Journal of the European

Communities, No L127, 20/5/88).

(30) 77/486/EEC, Official Journal of the European Communities, No L199, 6/8/77.

(31) Case 24/86, Vincent Blaizot and others v. University of Liege and others. Judgment 2/2/88. ECR (1988), 593, p.379 and Case 197/86, Steven Brown v. The Secretary of State for Scotland, Official Journal of the European Communities, No C193, 22/7/88.

(32) Council Regulation (EEC) No 3/84, Official Journal of the European Communities, No L2, 4/1/84. Council Regulation (EEC) No 1751/84, Official Journal of the European Communities, No L171, 29/6/84.

(33) A People's Europe: Communication from the Commission - COM(88) 331 final, p.30.

(34) Second programme, see Official Journal of the European Communities, No L185, 21/7/79. Third programme see COM(84) 265 final - Official Journal of the European Communities, No C153 and Decision No 84/636/EEC, Official Journal of the European Communities, No L331, 19/12/84. Also Report on Third Programme - COM(90) 79 final.

(35) Blakely, G. (1990) Youth Policy, Spicers European Policy Reports, Routledge. ISBN 0-415-03832-4.

(36) See for example Kindleberger, C.P. (1967) Europe's Post-war Growth - The Role of Labour Supply, Harvard University Press.

(37) The real number of inhabitants who originate from outside Western Europe is in fact larger than indicated in this table as a substantial proportion of both first and second generation immigrants are likely to have acquired citizenship in the host country, and therefore stop appearing in the statistics as aliens.

Employment Policy

(38) European Parliament Resolution on discrimination against immigrant women and female migrant workers in legislation and regulations in the Community, Official Journal of the European Commmunities, No C305, 1987, European Parliament Doc. A 2-133/87.

HEALTH AND SAFETY

There are three main reasons for Community involvement in the area of occupational health and safety:

- to equalize labour costs for employers in different countries;
- to avoid social dumping with employers setting up in those countries where health and safety protection is least developed;
- to ensure free movement of goods by harmonizing safety standards for machinery and other industrial equipment.

Health and safety is an area where the Community institutions are empowered to act by the Treaties. Health and safety is included both in the original Treaty and in clauses adopted as a consequence of the adoption of the Single European Act. Some legislation was adopted during the 1960s but real progress was made as a consequence of the adoption of a Health and Safety Action Programme in 1978. The current Commission Action Programme is the third and describes forty proposals to be adopted before the end of 1992 (1). The method of European legislation in this field has changed from detailed regulation of specific workplace hazards to setting more general minimum standards. As in most other Community social legislation, countries may maintain higher standards than the minima prescribed in European Directives.

The Treaty

Article 118 of the EEC Treaty states **'the Commission shall have the task of promoting close co-operation between Member States in the social field, particularly in matters relating to: ...prevention of occupational accidents and**

diseases'. In other words, the Commission is authorized by the Treaty to take initiatives in this field. The Single European Act introduced a new sub-clause in the Treaty specifically dealing with health and safety in **Article 118A** which requires the Member States to **'encourage improvements in the working environment as regards the health and safety of workers with the objective to achieving harmonization while maintaining improvements'. Article 118A** includes a provision that Directives shall avoid imposing administrative, financial and legal constraints in a way which would hold back the creation and development of small and medium sized undertakings. Whether this means that future European health and safety legislation may exempt SMEs from some provisions is unclear.

The area of health and safety is an area where joint Community action is required for competition reasons. Health and safety measures are often expensive. Employers in member countries with high standards have a clear interest in harmonization of legislation to impose the same cost on all Community employers. However, in the 1980s general welfare objectives have also entered the discussion. The aim for European legislation is now not only harmonization but general improvement of standards across the Community. Improved health and safety standards are an important part of the social dimension of the single market and of the People's Europe programme which aims to make the EC relevant to ordinary citizens.

One reason why health and safety forms a large part of the social part of the single market programme is that it has already been accepted as a legitimate area of EC activity. While Member States may argue about the precise provisions in EC legislation in this area, the Commission's competence to submit proposals on health and safety is not disputed.

The Commission started to legislate in the area of health and safety in the early 1960s. The motivation was, from the beginning, to equalize the cost of health and safety measures for employers across the Community. The first step was the issuing of a proposal for a Community-wide list of occupational diseases for which compensation would be paid. All six member countries had legislation on compensation for certain occupational diseases but the diseases included on the different national lists varied considerably. The first proposal was tabled in 1962, and failed to be adopted by the Council of Ministers. The Commission made a second attempt in 1966. This proposal also failed. Not until now has the Commission returned to this problem. A new proposal for a uniform list containing some twenty-five diseases is being prepared by the Commission (2).

The next Commission initiative came in the late 1960s when a Directive on the classification, packaging and labelling of dangerous substances (3) and a Directive on safety signs at work were adopted (4). The latter has since been amended six times (see Section III) mostly in terms of changing the specifications for some signs and introducing new safety signs for new hazards such as lasers. As the EC customs union led to increasing transnational trade, agreed signs for dangerous products were an obvious area of Community legislation.

In the 1970s there followed the first action programme on safety and health at work (5). The programme proposed improvements in the collection of statistics about accidents, sickness and mortality at work, and a series of Directives to provide standards of protection against dangerous substances, on the prevention of dangers from machines and on standards for monitoring and inspection. A series of Directives dealing with specific workplace hazards followed: on the use of electrical equipment in potentially explosive atmospheres (1976), safety signs at the workplace (1977), protection of workers exposed to vinyl chloride monomer (1978), Euratom Directive on radiation risks (1980), accident hazards in certain industrial activities (1982), protection of workers exposed to lead (1982), protection of workers exposed to asbestos (1983), marketing and use of asbestos (1983), protection of workers exposed to hazardous agents, protection of workers exposed to noise and the banning of certain activities and/or agents (1988) (6).

The Single Market

In October 1987 the Commission adopted a new programme

concerning safety, hygiene and health at work. This programme is a timetable for the implementation of the commitment to improve and harmonize national health and safety provisions which was made in both the single market programme and the People's Europe document.

The inclusion of health and safety into the single market programme has led to a change of approach from legislation on specific workplace hazards to setting more general minimum standards. This has been done through the adoption of a framework Directive on 'the introduction of measures to encourage improvements in the safety and health of workers at the workplace' submitted by the Commission to the Council of Ministers in March 1988 and adopted in June 1989 (7). At the same time the Commission submitted proposals for five Directives on specific subjects within the terms of the framework Directive: these concern minimum health and safety provisions for the workplace, minimum safety rules for the use of work equipment and personal protective equipment minimum requirements for work with visual display units and for handling heavy loads. These have also now been adopted (8).

In addition the Commission has submitted some proposals over the last decade which have so far failed to be adopted by the Council, but which may reappear on the legislative agenda. The Commission made a proposal on harmonization of the limits of the levels of benzene permitted in the air of the workplace in November 1985. The Parliament made use of its powers under the Single European Act to demand that the limits should be reduced further than the Commission had proposed. Under the new rules the Council could now only overrule the Parliament by a unanimous vote. The Council failed to achieve unanimity. The new rules stipulate that the proposal lapses if the Council fails to act within three months. However, the Council agreed that benzene should be included in the draft Directive on the protection of workers against carcinogens. This Directive was adopted by the Council on 28 June 1990 (9). A Directive on the risks posed by biological agents was submitted in 1988 and the Council has also reached a common position on this proposal (10).

The Social Charter and Action Programme

The Social Charter contains a rather vague commitment to a right of every worker to enjoy satisfactory health and safety conditions in his working environment. The Charter also demands further harmonization **'while maintaining the improvements made'**. Harmonization should take account in particular of the need for training, consultation and participation of workers in health and safety provisions.

By contrast the Commission's action programme is proposing a number of new Directives in this field. These include:

- improved medical assistance on ships;
- minimum health and safety provisions on temporary and mobile work sites;
- improved health and safety provisions in quarries and open-cast mining;
- improved health and safety in the drilling industries;
- minimum health and safety provisions on fishing vessels;
- the adoption of a 'European schedule of industrial diseases';
- minimum requirements for health and safety signs at the workplace - an update of existing Directives;
- definition of a system of specific information for workers exposed to dangerous industrial agents;
- minimum health and safety requirements regarding the exposure of workers to risks caused by physical agents (such as vibration, electromagnetic radiation);
- amendment of the Directive on asbestos at work;
- minimum health and safety provisions for the transport sector;
- the establishment of a European safety, hygiene and health agency.

This list is partly an exercise in adapting the basic provisions in the general Directives to specialist industries. Partly it demonstrates the fact that health and safety is an area where legislation has to be continually updated and amended to keep pace with technological change.

The proposed European safety, hygiene and health agency is intended to provide advice and assistance to industry on how to implement European health and safety provisions uniformly. It is also intended to examine ways of improving the exchange of information and experience and to study the repercussions at national level of Community measures in this field.

Decision-making on health and safety

It is important to remember that all health and safety legislation now falls under the procedural arrangements of the Single Act. This means that Parliament sometimes may succeed in amending legislation, for example, in terms of imposing stricter standards than the Commission has proposed and the Council accepted in its common position. If Parliament does not succeed in convincing the Council to accept its amendment it is still likely to be able to block the adoption of the whole Directive if the Council cannot achieve a unanimous rejection of the Parliament's amendment. Sometimes this may of course be counter-productive as it may mean that there will be no Community legislation at all in the area under discussion. However, it is often very difficult to amend Community legislation once adopted. Subjects covered by Directives are immune to later amendments for years or even decades as the Council is unwilling to re-open a debate where attitudes of Member States are fixed and well known. It may therefore be an advantage for the reformers if the Parliament succeeds to stop a proposal altogether if the minimum standards proposed are deemed not to go far enough. A new initiative may then be taken by the Commission a few years later.

The Commission has published a number of background reports in the field of health and safety. Some of these contain surveys of legislation and practice in the Member States. These are listed in Sections II and III. The European Foundation for the Improvement of Living and Working Conditions has also published reports on health and safety.

Institutions

Health and safety issues are handled by the Commission's Directorate V on 'Employment, Industrial Relations and Social Affairs' and by the European Parliament's Committee on Social Affairs. The Commission's activities in the health area cover a wider area than has been discussed in this chapter, and include health and safety aspects of consumer protection and environmental protection.

The Commission has a number of advisory committees established under the various health and safety Directives. The most important is the Advisory Committee on Safety, Hygiene and Health Protection at Work, established in 1974 as a consequence of the 1974 social action programme. This committee has seventy-two members including two representatives from the trade unions and two from the employers' organizations in each member country. The Committee is consulted about all new initiatives in this field and provides a sounding board for the Commission in the choice of Community priorities and measures. It is also the channel through which the two sides of industry in the member countries keep in touch with thinking and development at the European level. The Commission has also established a Community information system for health and safety at work called JANUS, which publishes a quarterly journal with information about developments in the field in the Community and in the Member States. The journal was started in 1990 and can be obtained free of charge for one year - for the address see the list in Appendix 2.

Notes

(1) COM(87) 520 final, Office of Official Publications, 23/10/87.

(2) Answer by Commissioner Marin to question in European Parliament 19/4/88 (Official Journal of the European Communities, No C229 p.29).

(3) Directive No 67/548/EEC, 1967.

(4) Amended by 77/576/EEC, Official Journal of the European Communities, No L229, 1977.

(5) Official Journal of the European Communities, No C165, 11/7/78.

(6) Potentially explosive atmospheres - 76/117/EEC, Official Journal of the European Communities, No L24, 1976.

Safety signs - Amended 77/576/EEC, Official Journal of the European Communities, No L229, 1977.

Workers exposed to vinyl chloride monomer - Official Journal of the European Communities, No L197, 1978.

Microwave risks - Official Journal of the European Communities, No C249, 1980.

Accident hazards - Official Journal of the European Communities, No L230, 1982.

Exposure to lead - Official Journal of the European Communities, No L247, 1982.

Exposure to asbestos - Official Journal of the European Communities, No L263, 24/9/83.

Marketing of asbestos - Official Journal of the European Communities, No L263, 24/9/83.
Protection of workers - Official Journal of the European Communities, No L179, 1988.

(7) 89/391/EEC, Official Journal of the European Communities, No L183, 29/6/89.

(8) Directives Nos 89/654/EEC, 89/655/EEC, 89/656/EEC all printed in Official Journal of the European Communities, L393, 30/12/89; Directives Nos 90/270/EEC and 90/260/EEC, Official Journal of the European Communities, No L156, 21/6/90.

(9) Directive 90/394/EEC, Official Journal of the European Communities, No L196, 26/7/90.

(10) COM(88) 165 final, Office of Official Publications, 5/4/88.

EMPLOYMENT AND WORKING CONDITIONS

Article 118 specifically gives the Commission the task of promoting close co-operation between Member States relating to labour law and working conditions.

The 1974 Social Action Programme contained two rather vague objectives relating to working conditions (1):

- the gradual elimination of physical and psychological stress;

- a reform of the organization of work giving workers wider opportunities, especially those of having their own responsibilities and duties and of obtaining higher qualifications.

No legislative action has followed directly from these objectives. The Foundation for the Improvement of Living and Working Conditions, which was established under the action plan, has, however, published a number of research reports on problems which involve workplace stress and the reorganization of work.

Directives

The Social Action Programme also contained a practical clause requesting the adoption of measures to protect workers' interests, in particular with regard to the retention of rights and advantages in the case of mergers, concentrations or rationalization of operations. This resulted in the adoption of three different Directives during the 1970s. These concerned:

- collective redundancies, 1975 (2);
- safeguarding workers' rights in the event of transfers of undertakings, 1977 (3);

- protection of employees in the event of insolvency, 1980 (4).

The main objective of these three Directives was to achieve approximation of the national rules concerning the rights of employees in the event of changes in the status of the employing company. In all three Directives the main obligation imposed on employers is to inform and consult with the workforce before the relevant action or event takes place. In the case of collective redundancies there is also an obligation to notify relevant national authorities.

As part of the action programme to implement the Social Charter, the Commission is proposing to extend European legislation on collective redundancies to those where the decisions are taken by a decision-making centre located in a member country other than that of the affected work force.

Atypical Work

In the early 1980s the Commission went on to draft two Directives on what the Commission now calls 'atypical employment contracts'. The purpose was to protect part-timers (5) and those on temporary contracts (6). The intention to legislate to protect workers on temporary contracts had been announced already in the 1974 Social Action Programme, but the draft Directive on part-time work was a new development. The intention with both Directives was to make employment conditions for employees with atypical employment contracts more comparable with those of full-time permanent employees. As more than nine-tenths of all part-time workers are women, the draft Directive on part-time work is an important potential instrument for achieving equal opportunities. The content of this draft is therefore discussed in more detail in the chapter on equal opportunities.

Both drafts were submitted in 1982. The part-time work Directive was discussed in the Council and then vetoed. The temporary work draft was never discussed, even in the relevant Council sub-committee. Now the Commission has published (June 1990) a proposal for new legislation including both areas in a more comprehensive Directive to cover all aspects of atypical work (7). This commitment is included in the Commission's action programme for the implementation of the Social Charter. In the face of the growth of many different forms of atypical work in the member countries, the Commission maintains that unless safeguards are introduced at the European level, **'there is a danger of seeing the development of terms of employment such as to cause problems of social dumping or even distortion of competition at Community level'.** Atypical work is mentioned in the Charter both in **Article 8** under the heading **'employment and remuneration'** and in **Article 10 'improvement of living and working conditions'.**

Working Hours

Article 10 of the Social Charter states **'The development of a European labour market must lead to an improvement in the living and working conditions of workers in the European Community...'** and then continues by enumerating the various areas where legislation ensuring 'approximation' of conditions is needed. Apart from protection for workers in atypical employment this list also includes legislation on:

- The organization and flexibility of working time, particularly by establishing maximum working hours.
- Work at unsocial hours, such as night work, shift work and systematic overtime.

The issue of working hours was tackled for the first time by the Commission in 1983 when it proposed a Council Recommendation with the purpose of reducing working hours and overtime to create more jobs, something which has been argued by trade unions for some time (8). This was discussed by the Council in 1984 (9) but no agreement was reached. The Commission is now proposing a Directive for the adaption of working time, which is intended not only to deal with reductions in working time and overtime but also to take account of recent developments in member countries in increasing flexibility of working time by, for example, introducing annualized working hours.

The Charter also lays down a right for every worker residing in the European Community to take annual paid leave, a weekly rest period or to a rest period at a regular rhythm to be agreed jointly by the two sides of industry. The implementation of this clause is however not included in the Commission's programme of work.

Proof of Employment

The final subsection in the Charter under the working conditions heading concerns the rights of workers to have their employment conditions stipulated in writing in an employment contract. The Commission is proposing to draft a Directive **'on the introduction of a form to serve as, proof of an employment contract or relationship'**. In particular, the document to be issued by firms will have to define the nature of employment, stipulate the duration of the contract, indicate the system of protection provided and contain a reference to the relevant law and/or collective agreement.

Pay

There has been no involvement at the European level in the issue of pay, with the exception of the legislation on equal pay for men and women. The Social Charter contains a complete innovation in **Article 8:** a right for workers to **'an equitable wage, i.e. a wage sufficient to enable them to have a decent standard of living'**. This implies some sort of assurance of a minimum wage. This is an area where the Council made changes to the Commission's original proposal. The original clause stated: **'To this effect, either by law or by collective agreement at national, regional, interoccupational, sectoral or company level or in accordance with national practices a decent wage shall be established, particularly at the level of the basic**

wage'. The final version of the clause says: **'All employment shall be fairly remunerated. To this effect, in accordance with agreements applying in each country: workers shall be assured of an equitable wage, i.e. a wage sufficient to enable them to have a decent standard of living'**. The new clause also adds protection for wages and salaries from being withheld or seized except in accordance with national law.

The Commission is not proposing legislation in this area: **'In the Commission's view, wage-setting is a matter for the Member States and the two sides of industry alone'**. The Commission points out that some member countries already have a minimum wage laid down in law (10). **'The fact remains however, that the difficulties encountered on the labour market have led to the development of wage practices which no longer afford those concerned a decent standard of living'**. The Commission therefore intends to deliver an opinion on this subject, which also will include the right to paid annual leave and sick pay.

Retirement

The retirement age varies from fifty-five for women and sixty for men in Italy to sixty-seven for both men and women in Denmark. Having a lower retirement age for women than for men is now the exception rather than the rule. Only Belgium, Greece, Italy and the UK still have this type of pension system (11).

Freedom of movement makes some basic harmonization desirable. In terms of equal opportunities, the lower retirement age for women practised in many member countries, discriminates against men - particularly in view of the fact that women live longer than men. In addition the earlier retirement age for women is an obstacle to earning a decent occupational pension, particularly for those who have had periods away from paid work for family reasons. However, lowering the retirement age, whether to give men the benefit of a lower pension age or to harmonize pension ages between countries is the most expensive of social security reforms. The Commission has therefore taken a different approach to the problem of varying retirement ages. In 1982 the Council on the proposal of the Commission adopted a Recommendation on the principles of Community policy with regard to retirement age (12) which recommends the progressive introduction of flexible retirement.

Notes

(1) Official Journal of the European Communities, No C13 12/2/74.

(2) 75/129/EEC, Official Journal of the European Communities, No L48, 22/2/75.

(3) 77/187/EEC, Official Journal of the European Communities, No L61, 5/3/77.

(4) 80/987/EEC, Official Journal of the European Communities, No L283, 20/10/80.

(5) Official Journal of the European Communities, No L18, 22/1/83.

(6) Official Journal of the European Communities, No C133, 21/5/84

(7) Official Journal of the European Communities, No C224, 8/9/90 and COM(90) 228 final.

(8) European Trade Union Institute, Reductions in Working Hours in Western Europe - Part One, ETUI, Brussels 1979. Part Two, ETUI, Brussels, 1980.

(9) Council meeting 7/6/84.

(10) France, Belgium, the Netherlands and Luxembourg.

(11) Comparative tables on the Social Security Systems of the Member States of the European Community (published by the European Commission every three years).

Employment Policy

(12) 82/857/EEC, Official Journal of the European Communities, No L357, 18/12/82.

SOCIAL POLICY

In the original six members and in Denmark the affluence of the 1960s led to improved social security systems, and poverty came to be regarded as a problem of small minorities with very special difficulties.

The rising tide of unemployment produced new poverty, but it was still generally assumed that recovery of economic growth would reduce poverty automatically. However, in the last few years when the growth rate in the Community has been 2.5 per cent to 3 per cent per annum rising to 3.5 per cent in 1988, the number of Community citizens who earn less than half of the average income per head in their country has risen from 38 million to 45 million or 14 per cent of the EC population (1). In developed Europe, unemployment caused by industrial restructuring in combination with a failure of social security benefits to keep in pace with inflation has led large new groups into poverty.

In the new Member States and in Ireland and southern Italy, where underdevelopment has produced large differences in living standards between rural and urban areas, poverty has been much more taken for granted as an inevitable consequence of underdevelopment. The proportion of the EC population who live in regions whose per capita GDP on the basis of purchasing power parity is less than one quarter of the EC average is 20 per cent, or 62 million people. The ratio between the GDP of rich and poor regions has now risen from 1:2 in the Community of six to 1:10 in the Community of twelve. Until recently the social security systems in the three new Member States were relatively less developed although the last fifteen years have seen efforts to extend the coverage of these systems.

The main causes of poverty, apart from living in an underdeveloped region, are unemployment, underemployment, badly paid work and single parenthood. Pensioners used to be a major group among the poor, but in the developed EC countries the proportion of pensioners among the under eighties on low income has been greatly reduced in the last two decades by the increasing proportion of people who have earnings-related occupational pensions. Germany illustrates this trend: in 1970 40 per cent of all social assistance recipient households were elderly, but in 1985 the proportion had been reduced to 13 per cent while at the same time the proportion of unemployed among social assistance claimants during the same period rose from 0.7 per cent to 26.4 per cent (2). However, large numbers of the over eighties were too old to benefit from the pension reforms of the 1960s and 1970s and this group shows the highest frequency of poverty. The elderly are still in some countries the largest group of people in poverty and in receipt of social assistance.

The great increase in the number of people in poverty is caused by unemployment. Despite the recent increase in employment, there are still 16 million unemployed people in the EC, of whom half have been out of work for more than one year. While unemployment benefit now is earnings-related in most Member States, this benefit is usually limited in time to one year of unemployment. Some countries have until recently had no income support systems for the long-term unemployed apart from social assistance. Long-term unemployment almost inevitably leads to increased debts and sometimes to homelessness. The situation is particularly serious for the young unemployed who have not had the opportunity to build up social security entitlement. Youth unemployment in the Community is still over 20 per cent.

Social change and changes in attitudes have led to a large increase in the number of one-parent families, more than nine-tenths of which are headed by women. Divorce is the largest cause of single parenthood despite the fact that in some countries divorce has only been made legal fairly recently - 1970 in Italy and 1981 in Spain. It is difficult to estimate the exact number of lone parents with dependent children. The most common estimate is that 10 per cent of children in the Community live in one-parent households, but the percentage may be higher because these figures date from the late 1970s.

Due to the high proportion of women who are long-term

unemployed and who receive low pay or are in part-time and temporary employment, as well as the prevalence of poverty among the over eighties (of whom the overwhelming proportion are women) and the rise in the number of single parents with low earnings, there is now a growing awareness of a **'feminization of poverty'**. It is not known what proportion of the population classified as living in poverty are women, or what proportion of European women are living in poverty, but it seems likely that women run greater risks of poverty than men. Another vulnerable group are migrants, whether from inside the Community or from third countries. A combination of discrimination by employers and low educational and skills levels mean that migrants are particularly vulnerable in times of recession. Another group with low incomes are the disabled. There are estimated to be 30 million EC citizens who suffer from physical or mental handicap, or 10 per cent of the total population. This is probably the group which meets most problems on the labour market. Within this group there are large differences in income and living standards depending on the cause of the handicap. Compensation for occupational accidents is more generous than compensation for other accidents. Usually no compensation at all is given to those who are born with a handicap.

From 1975 to 1985 poverty increased in most of the EC Member States. The exceptions were France and Belgium where poverty was reduced and Luxembourg and Greece where it remained stable. The largest increase in poverty took place in the UK which has the lowest levels of social security protection among the developed EC countries.

Current estimates of poverty levels should be seen against the fact that, although social spending has been increased in most countries by the increase in the number of people in receipt of unemployment benefit, social spending as a proportion of GDP has been reduced during the last decade (3).

Until recently EC policies in the social sphere have been mostly directed at employment-related issues. However, the Social Charter includes sections with recommendations on minimum living standards for the elderly, the disabled and for those who have no other income. The first Council Decision concerning social issues outside the field of employment and self-employment was the 1974 Social Action Programme. Amongst a large number of clauses concerning employment, training, social dialogue, health and safety and equal opportunities there are three clauses proposing action for the handicapped, social protection for those not covered by social security, better conditions for migrants and pilot schemes on specific measures to combat poverty. The Social Action Programme led to the first anti-poverty programme. The third was launched in 1989. Recent programmes of action or study have been adopted for the disabled and for single parents.

The Poverty Programmes

The first Poverty Programme ran from 1975 to 1980 and consisted of forty-nine local projects. The second Action Programme did not start until 1984 and ran for four years until 1988. The purpose of both programmes was to fund **'action research projects designed to test and develop new methods to help people suffering from or threatened by poverty'**. The projects had as far as possible to be drawn up and carried out with the participation of the people for whom they were designed. They had to be addressed to problems common to several Member States. There was also funding for dissemination and exchange of the experiences of the different projects and for the collection of comparable data on poverty in the EC.

The programme was allocated ECU 25 million with a further 4 million allocated for Spain and Portugal in 1986. It funded ninety-one projects across the Community targeted at different social groups: the long-term unemployed, young unemployed, the elderly, single-parent families, migrants and refugees, people without fixed abode - called marginals in the programme - underprivileged people in inner cities and in rural areas. Most of the projects were new, but some were further developments of projects financed under the first Poverty Programme. The majority of the projects were sponsored and run by different types of voluntary organizations from churches to local community organizations and national voluntary organizations. Forty of the projects were located in areas with low per capita GNP.

Part of the administration of the programme was contracted out to the Institut ISG Sozialforschung und Gesellschaftpolitik in Cologne which had the task of 'Animation and Dissemination' of the projects, and the evaluation was further subcontracted to the Centre for Analysis of Social Policy at the University of Bath. References to the various reports published on the Programme are found in Section III.

The third Poverty Programme was adopted by the Council in July 1989 and will cover the period 1990 to 1995 (4). The budget allocation has more than doubled to ECU 70 million. In its communication to the Council on the draft Programme, the Commission emphasises that poverty is multi-dimensional and that solutions cannot be limited to providing material aid. The Commission also stresses the need for partnership with the people for whom the projects are designed.

The new programme is more ambitious in the projects it aims to set up. Instead of the individual 'micro-projects' which made up the second Programme, the new projects are intended to be fewer but on a larger scale and to cover all action for underprivileged groups within a given territory. Instead of relying on voluntary organizations, the Commission wants a committee of national, local and regional actors to be set up.

The most profound criticism by the project leaders themselves of the projects under the second Programme was that local voluntary action could not compensate for problems which had their roots in national government policies such as deficiencies in the education or social security systems (5). The Commission is therefore intending to get government bodies at both the national and local levels firmly committed to the new macro projects. The Commission calls these new type of projects 'prototype experiences'. Part of the purpose of the Programme is to develop new organizational models for the economic and social integration of the least privileged. Funding will still be available for some smaller projects which address groups with particular problems such as the single homeless. There is also funding of dissemination and exchanges. The new programme is managed by a group called 'Anitmation et Rechereche' consisting of the previous managers: ISG and the Centre for Analysis and Social Policy at the University of Bath, and a number of other organizations (for addresses see the address list).

In September 1989 the Council and the Ministers for Social Affairs adopted a Resolution on combating social exclusion (6). The Resolution marks an awareness that poverty is not only a matter of low income but of exclusion from the minimum acceptable way of life in their country due to a lack of material, cultural and social resources. In 1977 the EuroBarometer survey was dedicated to the issue of poverty. This Europe-wide survey reveals interesting differences in public attitudes to poverty in different member countries, and also differences in perceptions of the quality of life of respondents (7).

The Social Charter

The Social Charter in contrast to other Community pronouncements deals with poverty entirely in terms of income. The chapter 'Right to Social Protection' states that **'every citizen of the European Community shall have a right to adequate social protection'**. The article then amplifies the initial statement by **'all workers, whatever their status...must enjoy adequate levels of social security...'** and a commitment to minimum income for those who have been unable either to enter or re-enter the labour market as well as a right to minimum income for the elderly supplemented by appropriate social assistance. The same theme is repeated in **Articles 27, 28** and **29**, which concern the right of **'every person in retirement'** to enjoy a decent standard of living, a right for elderly people without adequate pension to a minimum income and medical and social assistance, and a right for all disabled persons whatever the origin and nature of the disablement to **'additional concrete measures aiming at improving their social and professional integration'**.

The Commission's action programme to implement the Social Charter, under the heading 'Social Protection', concentrates on the need to harmonize social security provisions further to facilitate freedom of movement, with a commitment to produce a Recommendation on the convergence of social protection. More relevant for the issue of poverty may be the promise of a Commission Recommendation on common criteria concerning sufficient resources and social assistance in the social protection systems. The Commission intends to propose a draft action programme for the elderly which will provide for pilot projects, exchanges of experience, and improved information between groups representing the elderly. The Commission also announces its intention to propose that 1993 be designated the year for the elderly.

Action for the Disabled

The first action programme in favour of the disabled ran from 1984 to 1987. This programme concentrated on exchanges of experiences between Member States, the provision of international experts giving advice to national and local projects, co-ordination and evaluation of activities. There was also funding for nineteen local projects.

The new action programme to promote social integration and independent living for disabled people, HELIOS, was proposed by the Commission in December 1987 and adopted by the Council after some initial difficulties in April 1988 (8). HELIOS has two objectives. This first is to take steps towards the development of an EC policy on disability, particularly with regard to mobility, access to public buildings, adapted employment and housing, integration in schools and the impact of new technology. The second objective is to support innovative projects and exchanges as well as to continue to support co-ordination between various activities at Community level. Three Community networks of projects will be established with eighty activities in total in the fields of:

- employment and vocational training and readaption;
- social integration, environment for independent living as well as general co-ordination;
- integration in schools.

Under the new programme the Commission will give priority to supporting voluntary organizations active at the European level and practising a policy of active involvement of disabled people. The Commission will also support model projects in independent living.

In a separate development the Commission has built up an information system on handicap problems called HANDYNET which includes a module on disability aids called HANDYAIDS. This information network is now incorporated into the HELIOS programme. In addition a journal on disability information is published in all EC languages.

An advisory committee on disability was set up as part of the HELIOS programme. The original Commission proposal included representatives of disabled people, but the Council limited the Committee to government experts. Instead a liaison group was set up consisting of two government representatives per Member State, nine representatives of disabled people and two representatives of the social partners (9).

Since 1971 the European Social Fund has also financed a number of training programmes and projects for disabled people in the Member States.

Disability in the Social Charter

As mentioned above, the Social Charter includes a short section on disability which lays down the right of disabled people to **'additional concrete measures aiming at improving their social and professional integration'.** The Charter goes on to point to priority areas for action: vocational training, ergonomics, mobility, transport and housing. In the action programme on the Social Charter the Commission proposes to draw up a proposal for a third action programme for the disabled for the period 1992 to 1995 and to draft a Council Directive on the introduction of measures aimed at promoting improvement in the travel conditions of workers with motor disabilities. This action was first proposed by the European Parliament in 1987. The Commission sees mobility as a key to access to vocational training and employment for disabled people.

Employment Policy

Family Policy

This is a new area of Community concern, apart from the occasional mention of the need to facilitate combining work with family commitment as part of the EC equal opportunities policy. Family policy which seems a natural preserve for the Member States has become a subject for discussion at the European level because of falling birth rates. The Council of Ministers responsible for family affairs adopted a resolution on family policies in September 1989 where the concern seems to be to increase the opportunities for women to return to the labour market to make up the demographic shortfall without causing a further reduction of the birth rate and without reducing the role of women as carers of the elderly. The Council modestly proposes a number of actions at the Community level which basically concern monitoring the development household formation and birth rates and the impact of other Community policies on family policy (10).

In the early 1980s the Commission requested a special report on single-parent households which was published in 1982. The report pointed to the lack of comparable data between member countries (11). The European Parliament's Committee on Women's Rights came to the same conclusion (12). A further report commissioned by the Community was carried out by Jo Roll and published in 1989 (13).

Notes

(1) See 'Poverty, unemployment and the European Community: lessons from experience' by John Benington in K. Dyson (ed.) Combating Long-term Unemployment, Routledge, 1989, p.84.

(2) Social Europe 'The Fight against Poverty' Supplement 2/89.

(3) Commission Report 'Medium-term projections of social protection expenditure and its financing - 1990 projections - Summary report'. COM(88) 655 final, 7/12/88.

(4) 89/457/EEC, Official Journal of the European Communities, No L224, 2/8/89.

(5) See 'Poverty, unemployment and the European Community: lessons from experience' by John Benington in K. Dyson (ed.) Combating Long-term Unemployment, Routledge, 1989.

(6) See Council Press Release 8773/89 of 29/9/89.

(7) See bibliography - statistics, Eurobarometer.

(8) 88/231/EEC, Official Journal of the European Communities, No L104, 23/4/88.

(9) See 'HELIOS: A new step towards integration and independent living for disabled people in the European Community', in Social Europe 2/89, p.62.

(10) Official Journal of the European Communities, No C277, 31/10/89.

(11) 'One-parent families and poverty in the EEC' (V/2541/1/82). See also Social Europe 1/89, 'Lone parent families in the European Communities', pp.87-9.

(12) Official Journal of the European Communities, No C227, 1986.

(13) Lone-parent families in the European Community. See bibliography for full title.

MEASURES TO COMBAT UNEMPLOYMENT

A comparison between EC and Member State measures to combat unemployment reveals fundamental differences in the ability to act between governments and EC institutions. Economic policy is still entirely managed at the national level. Member States still have a capacity to act both in the public and private sector within their territory which is not matched by the EC. In addition, the EC budget is only a fraction of the size of the budget of even the smaller Member States, and nearly two-thirds of this budget is still devoted to the Common Agricultural Policy. Community action has therefore been limited to exhortation on co-ordination of Member State policies, limited funding of infrastructure investment in under-privileged regions and funding of training projects. It cannot be said that the European Community has a comprehensive employment policy. The Community's role is very much subsidiary to action at local regional and national level. The European Social Fund's overall contribution to national training programmes has been limited, partly because the ESF is small in relation to the unemployed population of the Community and partly because governments have used ESF funding to finance their own training programmes rather than to create additional training facilities. However ESF has been useful in helping to promote initiatives and innovations in local government and voluntary sector programmes.

The various action plans and recommendations adopted by the Commission and Council on action to combat unemployment have not made a very large impact on Member State action but have gone some way to achieve at least exchange of information and some co-operation between national institutions in the training field.

Apart from macro-economic measures to achieve economic growth, national governments have in the last two decades taken a number of different actions of a micro-economic nature to alleviate unemployment. These measures fall roughly into three categories:

- job creation in the public sector through cultural and community work;

- job creation in the private sector through financial incentives in the form of wage subsidies or other grants. Reduction of charges on employment such as the employer's contribution to social security can also be included here;

- improvement of labour exchanges and the provision of counselling, training and retraining;

- measure to support unemployed person, who want to set up their own business.

Community action is for obvious reasons very limited indeed in the first two categories, although there are provisions in the Social Fund Regulations for funding employment subsidies. Practical action at the European level is mainly concentrated on the funding of special projects in the area of training, counselling and otherwise facilitating the entry or re-entry to the labour market of individual unemployed persons.

Measures to combat unemployment, particularly that which resulted from the restructuring caused by European policies go back to the European Coal and Steel Community which had and has extensive powers to assist employees in the coal and steel industries to overcome employment problems caused by rationalization. These measures ranged from redundancy payments to the funding of retraining, counselling and measures to create new employment. The ECSC has still got greater powers to take action both in terms of funding and in terms of regulation of production in the area of coal and steel than in any other sector.

The EEC was given a Social Fund in the Treaty, modeled on the ECSC Social Fund, to promote training in other industrial sectors. The Guidance section of the European Agricultural Guarantee and Guidance Fund (EAGGF) was established to help farmers who were threatened with loss of livelihood from the restructuring and modernization of farming. This is done both by funding early retirement, withdrawal of productive capacity and funding modernization of individual farms and of food processing plants. In 1975 a large fund for regional development - ERDF was established. ESF, EAGGF and ERDF and the various ECSC instruments are the EC Structural Funds. There is a detailed account of the role and activities of the Regional Fund in Regional Policy (1990). The subject for this book is the Social Fund. However, some discussion of the structural funds has to be included in this chapter as recent reforms of the structural funds involve the three main funds together and the new Social Fund provisions have to be seen in this context.

Until the mid-1970s EC action on unemployment was entirely concentrated on the areas of coal, steel and agriculture. The recession led to a gradual development of policies to combat unemployment in general. This took the form of reforms of the ESF, and in 1988 a comprehensive reform of consecutive three main structural funds and of the development of a number of action programmes mainly on vocational training launched in the late 1970s and throughout the 1980s. These action programmes consist mainly of recommendations to Member Governments of co-ordinated action and pump-priming funding through the ESF and other financial programmes. In order to understand the development of EC policies in this field it is necessary to understand the development of unemployment in the EC area.

The Structure of European Unemployment

It is sometimes difficult to remember that throughout the 1960s and the first years of the 1970s unemployment was not a major problem in the industrialized world. From the early 1970s a rapid rise in unemployment occurred across Western Europe triggered by a number of outside events, in particular the oil crisis of 1974. Since then unemployment has increased steadily from a European Community average of 1.8 per cent in 1970 to 11.7 per cent in 1989 (Figures 9 and 10) which has meant a doubling or trebling of the unemployment rates in all EC countries although the absolute rate varies greatly between countries with the current unemployment rate in Ireland and Spain running at nearly 17 per cent and 16 per cent respectively but at 1.5 per cent in Luxembourg. Not until the late 1980s did the European Community experience a general decline in unemployment.

Unemployment has been very unevenly distributed between sectors of industry, regions and social classes. Europe has experienced a massive reduction of employment in manufacturing industry and an almost equally massive expansion of the service sector. Traditional smoke stack industries have been particularly hit. Employees made redundant by traditional industry and in declining regions have not been able to compete for the new jobs created in the service sector and in expanding regions. At the same time Ireland and southern Europe have experienced a dramatic move from jobs in agriculture and rural areas into urban areas. In southern Europe this flight from the countryside to urban areas and to industrial jobs in northern Europe has now almost ceased but Ireland still has a large emigration, mainly to the UK.

This dramatic and continuous increase in unemployment has been far higher in the European Community than in other industrialized nations (Figure 25). Not only have the United States and Japan suffered less, but the EFTA countries have also had much lower unemployment rates than all the EC countries with the exception of Luxembourg. Interestingly the economic policies of the EFTA countries vary a great deal from the interventionist, Keynsian approach of the Nordic countries to the traditional balanced budget of Switzerland.

One common feature of national employment policies contributes to the particular profile of modern European unemployment patterns. Employment protection legislation in all countries now stops employers from shedding older workers except through fairly expensive early retirement schemes. This, although a desirable development, has led to proportionately fewer jobs being available for new entrants to the labour market. In consequence women returners and school leavers therefore experience a higher unemployment rate than men in nearly all EC countries.

There are currently over 5 million unemployed under the age of twenty-five in the Community (Figures 12 and 14). The EC unemployment rate for people under twenty-five is 22 per cent or double the unemployment rate for all workers. It is likely that sex discrimination also plays a role in producing a relatively higher unemployment rate for women (Figure 11) and for girls under twenty-five. In addition employers seem to apply a 'last out first back' recruitment policy preferring jobseekers who are employed to those who are unemployed, in particular discriminating against the long-term unemployed. As a result the proportion of long-term unemployed on the unemployment registers has gradually risen over the last decade and a half. People who have been unemployed for more than one year now make up between just under half to more than two-thirds of the unemployed or nearly 6 million in all European Community countries.

The need for special action to improve the employment prospects of women, people under twenty-five, the disabled and migrant workers was recognized in the 1970s. Action particularly targeted at the long-term unemployed was not developed until the early 1980s. Previously it was assumed that long-term unemployment would be reduced at the same time and pace as the overall unemployment rate. However, the rising proportion of the long-term unemployed in the total number of unemployed during the second half of the 1980s when overall unemployment rates have declined indicates that the long-term unemployed will take longer to benefit from an economic up-turn and may need special assistance.

The need for comprehensive training policies is also made more urgent by the reduction in apprenticeship training provided by industry which has taken place in many member countries, notably Germany. Instead the education sector in many countries has expanded and become the main provider of occupational and vocational training.

The Social Action Programme

The Social Action Programme of 1974 was partly an effort to develop a co-ordinated response to the rise in unemployment, although action specifically targeted on unemployment is confined to a few clauses basically concerning the co-operation and co-ordination of national policies:

- consultation between Member States on employment policies;
- promotion of co-operation between national employment services;
- implementation of a common vocational training policy.

A number of efforts have been made to co-ordinate national employment policies. In addition co-operation between national employment services has been developed. A centre for research and development of vocational training, CEDEFOP, was established in 1975. Initiatives have been taken to promote initiatives to ease the transition from school into working life for school-leavers.

European Social Fund reforms 1971-1983

The European Social Fund was established by the Treaty of Rome, with the task of contributing 50 per cent of the funding for schemes which ensure **'productive re-employment of workers'** by means of vocational retraining and resettlement allowances and other assistance. Until 1971 the Fund played a limited role. The Fund was then reformed a number of times, the latest reforms being part of the single market initiative. ESF is the main vehicle for EC action to combat unemployment but the fund's total resources are still very limited both in relation to the number of unemployed in the Community and in comparison with the spending of national governments. The early 1970s also saw the creation of a much larger fund, the European Regional Development Fund (ERDF) which funds development initiatives in underdeveloped or declining regions. One of the main strands of the social dimension of the single market programme is now a large expansion in the funding of all three Structural Funds - including the agricultural guidance fund, EAGGF - and a programme to co-ordinate and concentrate the work of all three funds on the most needy regions and groups of unemployed.

ESF - development 1971-1983

The legal base of the ESF is found in **Articles 123** to **128** of the EEC Treaty. According to **Article 123** the purpose of the Fund is to **'improve employment opportunities for workers in the common market and to contribute thereby to raising the standard of living'** and **'rendering the employment of workers easier and of increasing their geographical and occupational mobility within the Community'**. Although the Fund has played an important role in promoting training for the unemployed it has hardly been able to live up to the Treaty's goal of contributing to raising the standard of living. Even after the most recent increase in the Fund's resources, the ESF budget amounts for 1990 only to ECU 4,075 million or around ECU 270 per unemployed person in the EC.

The Social Fund finances two types of action: occupational training and employment subsidies.

The Fund is administered by the Commission, which is 'assisted' by a Committee of representatives of national Governments trade unions and employer's organizations chaired by the Commission. Council decisions concerning the fund take the form of Regulations. Originally the funds for the ESF were contributed by Member States, but since 1971 the fund is financed from the Community's own resources.

Originally the Fund could only support government training schemes. The 1971 reform opened the door to funding of training projects in the private and voluntary sector. The main objective of the fund was to assist with the retraining needs which arise from industrial restructuring caused by Community policies. Large special aid programmes were launched in the 1970s to give training to people leaving agriculture, the textile and clothing industry and shipbuilding. These programmes were terminated in 1985. Certain groups of unemployed persons with particular problems were given priority: migrant workers, young unemployed persons, women and the handicapped. The Fund quadrupled between 1973 and 1976, and at the same time the number of applications rose as the fund became better known. In an effort to support as many training initiatives as possible the proportion of ESF funding for each project was cut down. As a result the limited ESF funds were sprinkled widely and thinly across the Community.

Nineteen eighty-three saw the first initiative to concentrate and target the funds efforts. First, 75 per cent of the spending of funds was allocated to schemes for unemployed young people under twenty-five. Secondly, 40 per cent of the Fund's spending on general schemes was directed to the least favoured regions: Ireland, Northern Ireland, Greece, Mezzogiorno and the French overseas departments. After the entry of Spain and Portugal this proportion was increased to 44.5 per cent.

Currently the ESF section at the Directorate General for Social Affairs employs only just over sixty civil servants who, until the 1988 reform, handled over 10,000 applications annually. Directorate General XVI Regional Affairs is equally stretched. There were many complaints from project managers, particularly in the voluntary and private sectors that the funds when approved were only paid at the end of the period which the grant was supposed to finance. In addition ESF funding was approved for one year only after which a new application had to be made, which made forward planning difficult for project managers. An important objective of the 1988 reform was to integrate the activities of all three Funds with the employment policies and regional development plans of the individual Member States.

The 1988 reform of the Structural Funds

The European Council meeting on February 11 to 13 1988 accepted the general principles of the Commission's proposals for a comprehensive reform of the three main structural funds presented in the document 'The Single Act: A new frontier for Europe'. As a result the new structural fund regulations were adopted by the Council of Ministers in June 1988.

The new objectives for the funds can be summarized as follows:

ERDF will fund:

- productive investment;
- the modernization of or creation of new infrastructure needed for the development of regions, frontier regions or parts of regions including employment areas or urban communities;
- measures to exploit the potential for internally generated development in such areas;
- studies or pilot schemes of physical planning at Community level, especially in frontier areas.

ESF will support projects and measures aimed at:

- combating unemployment among young people and the long-term unemployed;
- providing workers with the vocational skills which lead to stability of employment;
- expanding employment opportunities.

EAGGF Guidance Section will support measures which:

- reorganize and improve agricultural structures;
- convert agricultural production for farmers in rural areas;
- ensure a fair standard of living for farmers;
- help develop the social fabric of rural areas, safeguard the environment and preserve the countryside.

The most important aspect of the 1988 reform was the concentration of the activities of both the Structural Funds, the ERDF and the EAGGF and the ESF on five objectives:

Objective 1: Structural adjustment and development of regions whose development is lagging behind.

These are the whole of Ireland, Greece and Portugal, parts of Spain and Italy, Northern Ireland, Corsica and the French overseas departments (1).

Objective 2: Conversion of regions and frontier regions seriously affected by industrial decline. The Commission is in charge of drawing up the list of regions which qualify for assistance under Objective 2 in accordance with objectives laid down in Article 9 (2) of the Structural Funds Regulation (EEC) No 2052/88 (2). All member countries have some areas which qualify. In Germany, for example some parts of the Ruhr and areas blighted until 1989 by the border with the German Democratic Republic are included. In Britain parts of Scotland, the North, the Midlands and the West Country qualify.

Objective 3: Combating long-term unemployment (3).

Objective 4: Facilitating the occupational integration of young people (under 25) (4).

Objective 5a: Speeding up the adjustment of agricultural structures.

Objective 5b: Development of certain rural areas. The Commission selects these regions on the basis of criteria laid down in the Regulations (5). The criteria include: a large proportion of jobs in agriculture, low income in agriculture, low level of socio-economic development and vulnerability to changes brought about by the Common Agricultural Policy.

Objective 5a involves only EAGGF, but all Funds may contribute to projects under Objectives 1, 2 and 5b, while only the ESF deals with Objectives 3 and 4.

In Objective 1 areas, the Community can now contribute up to 75 per cent of the costs of a scheme and up to 50 per cent of eligible public expenditure attached to a project or programme, while the upper limit for assistance from the Funds in all other cases is 50 per cent of expenditure and 25 per cent of eligible public expenditure. The finance from the three funds to Objective 1 regions will have doubled in real terms from 1987 to 1993 from ECU 7,000 million to ECU 14,000 million per annum - a sum which does not include the finance which some projects and regions will borrow from the European Investment Bank. This is beginning to amount to real transfer of resources from the wealthy to the underdeveloped regions, compared to earlier fund activities which were more in the nature of seed money. Some people are now talking about this programme with some justification (6) as the second Marshall Aid.

The 1988 reform seeks to alleviate congestion in the Commission and achieve a more coherent and concentrated use of funds. Governments now have to produce a national plan including a comprehensive analysis of national and regional skills shortages with clear priorities. All individual projects applying for funding have to be supported by the national government and be fitted into the national programme. The Member States' plans will be assessed by the Commission in the light of their consistency with the objectives. The Commission will then draw up the 'Community support framework' in agreement with each Member State concerned. One of the most important innovations from the point of view of project managers, particularly in voluntary organizations, is the fact that all approved projects now are more or less guaranteed finance for several years.

Three target groups, migrant workers, the disabled and women have been excluded from the new regulations, but after protests from the European Parliament the Commission has instead included these three groups in the new guidelines which lay down the criteria for eligible projects. Operations involving training for categories facing particular difficulties on the labour market such as migrants, women and disabled people will receive preferential treatment. This also applies to innovative and transnational projects, training in advanced technology and training designed to modernize production and marketing systems of businesses in economically promising sectors.

Another change in the ESF guidelines applies to the nature of the training schemes supported. In the past some training schemes involved general confidence building and access courses, which prepare participants to take up occupational training in the future. Now training schemes should provide the skills necessary to carry out specific types of employment, which often will mean training which leads to a recognized qualification. There used to be a requirement that schemes should include at least two hundred hours training of which forty hours must be devoted to new technology, but this has been deleted from the new guidelines. Finally the training should be likely to lead to employment. Projects intended for the long-term unemployed should be tailored specifically to the needs of this group. These are more exacting requirements on training providers.

In addition to training measures and vocational guidance there are a number of new measures included for the first time among eligible types of projects. Among these are help to finance reports and studies, technical assistance, exchange of information and the monitoring and evaluation of projects which have been given assistance. ESF can now also fund career guidance services for the long-term unemployed, and transnational projects 'within the framework of the social dialogue' aimed at employees concerning the transfer of special knowledge of relevance to the modernization of the production apparatus (7).

One problem which is unlikely to be solved by the latest reforms is the enforcement of the Treaty provisions that finance from the Funds should be additional or complementary to the spending by national governments. In reality, most governments treat EC development finance as a contribution to their own development spending. The largest amount of ESF funds has been used to finance national employment programmes. In the UK approximately 177 million or 52 per cent of UK share of ESF money goes to the Training Agency to finance the Employment Training and the Youth Training programmes.

Other Employment and Training Action programmes

The first resolution urging the development of a common EC vocational training policy was adopted in 1963. The 1974 Social Action Programme contains the first commitment to a number of recurring themes: the need to ease the transition from school to working life; the need for member governments to consult on employment policy; and the promotion of better co-operation between national employment services. In addition the action programme reiterates the commitment to the implementation of a common vocational training policy.

In the 1980s, as unemployment continued to rise and a growing reluctance among governments to take on further commitments in the social field or to burden industry with more costs stopped further development of European social legislation, Council efforts in the social sphere became focused on resolutions and action programmes on practical measures to combat unemployment, and, in particular, initiatives to develop and improve vocational training. The list below shows the development of EC policy on unemployment and training:

1963 Council Decision on Vocational Training which laid down the general principles for implementing a common vocational training policy for the EC (8).

1974 The Social Action Programme.

1975 Establishment of the European Centre for the Development of Vocational Training - CEDEFOP.

1979 Council Resolution on linked work and training for young people established the first Community-funded programme for funding projects to make the transition from school to work easier for school leavers.

1983 Council Resolution on vocational training in new information technology (9) established a five-year programme for the purpose of creating a network of demonstration projects.

Employment Policy

1983 Council Resolution on training policies for the 1980s (10), a resolution which reiterates familiar themes of innovation and improvement of national training systems, Community support for pilot projects and the training of trainers.

1984 Council Resolution on the contribution made by local employment initiatives to combating local unemployment. Local employment initiatives are businesses, co-operatives and community businesses which operate on the basis of small-scale local community development. The Commission offers assistance both to individual businesses of this kind in certain areas and to agencies which promote the setting up of LEIs.

1985 The establishment of ELISE - the European information exchange network on local employment initiatives - which aims to make information about LEIs available to all who are involved in local development.

1985 EUROTECNET I a three-year programme lasting from 1985 to 1988 on action to promote continuing vocational training in technology (11).

1986 Council Action programme on employment growth (12) which concentrates on ways of promoting survival and growth among small and medium sized businesses but contains a number of clauses on training. In this Resolution the Council mentions the development of local employment initiatives for the first time. The Resolution reveals its ideological origins in ideas on the promotion of enterprise through deregulation, by being the only Council Resolution in the social sphere which advocates further deregulation of atypical work. It also establishes for the first time that it is EC and Council policy that all young people should have a right to one or two years of vocational training after leaving school leading to recognized vocational qualifications.

Employment Policy

1986 ENGLEI - the European group for local employment initiatives - was established by the Commission. It is an annual exchange programme for local development agencies, mainly local authorities.

1986 Research action programme on local development of the employment market. This was a study of pilot projects in twelve different regions published in 1988.

1986 COMETT, Programme of the Community in education and training for technology. This is a programme of grants to promote co-operation between universities and industry to improve training in advance technology

1986 SME action programme on small and medium sized enterprises - this programme contains a strong component of training both for SME managers and employees (13).

The Commissions scheme under this programme for financial support for SME training focuses on experimental schemes.

1987 PETRA - the action programme for the vocational training of young people and their preparation for adult and working life (14). This programme includes funding for pilot projects in Member States to facilitate the transition from school to work. Grants are available for projects run by young people themselves and for exchange projects. New proposals for an expansion of PETRA are expected to be published in the autumn of 1990.

1987 IRIS network on vocational training for women (15).

1988 Commission introduced a small programme of support for local employment initiatives by women. In 1988 grants were given to 128 new businesses established by women.

1988 DELTA - Developing European Learning Through

Technological Advance - an action programme to develop learning technology with the aid of a programme of grants for consortia of industry, universities and publishers working to develop distance learning (16).

1989 SPRINT - the Strategic Community Programme for Innovation and Technology Transfer includes a training element (17).

1989 EUROTECNET II - the second and larger programme to promote vocational training (18). The programme includes a strong element of information exchange and dissemination. The old Eurotecnet project had by 1988 developed 135 different projects.

1989 COMETT II - the programme for co-operation between industry and university regarding vocational training in the field of advanced technology (19).

1989 The Social Charter states that all workers have the right to lifelong continuing vocational training.

1989 FORCE - this is the first comprehensive programme on training directed at people in employment rather than the unemployed. The actual format of the support measures has not yet been presented by the Commission. It is expected that some of the funding for this programme will come from the ESF, but it is not yet clear whether ESF rules apply to these grants.

Running through all these programmes are a number of common themes: vocational training as an essential component in employment growth, equal opportunities, emphasis on co-operatives, special emphasis in most programmes on small and medium sized enterprises, support for innovation and pilot projects and for transnational projects, the need to exchange experiences and information between Member States, the need to co-ordinate national employment policies and the need for co-operation between education and the world of work, between universities and industry. The demand for all young people to be given the opportunity of one to two years of vocational training after leaving school turns up for the first time in the 1986 action programme for employment growth. In later statements the Commission and Council unequivocally favour a minimum of two years vocational training.

The trend over the 1980s has been a development from the promotion of small innovative projects to support for larger scale projects with the involvement of all the different actors in a particular geographical area. There has also been a move towards greater emphasis on recognized qualifications rather than access courses, something which worries organizations working with underprivileged groups. The previous focus on training for the unemployed is now shifting towards training for school leavers and continuous training for people in employment. Overall there is a change of EC focus from individuals outside or on the margins of the national training systems to the education and training systems themselves.

It is difficult to assess the effect of Community policies and initiatives in the area of employment growth and training on the Member States because EC policy is conducted through recommendation and funding rather than through legislation. The different programmes of grant support for projects in the Member States - particularly when given to local authorities and the private and voluntary sector have quite clearly provided additional resources for certain activities and will have assisted the development of innovation and new ideas. Many of the programmes have very limited budgets, but the Social Fund has now got substantial resources. It is likely that Community funding has meant that many institutions around Europe have been given opportunities they would not otherwise have had and that the possibility of funding have led some institutions to take an interest in projects they would otherwise not have developed. Many of the newsletters serving the larger programmes such as EUROTECNET and INFORMISEP have a fairly wide distribution among training institutions and authorities and serve to inform non-participant institutions about new policy initiatives.

It is much more difficult to establish what effect the different Community recommendations for Member State action have had on government policy. The fact that the ministers of employment and education meet regularly and report on action taken at the national level must at least mean that new ideas and initiatives are spread across Europe faster than would have happened. The fact that governments backing Community policy by unanimously adopting resolutions on these policies in the Council ought to influence policy development at the national level at least in the long run.

Comparative employment statistics

It should be noted that national statistics on employment and particularly the unemployment of certain sub-groups such as the long-term unemployed should not be used for exact comparisons between Member States. The Statistics Office of the Commission issues recommendations on how to achieve a common base for the collection of statistics throughout the Community, and EC legislation does lay down ground rules for harmonizing definitions in certain fields, but particular definitions of long-term unemployment vary. However, this type of statistics usually give a fairly accurate measure of changes over time in individual countries. The main tool for employment statistics in the member countries is the annual Labour Force Surveys.

The European Social Fund is managed by a subsection of DG V - Employment and Social Affairs. Most other training programmes are managed by the Human Resources Taskforce, set up in 1989, as an autonomous service within the Commission to provide a more flexible and informal administrative framework to manage and develop EC training policy. The Taskforce reflects the high priority now given to the development of human resources within the Community. COMETT, FORCE, ERASMUS, LINGUA, PETRA, EUROTECNET, Youth for Europe are all managed by the Task-force. In addition the Taskforce has the responsibility for the development of EC vocational training policy, for co-operation in education and for the development of better links between Member States on training. The Taskforce is also in charge of CEDEFOP.

Notes

(1) See Regulation (EEC) No 2052/88, Article 8(1), (2) and (3) and list of regions in appendix to the Regulation. Official Journal of the European Communities, No L112, 25/4/89 p.19.

(2) Official Journal of the European Communities, No L112, 25/4/89 p.19.

(3) Article 1, Regulation (EEC) No 2052/88, Official Journal of the European Communities, No L112, 25/4/89.

(4) Article 2, Regulation (EEC) No 2052/88, Official Journal of the European Communities, No L112, 25/4/89.

(5) Article 11(2), Regulation (EEC) No 2052/88, Official Journal of the European Communities, No L112, 25/4/89 and Article 4, Regulation (EEC) 4253/88, Official Journal of the European Communities, No L198, 12/7/89.

(6) See for example P. Venturini, 1992: The European Dimension, European Commission, 1989, p.42.

(7) A summary of the new regulations for the Structural Funds and the new guidelines for ESF projects is found in Kolotourou, Vali, 'The reform of the Structural Funds and the European Social Fund', Social Europe, 3/89, p.87.

(8) 63/226/EEC, Official Journal of the European Communities, No 63, 20/4/63.

(9) Official Journal of the European Communities, No C166, 25/6/83.

(10) Official Journal of the European Communities, No C193, 20/7/83.

(11) COM(85) 167 final.

(12) Official Journal of the European Communities, No C340, 31/12/86.

(13) Official Journal of the European Communities, No C287, 14/11/86.

(14) 87/569/EEC, Official Journal of the European Communities, No L346, 16/12/87.

(15) 87/567/EEC, Official Journal of the European Communities, No L342, 4/12/87.

(16) 88/417/EEC, Official Journal of the European Communities, No L206, 30/7/88.

(17) 89/286/EEC, Official Journal of the European Communities, No L112, 25/4/89.

(18) COM(89)355 final - Official Journal of the European Communities, No C242, 22/9/89.

(19) 89/657/EEC, Official Journal of the European Communities, No L393, 30/12/89.

(20) 89/27/EEC, Official Journal of the European Communities, No L13, 17/1/89.

Figure 1 Labour force participation rates, men and women, 1986

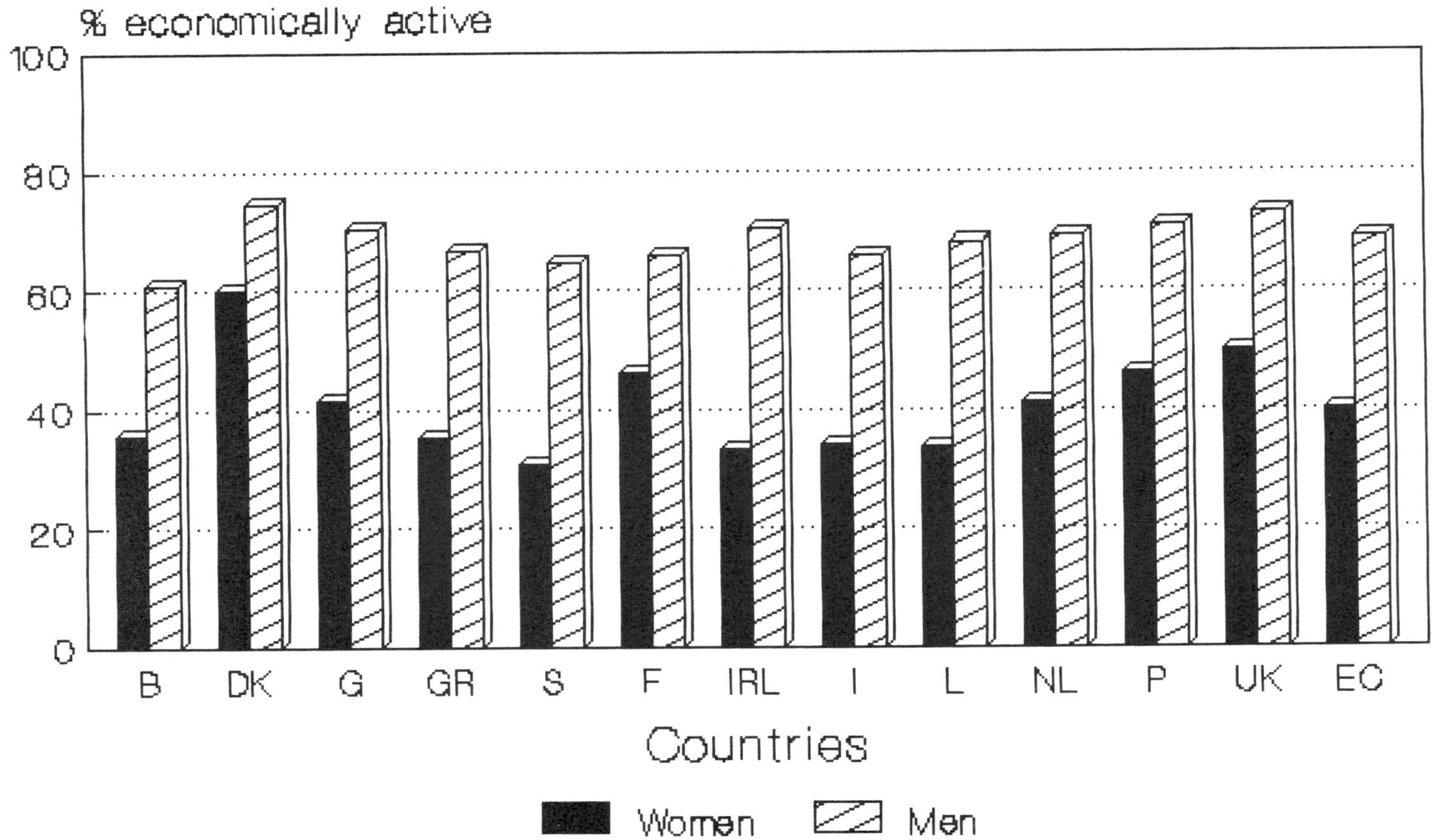

Source: Eurostat, Labour Force Survey, 1986

Figure 2 Percentage of women in the labour force, 1986

Countries	% females
Belgium	40
Denmark	46
Germany	39
Greece	34
Spain	30
France	42
Ireland	30
Italy	36
Luxemburg	36
Netherlands	35
Portugal	41
U K	41
E C	38

Source: Eurostat, Employment and Unemployment, 1986

Figure 3 Labour force participation of men and women between the ages of 25 and 49

Source: Eurostat, Labour Force Survey, 1986, pp. 82-3

Figure 4 Birth rates and death rates in the EC Member States

Countries	Birth rates	Death rates
Belgium	12.1	10.6
Denmark	11.5	11.5
Germany	11.1	11.2
Greece	10.8	9.1
Spain	10.8	8.2
France	13.8	9.4
Ireland	15.4	8.9
Italy	10.1	9.4
Luxemburg	12.4	10.3
Netherlands	12.7	8.4
Portugal	11.9	9.6
United Kingdom	13.8	11.4
European Community	12.0	9.9

Figures from Spain 1987

Source: Eurostat, *Rapid Reports Population*, 1/89

Figure 5 Average number of children per woman in the EC countries, 1988

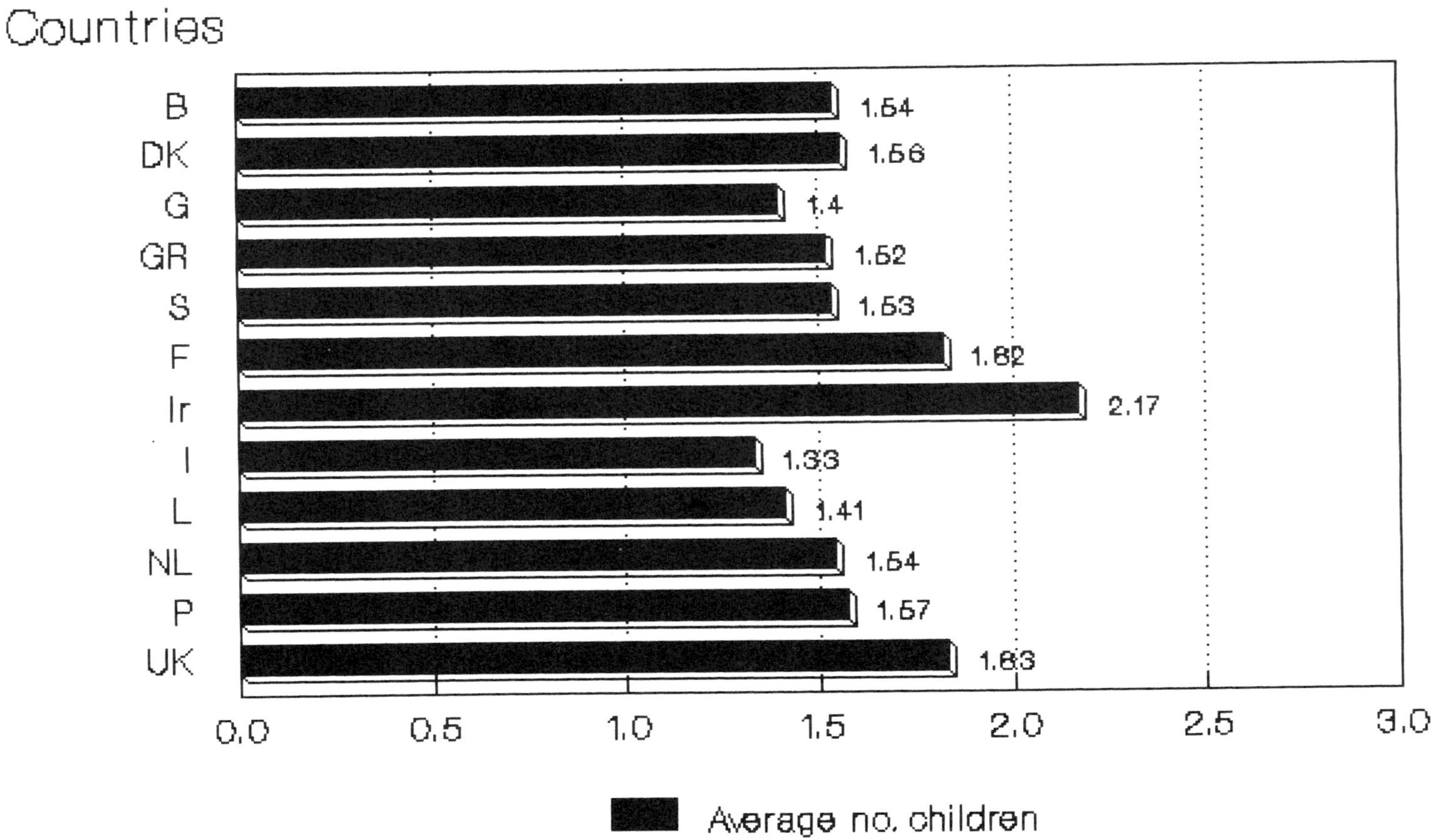

Source: Eurostat, Rapid Reports Population, 1/89

Figure 6 Third or higher order births as a percentage of total number of births

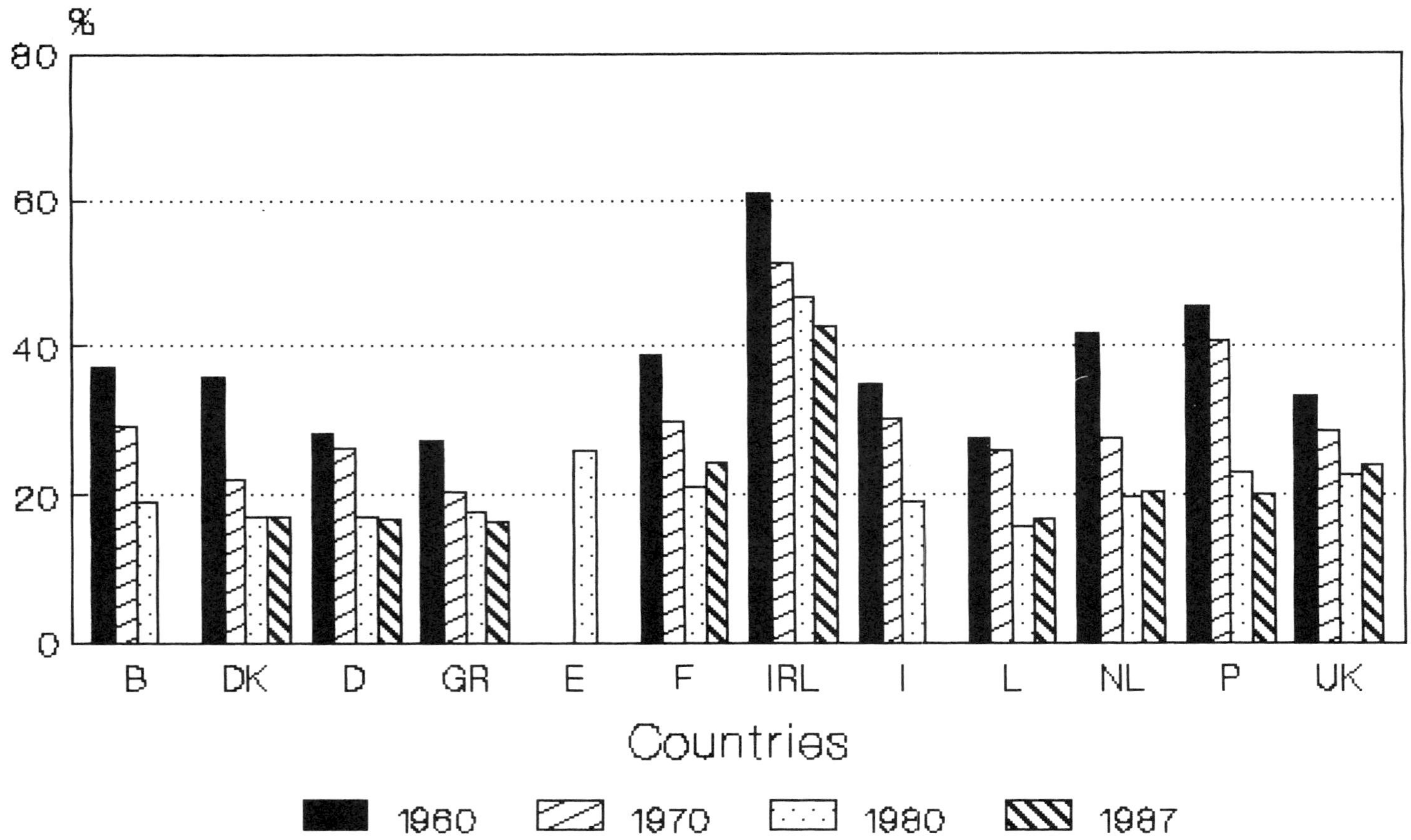

Source: Eurostat, Rapid Reports Population, 1/89

Figure 7 Percentage of employed men and women in part-time work, 1988

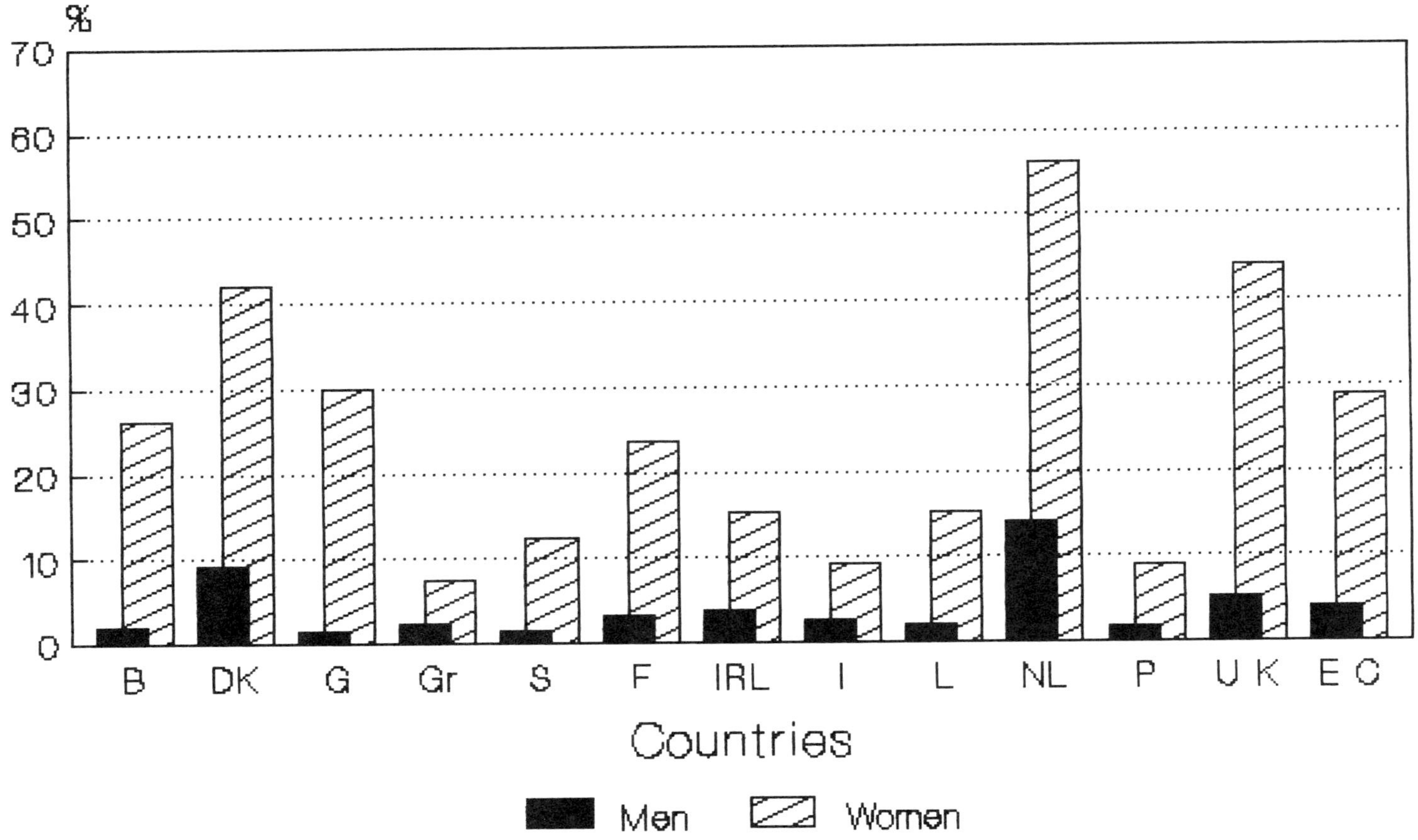

Source: Eurostat, Labour Force Survey, 1988

Figure 8 Proportion of women employees in part-time work, 1986

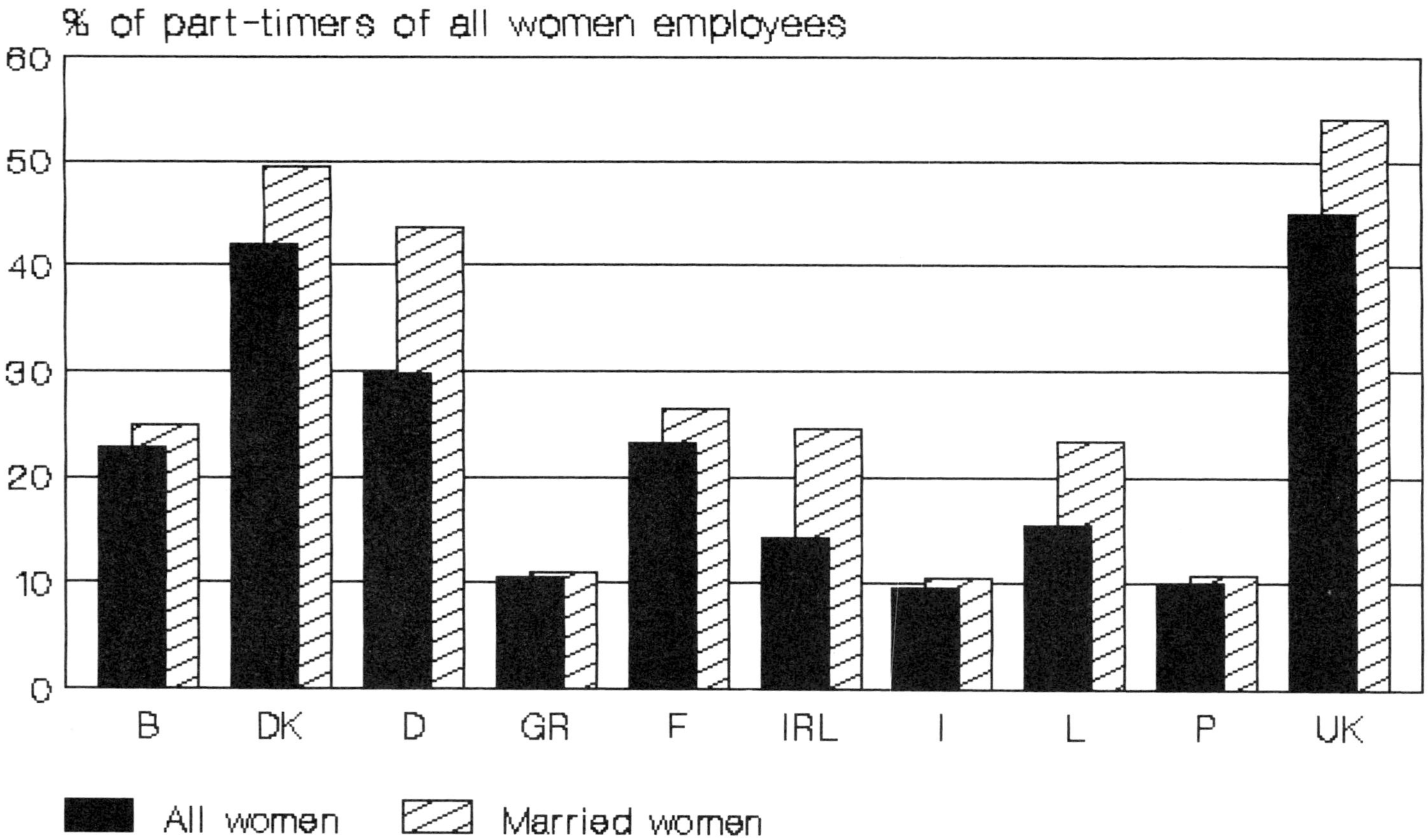

Source: Eurostat, *Labour Force Survey*, 1986

Figure 9 Average unemployment rates, 1989

Countries	Unemployment rate %
Belgium	9.5
Denmark	6.7
Germany	5.5
Greece	7.8
Spain	16.9
France	9.5
Ireland	17.0
Italy	11.0
Luxembourg	1.8
Netherlands	9.3
Portugal	5.0
United Kingdom	6.7
European Community	9.0

Source: Eurostat, *Unemployment Monthly*, 1/90

Figure 10 Unemployment rates in the EC, 1970-1986

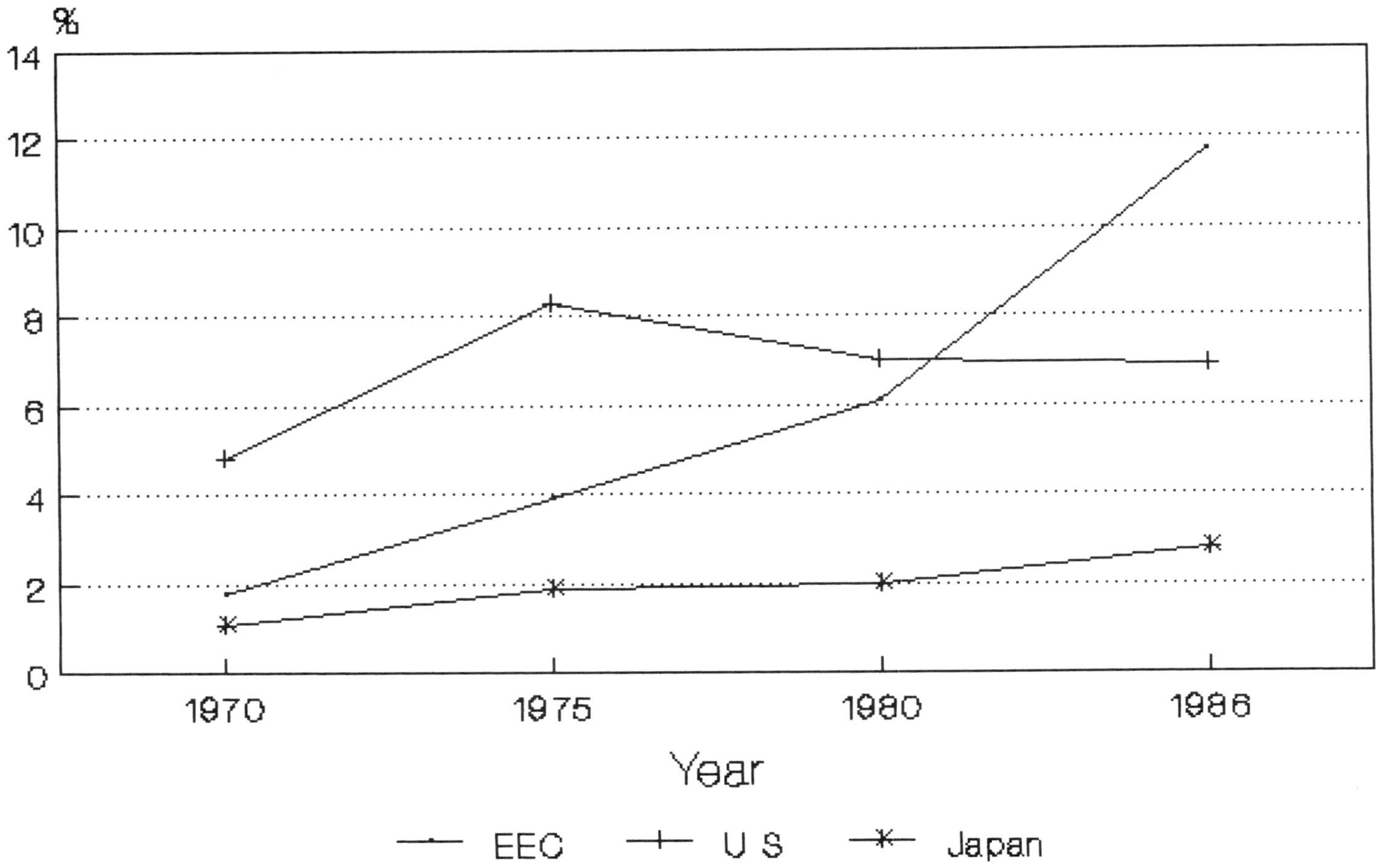

Source: Eurostat, Rapid Reports Population, 1/89

Figure 11 Male and female unemployment rates, 1989

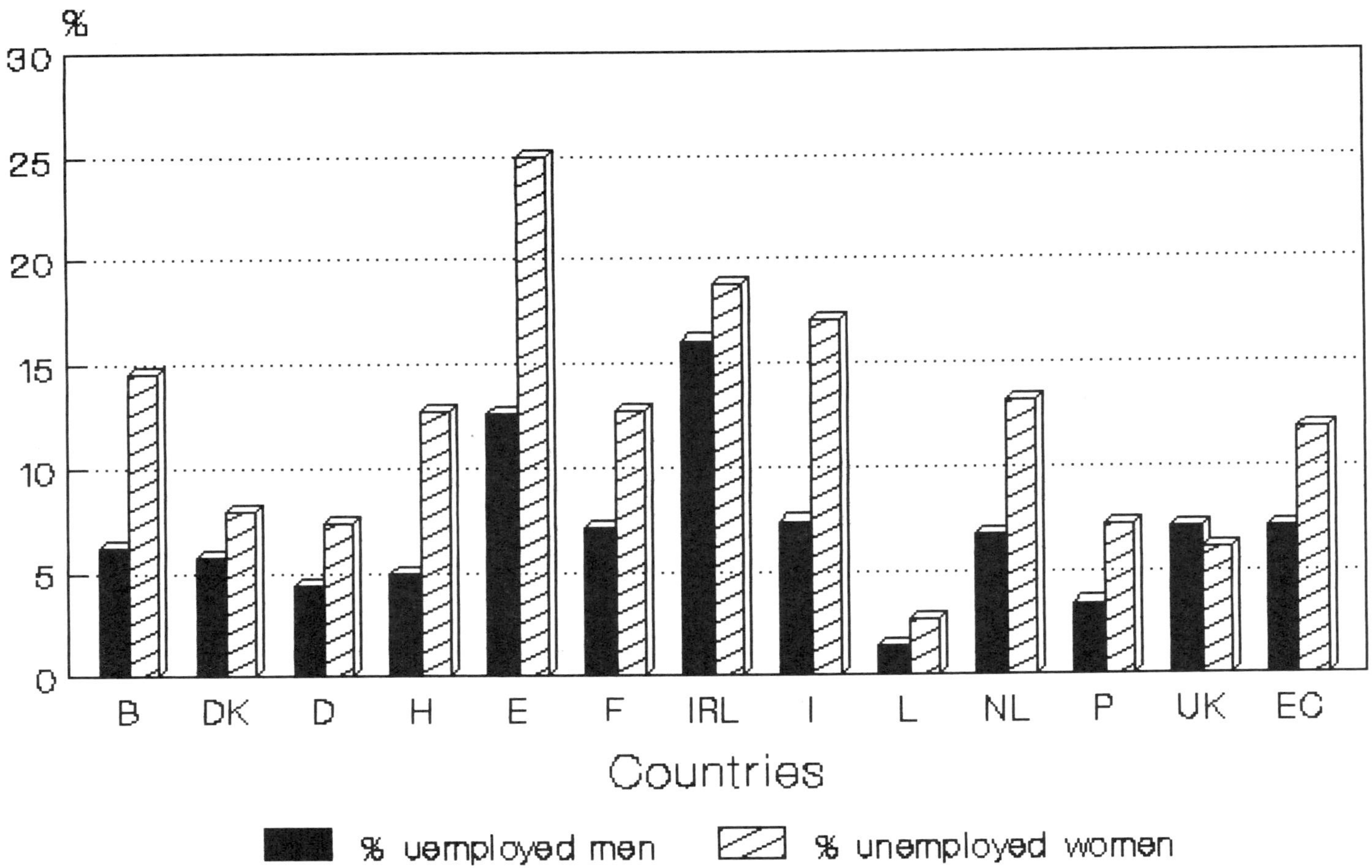

Source: Eurostat, Unemployment Monthly, 1/90

Figure 12 Unemployment rates among people under the age of 25, 1989

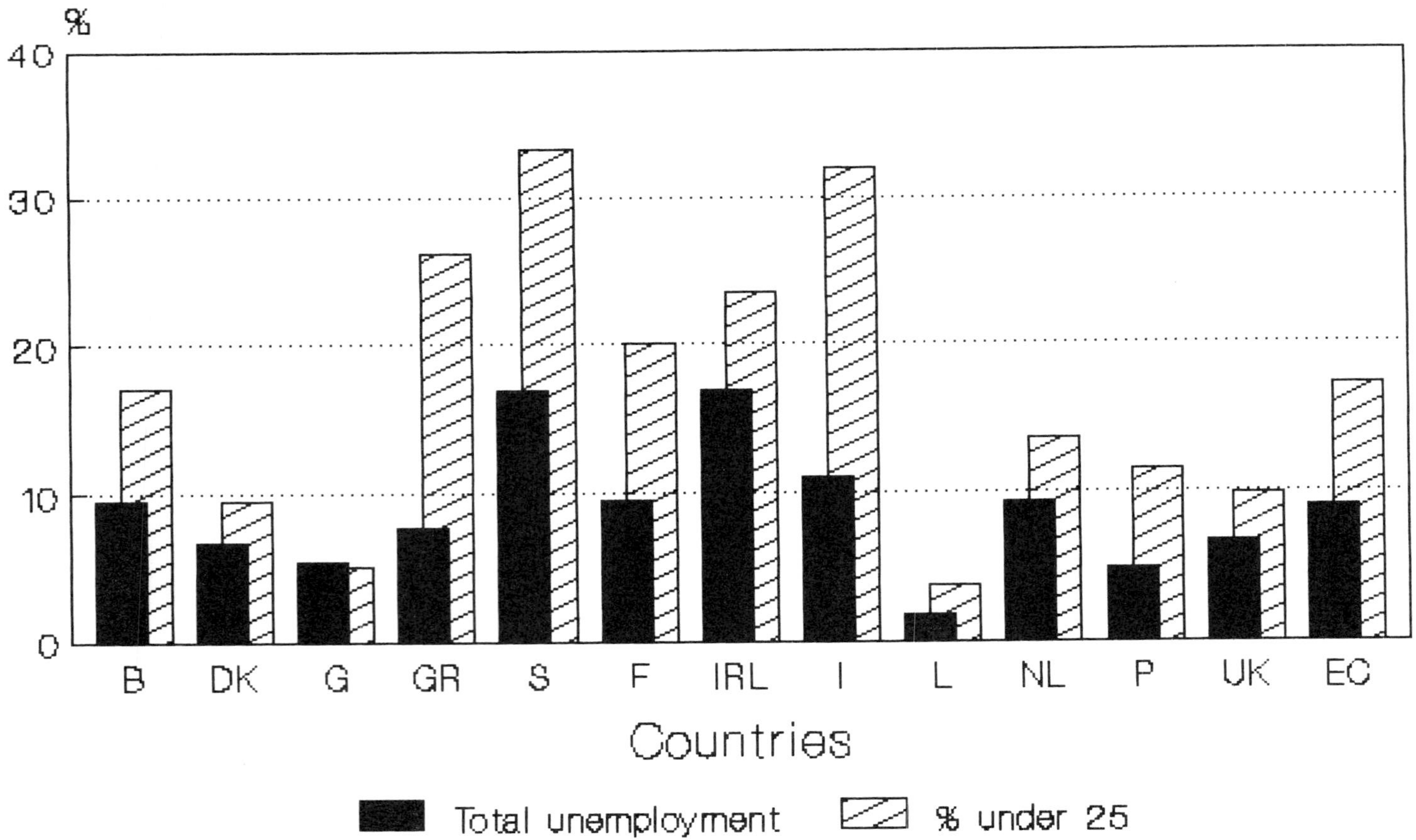

Source: Eurostat, Unemployment Monthly, 1/90

Figure 13 Proportion of unemployed who have been out of work for a year or more, 1987

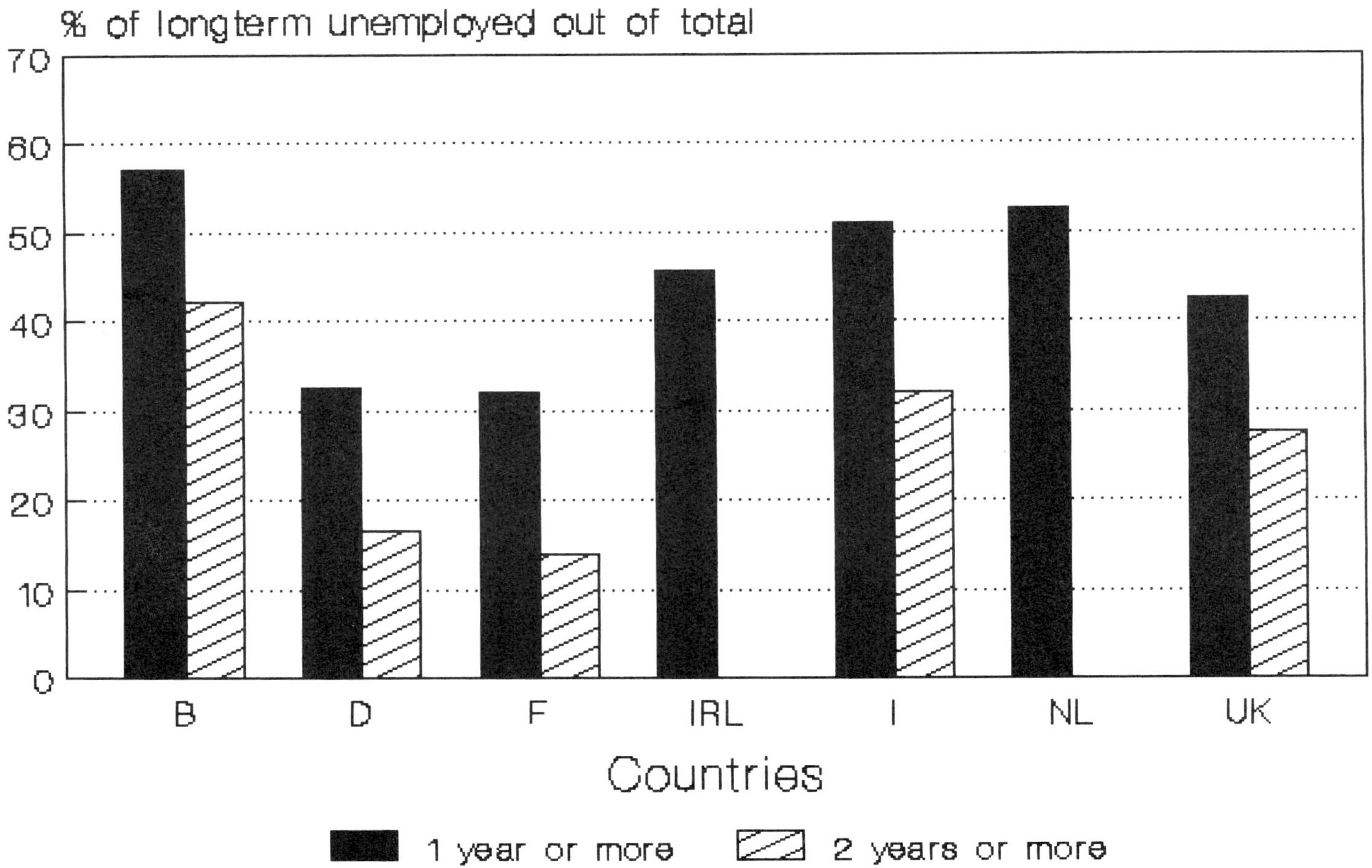

Source: Eurostat, Long Term Unemployment, 1988

Figure 14 Unemployment rates among men and women under the age of 25, 1989

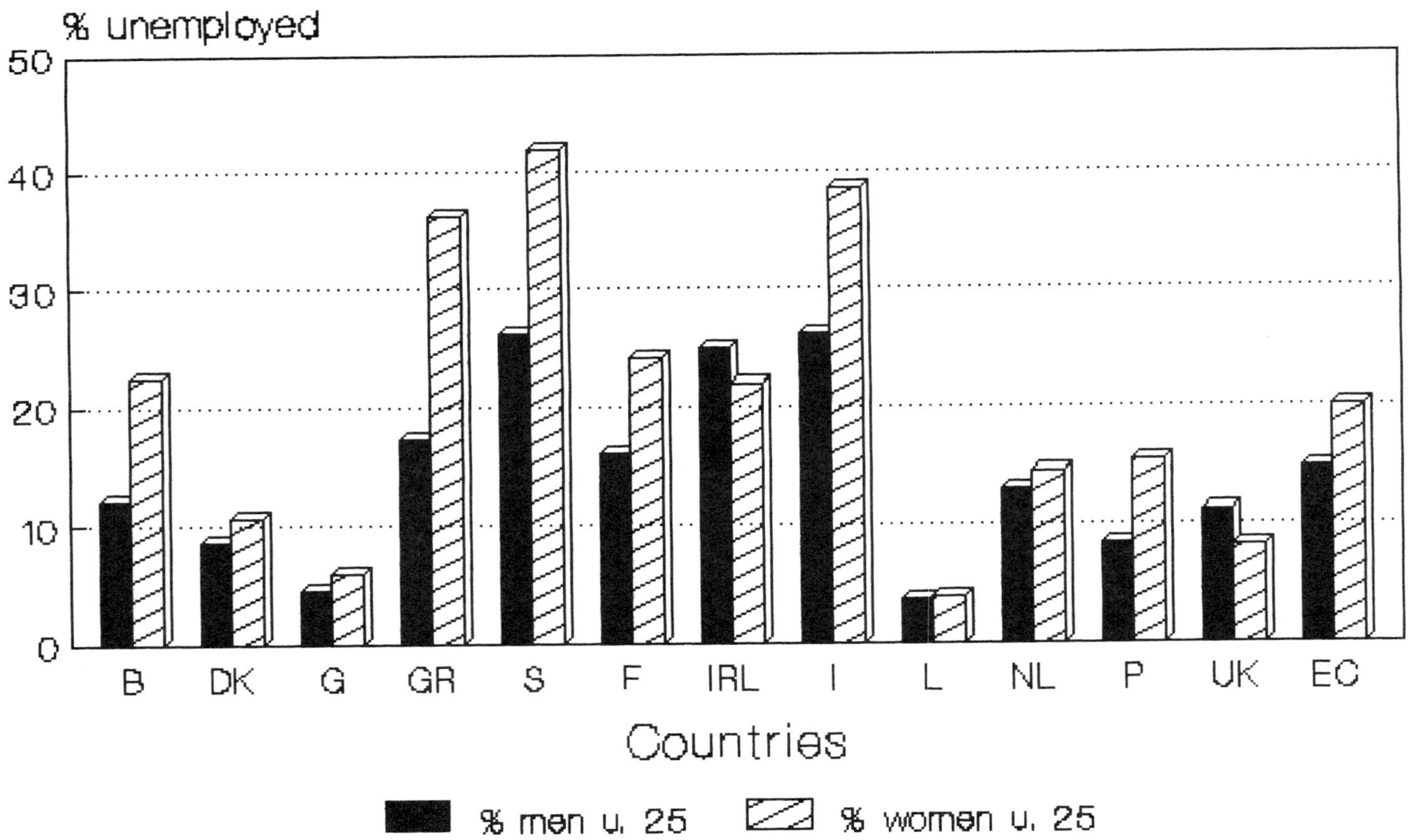

Source: Eurostat, Unemployment Monthly, 1/90

Figure 15 Structure of labour markets in EC Member States

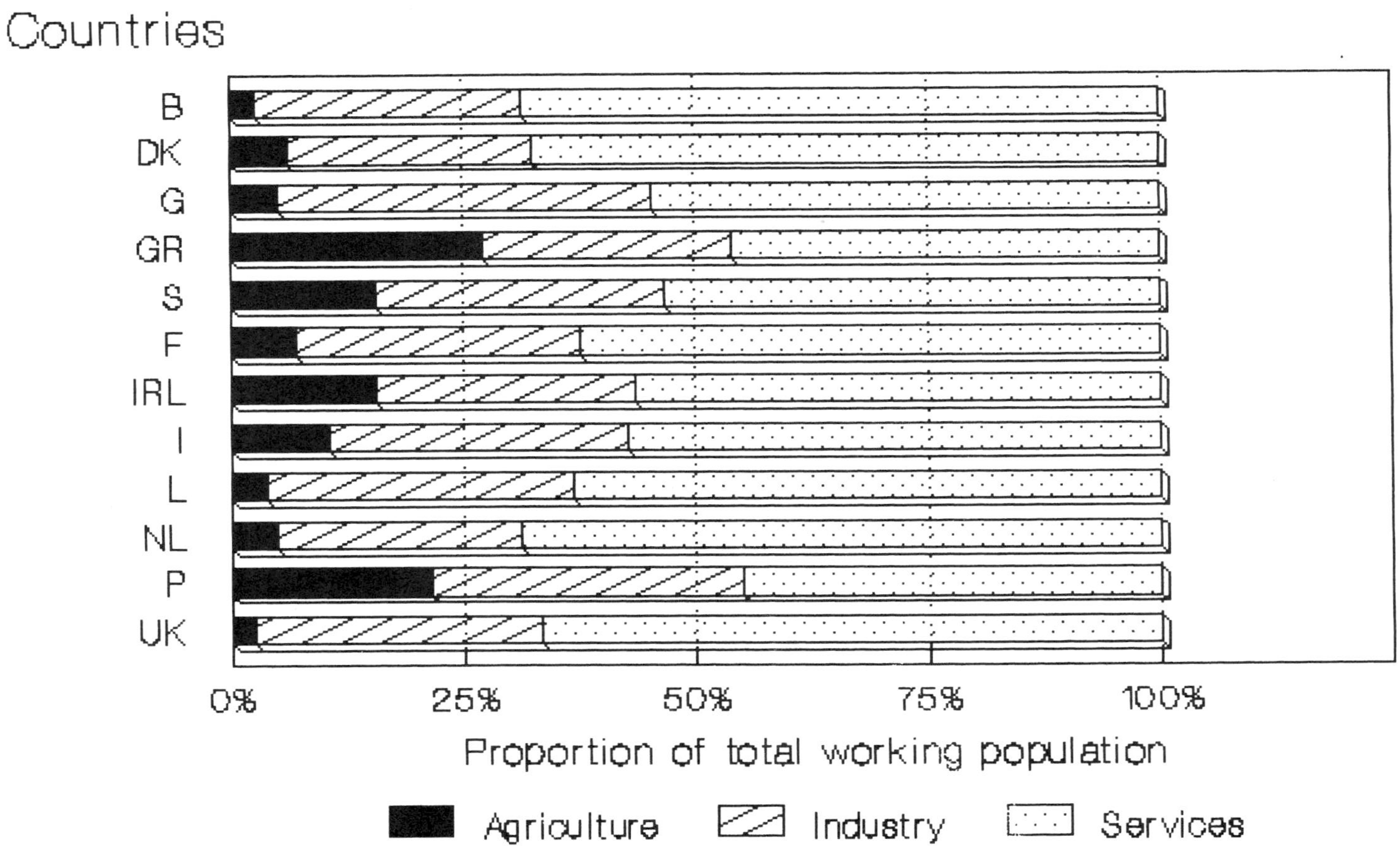

Source: Eurostat, Rapid Reports Population, 1/89

<u>Figure 16</u> Men and women employees by sector in the EC, 1986

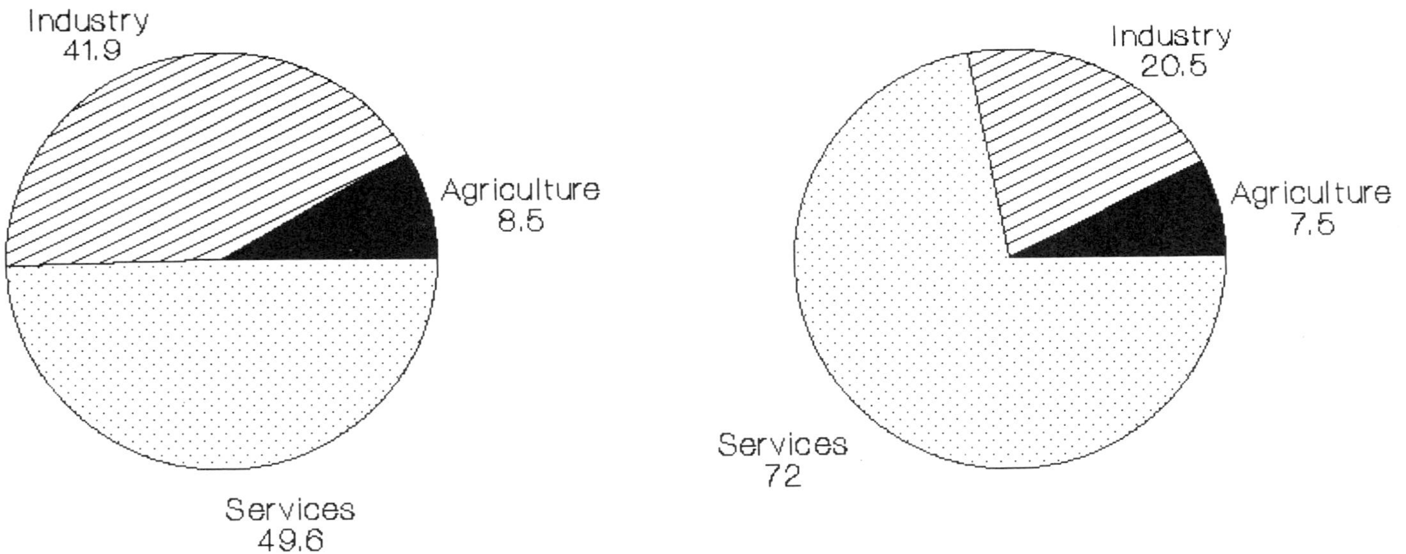

Source: Eurostat, *Labour Force Survey*, 1986

Figure 17 Percentage of persons who are self-employed, employed and family workers, 1988

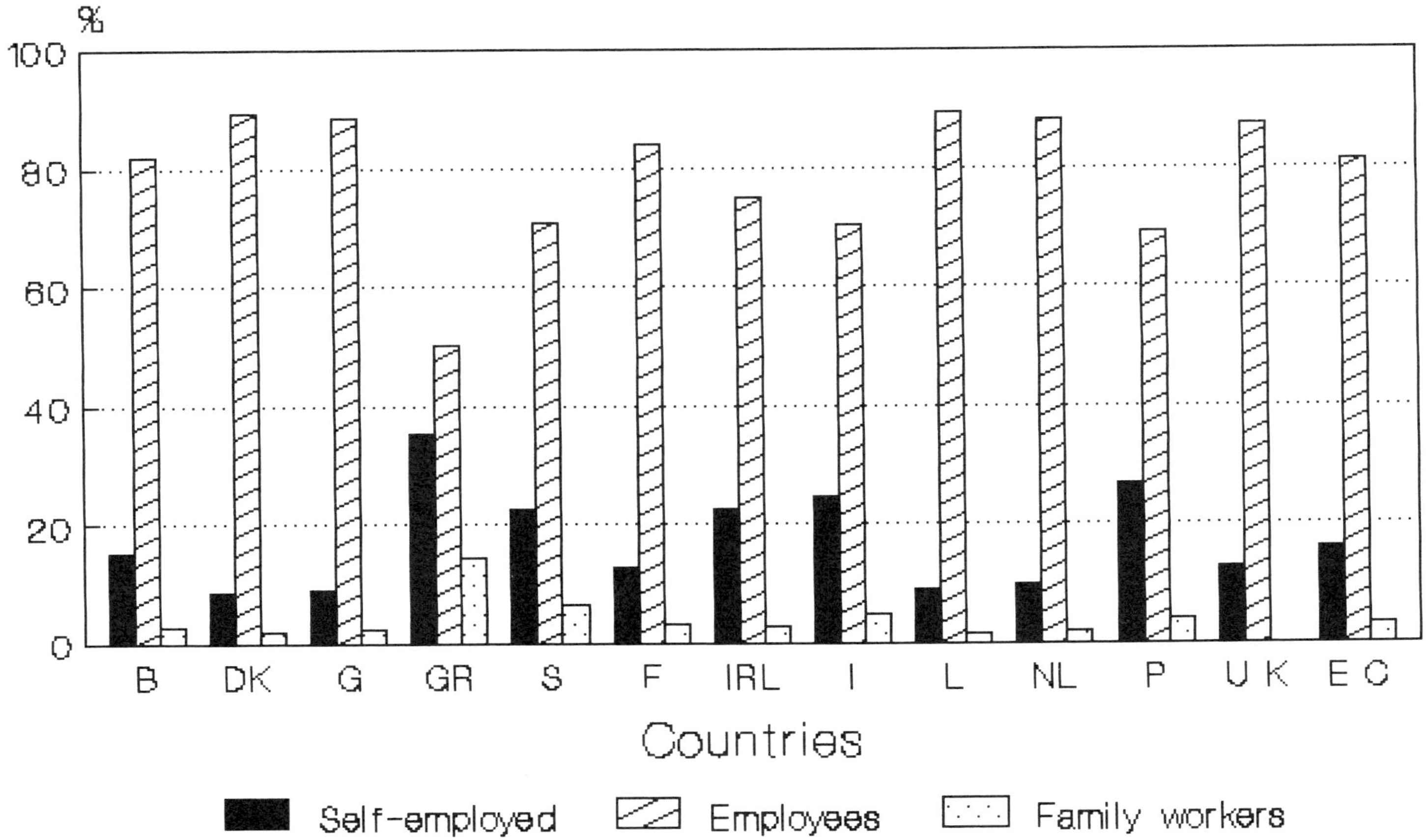

Source: Eurostat, Labour Force Survey, 1988

Figure 18 17- and 18-year-old boys in full-time education

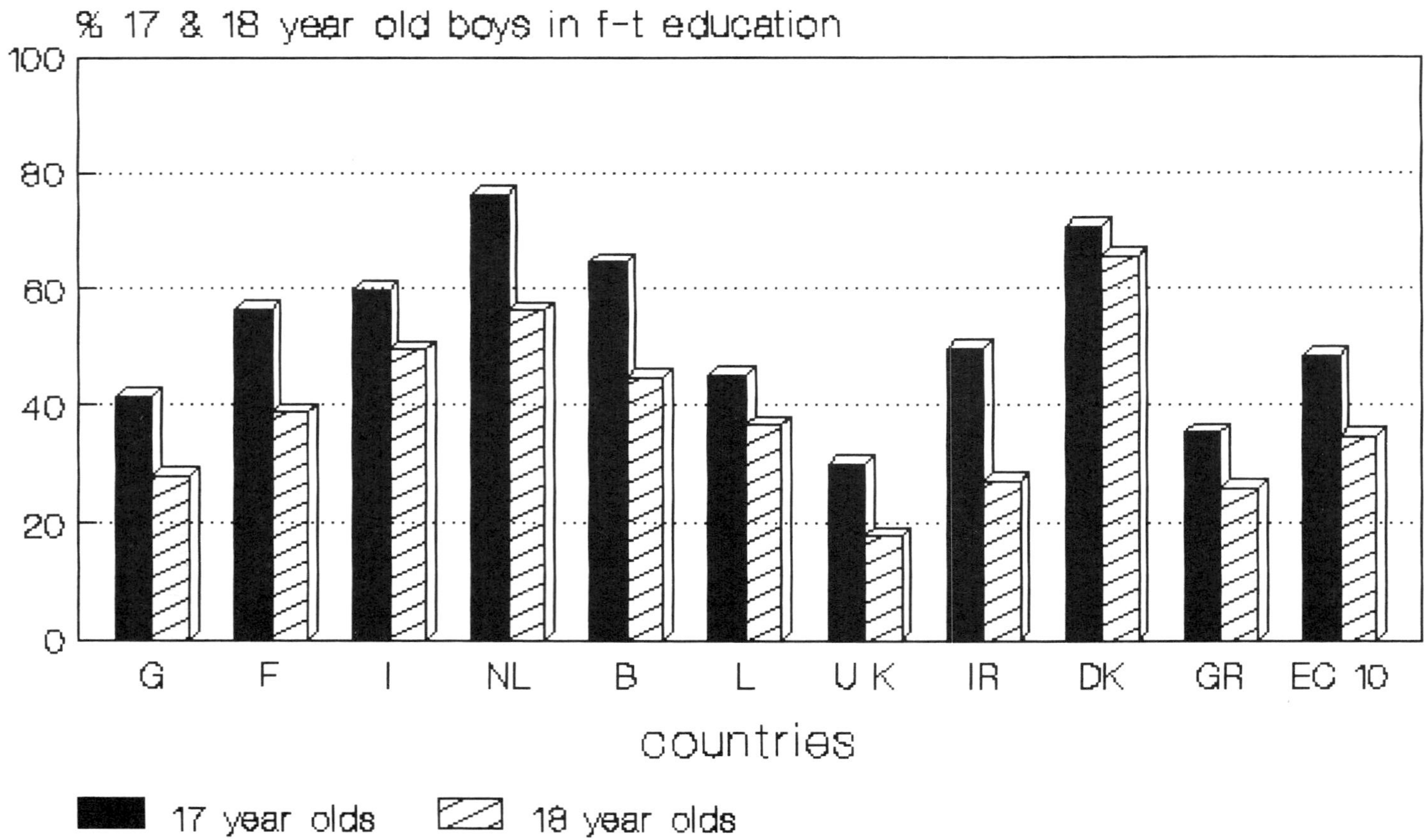

Source: Eurostat, Education and Training, 1985

Figure 19 Number of students at universities and polytechnics in the EC countries, 1985

Countries	Students 000	% of population
Belgium	247	2.5
Denmark	127	2.5
Germany	1530	2.5
Spain	935	2.4
France	935	2.4
Ireland	55	1.6
Italy	1118	2.0
Netherlands	308	2.1
U K	600	1.1
U S A	12247	5.1
Japan	2403	2.0

Source: Eurostat

Figure 20 Current expenditure on social security as a percentage of GDP, 1988

Countries	% of GDP
Belgium	28.7
Denmark	28.5
Germany	28.1
Spain	17.7
France	28.3
Ireland	22.5
Italy	22.9
Luxemburg	26.6
Netherlands	30.7
Portugal	17.0
U K	23.6

Figures for Belgium, Spain and UK 1987

Structure of finance of social security in the Member States of the EC, 1988

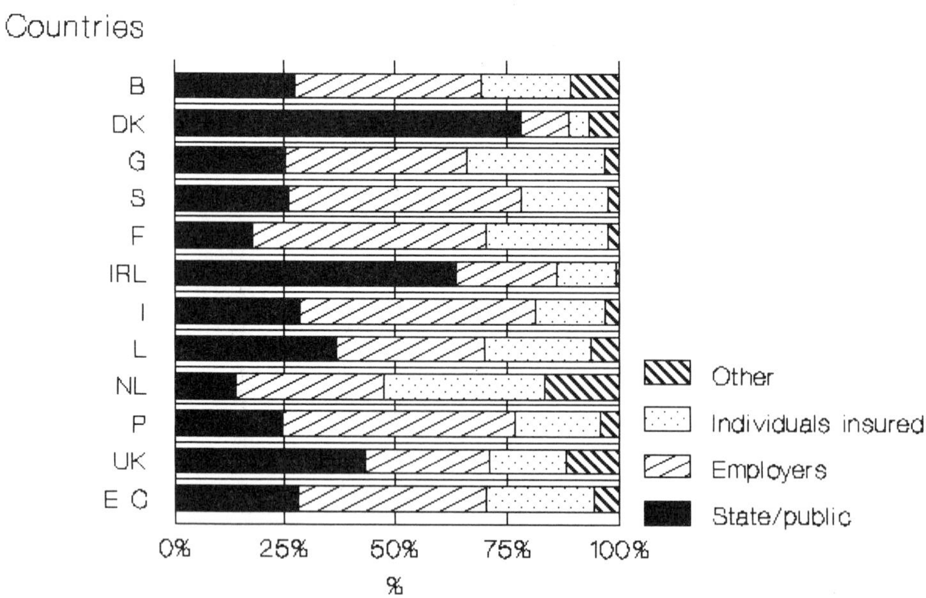

Source: Eurostat, Rapid Reports Population and Social Conditions, 3/90

Figure 21 Weekly working hours in EC Member States by law and agreement

Countries	Law	Collective Agreement
Belgium	40	38
Denmark	39	37
Germany	48	37
Greece	40	40
France	39	36 - 38
Ireland	48	40 BC 38 WC
Italy	48	38
Luxemburg	40	40
Netherlands	48	38
Portugal	48	40 - 44 BC 35 - 40 WC
Spain	40	40
U K	No law	39

Collective agreements valid for the largest number of workers in each state

BC = Bluecollar, WC = Whitecollar

Sources: COM(89) 360 final, European Industrial Relations Review, IDS European Reports

Figure 22 Proportion of employed men working on average 40+ hours/week

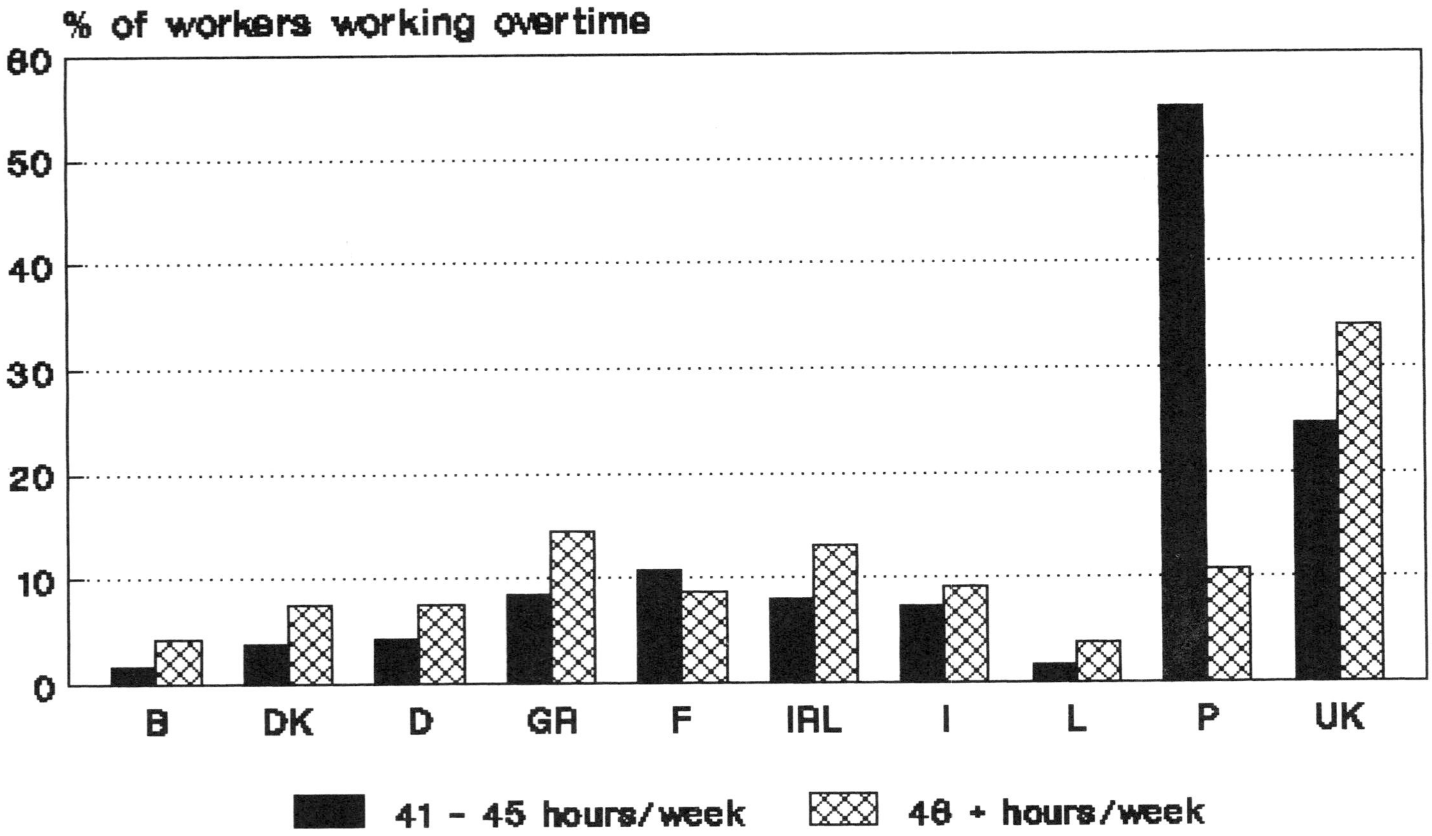

Source: Eurostat, Labour Force Survey, 1986

Figure 23 Foreign employees in the EC, 1986 (1,000s)

Countries	Other EC	Non-EC
Belgium	140.7	46.4
Denmark	11.6	27.7
Germany	498.3	1048.3
Greece	6.9	17.6
France	589.6	583.0
Ireland	16.1	4.4
Luxemburg	52.1	2.8
Netherlands	76.2	92.4
Portugal	6.7	23.2
UK	398.2	422.6

Source: Eurostat, Labour Force Survey, 1986

Figure 24 Net migration rates 1988. Immigrants/emigrants per 1000 population

Country	Net migration rate
Belgium	0.0
Denmark	0.1
Germany	7.6
Greece	0.0
France	0.0
Ireland	- 9.0
Italy	1.1
Luxemburg	11.3
Netherlands	2.4
Portugal	1.0
United Kingdom	0.0
European Community	1.8

Source: Eurostat, *Rapid Reports Population*, 1/89

Figure 25 EC unemployment rate 1970-1986. International comparison

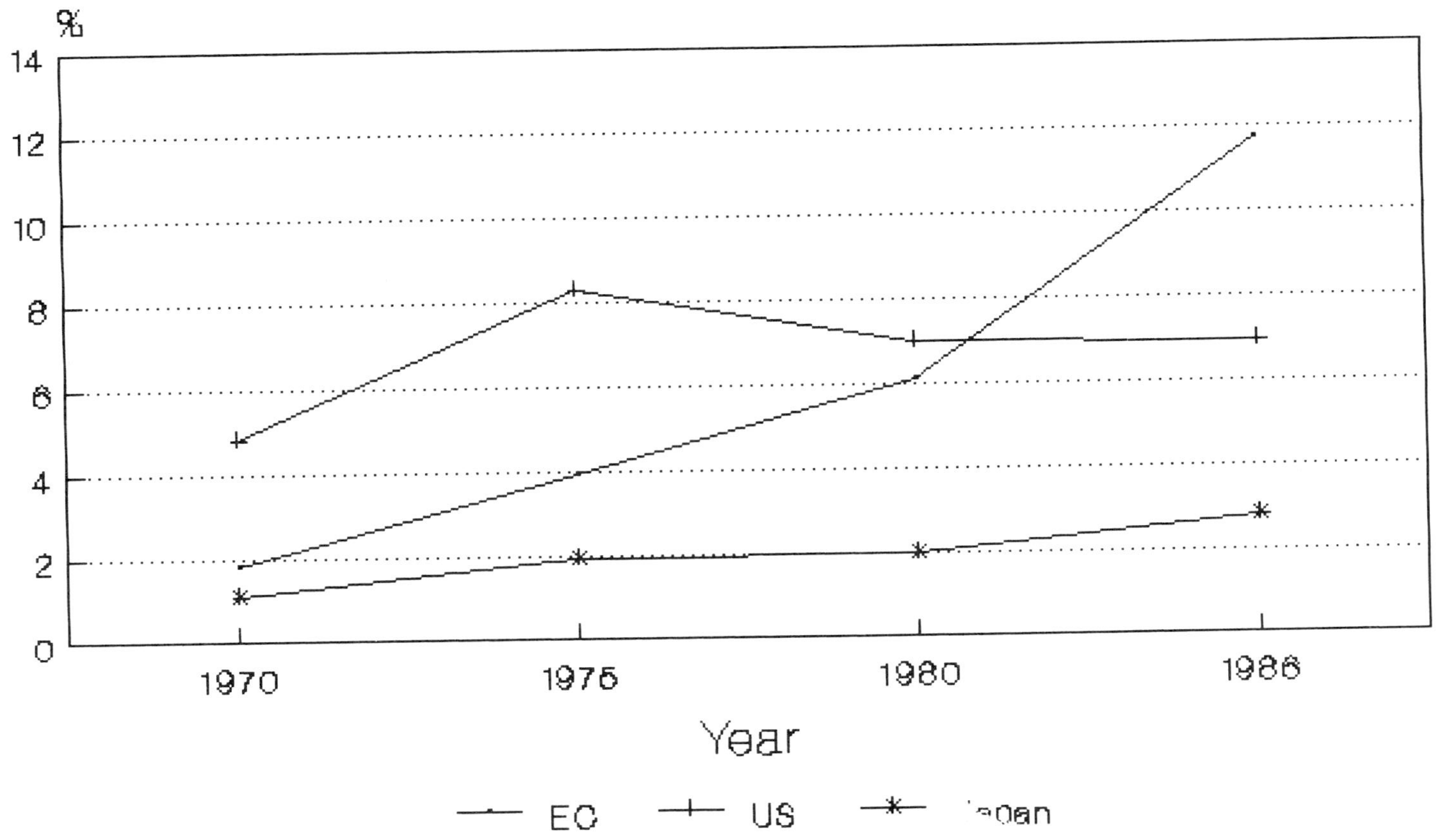

Source: Eurostat, Rapid Reports Population, 1/89

SECTION II
KEY DOCUMENTS ON EMPLOYMENT POLICY

GENERAL

Treaties

Article 3C

The abolition, as between Member States, of obstacles to freedom of movement of persons, services and capital.

Article 7

Within the scope of application of this Treaty, and without prejudice to any special provisions contained therein, any discrimination on grounds of nationality shall be prohibited.

The Council may, on a proposal from the Commission and in co-operation with the European Parliament, adopt, by a quality majority, rules designed to prohibit such discrimination.

Article 100

The Council shall, acting unanimously on a proposal from the Commission, issue directives for the approximation of such provisions down by law, regulation or administrative action in Member States as directly affect the establishment or functioning of the common market.

The European Parliament and the Economic and Social Committee shall be consulted in the case of directives whose implementation would, in one or more Member States, involve the amendment of legislation.

Article 100a (SEA)

1. By way of derogation from Article 100 and where otherwise provided in this Treaty, the following provisions shall apply for the achievement of the objectives set out in Article 8a. The Council shall,

acting by a qualified majority on a proposal from the Commission in co-operation with the European Parliament and after consulting the Economic and Social Committee, adopt the measures for the approximation of the provisions laid down by law, regulation or administrative action in Member States which have as their object the establishment and functioning of the internal market.

2. Paragraph 1 shall not apply to fiscal provisions, to those relating to the free movement of persons nor to those relating to the rights and interests of employed persons.

3. The Commission, in its provisions envisaged in paragraph 1 concerning health, safety, environmental protection and consumer protection, will take as a base a high level of protection.

4. If, after the adoption of a harmonization measure by the Council acting by a qualified majority, a Member State deems it necessary to apply national provisions on grounds of major needs referred to in Article 36, or relating to protection of the environment or the working environment, it shall notify the Commission of these provisions.

The Commission shall confirm the provisions involved after having verified that they are not a means of arbitrary discrimination or a disguised restriction on trade between Member States.

By way of derogation from the procedure laid down in Article 169 and 170, the Commission or any Member State may bring the matter directly before the Court of Justice if it considers that another Member State is making improper use of the powers provided for in this Article.

5. The harmonization measures referred to above shall, in appropriate cases, include a safeguard clause authorizing the Member States to take, for one or more of the non-economic reasons referred to in Article 36,

provisional measures subject to a Community control procedure.

Article 117

Member States agree upon the need to promote improved working conditions and an improved standard of living for workers, so as to make possible their harmonization while the improvement is being maintained.

They believe that such a development will ensue not only from the functioning of the common market, which will favour the harmonization of social systems, but also from the procedures provided for in this Treaty and from the approximation of provisions laid down by law, regulation or administrative action.

Article 118

Without prejudice to the other provisions of this Treaty and in conformity with its general objectives, the Commission shall have the task of promoting close co-operation between Member States in the social field, particularly in matters relating to:

- employment;
- labour law and working conditions;
- basic and advanced vocational training;
- social security;
- prevention of occupational accidents and diseases;
- occupational hygiene;
- the right of association, and collective bargaining between employers and workers.

To this end, the Commission shall act in close contact with Member States by making studies, delivering opinions and arranging consultations both on problems arising at national level and on those of concern to international organizations.

Before delivering the opinions provided for in this Article, the Commission shall consult the Economic and Social Committee.

Employment Policy

<u>Article 118A (SEA)</u>

1. Member States shall pay particular attention to encouraging improvements, especially in the working environment, as regards the health and safety of workers, and shall set as their objective the harmonization of conditions in this area, while maintaining the improvements made.

2. In order to help achieve the objective laid down in the first paragraph, the Council, acting by a qualified majority on a proposal from the Commission, in co-operation with the European Parliament and after consulting the Economic and Social Committee, shall adopt, by means of directives, minimum requirements for gradual implementation, having regard to the conditions and technical rules obtaining in each of the Member States. Such directives shall avoid imposing administrative, financial and legal constraints in a way which would hold back the creation and development of small and medium sized undertakings.

3. The provisions adopted pursuant to this Article shall not prevent any Member States from maintaining or introducing more stringent measures for the protection of working conditions compatible with this Treaty.

<u>Article 118B (SEA)</u>

The Commission shall endeavour to develop the dialogue between management and labour at European level which could, if the two sides consider it desirable, lead to relations based on agreement.

<u>Article 121</u>

The Council may, acting unanimously and after consulting the Economic and Social Committee, assign to the Commission tasks in connection with the implementation of common measures, particularly as regards social security for the migrant workers referred to in Articles 48 to 51.

Employment Policy

Article 122

The Commission shall include a separate chapter on social developments within the Community in its annual report to the European Parliament. The European Parliament may invite the Commission to draw up reports on any particular problems concerning social conditions.

Article 130A (SEA)

In order to promote its overall harmonious development, the Community shall develop and pursue its actions leading to the strengthening of its economic and social cohesion.

In particular, the Community shall aim at reducing disparities between the various regions and the backwardness of the least-favoured regions.

Article 130B (SEA)

Member States shall conduct their economic policies, and shall co-ordinate them, in such a way as, in addition, to attain the objectives set out in Article 130A. The implementation of the common policies and of the internal market shall take into account the objectives set out in Article 130A and in Article 130C and shall contribute to their achievement. The Community shall support the achievement of these objectives by the action it takes through the Structural Funds (European Agricultural Guidance and Guarantee Fund, Guidance Section, European Social Fund, European Regional Development Fund), the European Investment Bank and the other existing financial instruments.

Article 130C (SEA)

The European Regional Development Fund is intended to help redress the principal regional imbalances in the Community through participating in the development and structural adjustment of regions whose development is lagging behind and in the conversion of declining industrial regions.

Employment Policy

Article 130D (SEA)

Once the Single European Act enters into force the Commission shall submit a comprehensive proposal to the Council, the purpose of which will be to make such amendments to the structure and operational rules of the existing Structural Funds (European Agricultural Guidance and Guarantee Fund, Guidance Section, European Social Fund, European Regional Development Fund) as are necessary to clarify and rationalize their tasks in order to contribute to the achievement of the objectives set out in Article 130A and Article 130C, to increase their efficiency and to co-ordinate their activities between themselves and with the operations of the existing financial instruments. The Council shall act unanimously on this proposal within a period of one year, after consulting the European Parliament and the Economic and Social Committee.

Article 130E (SEA)

After adoption of the decision referred to in Article 130D, implementing decisions relating to the European Regional Development Fund shall be taken by the Council, acting by a qualified majority on a proposal from the Commission and in co-operation with the European Parliament.

With regard to the European Agricultural Guidance and Guarantee Fund, Guidance Section and the European Social Fund, Articles 43, 126 and 127 remain applicable respectively.

Article 193

An Economic and Social Committee is hereby established. It shall have advisory status. The Committee shall consist of representatives of the various categories of economic and social activity, in particular, farmers, carriers, workers, dealers, craftsmen, professional occupations and representatives of the general public.

Employment Policy

Article 194

The number of members of the Committee shall be as follows:

Belgium - 12
Denmark - 9
Germany - 24
Greece - 12
Spain - 21
France - 24
Ireland - 9
Italy - 24
Luxembourg - 6
Netherlands - 12
Portugal - 12
United Kingdom - 24

The members of the Committee shall be appointed by the Council, acting unanimously, for four years. Their appointments shall be renewable.

The members of the Committee shall be appointed in their personal capacity and may not be bound by any mandatory instructions.

Article 195

1. For the appointment of the members of the Committee, each Member State shall provide the Council with a list containing twice as many candidates as there are seats allowed to its nationals.

   The composition of the Committee shall take account of the need to ensure adequate representation of the various categories of economic and social activity.

2. The Council shall consult the Commission. It may obtain the opinion of European bodies which are representative of various economic and social sectors to which the activities of the Community are of concern.

Article 196

The Committee shall elect its chairman and officers from among its members for a term of two years.

It shall adopt its rules of procedure and shall submit them to the Council for its approval, which must be unanimous.

The Committee shall be convened by its chairman at the request of the Council or of the Commission.

Article 197

The Committee shall include specialized sections for the principal fields covers by this Treaty.

In particular, it shall contain an agricultural section and a transport section, which are the subject of special provisions in the Titles relating to agriculture and transport.

These specialized sections shall operate within the general terms of reference of the Committee. They may be consulted independently of the Committee.

Sub-committees may also be established within the Committee or prepare on specific questions or in specific fields, draft opinions to be submitted to the Committee for its consideration.

The rules of procedure shall lay down the methods of composition and the terms of reference of the specialized sections and of the sub-committees.

Article 198

The Committee must be consulted by the Council or by the Commission where this Treaty so provides. The Committee may be consulted by these institutions in all cases in which they consider it appropriate.

The Council or the Commission shall, if it considers it necessary, set the Committee, for the submission of its opinion, a time limit which may not be less than ten days from the date which the chairman receives notification to this effect. Upon expiry of the time limit, the absence of an opinion shall not prevent further action.

The opinion of the Committee and that of the

specialized section, together with a record of the proceedings, shall be forwarded to the Council and to the Commission.

Action Programmes and Council Resolutions

Council Resolution of 21 January 1974 concerning a Social Action Programme - Official Journal of the European Communities, No C13, 12/2/74.

The **Social Action Programme** contained the following objectives:

- **full and better employment;**
- **improvement of living and working conditions to make harmonization possible while maintaining improvements;**
- **increased involvement of management and labour in the decisions of the Community;**
- **increased involvement of workers in their undertakings.**

The Council stated that these objectives should be achieved by means of Community measures **'without however seeking a standard solution to all social problems or attempting to transfer to the Community level any responsibilities which are assumed more effectively at other levels'**.

Under the heading **employment** the Programme proposed various measures for consultation between Member States on employment policies and training, and legislation on equality between men and women in pay and employment. This proposal was quickly followed by the adoption of the important equal pay and equal treatment Directives in 1975 and 1976. The Council Resolution also stresses that it is important to ensure that **'the family responsibilities of all concerned may be reconciled with their job aspirations'**. This clause is now included in a slightly different form in the Social Charter. The Commission has in the last few years made a number of proposals in this area in the form of Recommendations, some of which have yet to be adopted by the Council.

The section on employment also contains a commitment

to adopt measures to protect workers hired through temporary employment agencies. This aim was fulfilled by the Commissions draft Directive on voluntary temporary work, submitted to the Council in 1982 which has so far failed to achieve approval by the Council. The Commission submitted a new draft Directive on atypical work which includes both temporary and part-time work in June 1990 as part of the Social Charter action programme.

The Council established the need for an action programme for **migrant workers**, including migrants from non-member countries and another action programme for the vocational and social integration of **handicapped people.** From the clauses on disability has followed a series of action programmes for the disabled, the latest being **HELIOS** adopted in 1988.

Under the heading '**improvement of living and working conditions**' are found:

- improvement in health and safety provisions;
- elimination of stress at work;
- reform of the organization of work to give opportunities for workers to have greater responsibility and to train for higher qualifications;
- measures to combat poverty.

A large number of **health and safety** Directives were adopted during the 1970s while more comprehensive legal instruments are now being adopted as part of the single market programme. Two programmes funding pilot projects to alleviate **poverty** were adopted in the 1980s. A new, more comprehensive scheme was adopted in 1989. The proposals to eliminate stress and improve working conditions have not been followed by legislative measures but have been part of the study programmes of the European Foundation for the Improvement in Living and Working Conditions which was set up in 1975, following the 1974 Action Programme.

The section on **'living and working conditions'** also contains a number of recommendations on improvement of social security provisions both for migrant workers and for **'adapting social security benefits to increased prosperity...'**. The improvement of social security rights for migrant workers is now taking place as part of the single market programme. This section also proposes measures to protect workers' interests in particular with regard to mergers and collective dismissals. These Directives were adopted in the mid-1970s. The Commission produced during the same period a number of recommendations with the aim of long-term harmonization of national provisions for example urging the adoption of a forty-hour working week, four weeks' paid holiday and job sharing schemes.

The Social Action Programme also contains a commitment to **worker participation.** The Commission drafted legislation in the context of company law on worker participation, but these initiatives failed to be agreed by the Council.

The Council further proposed to set up a European Trade Union Institute, which was established in Brussels in 1978. This institute has produced a large number of comparative studies of working conditions in member countries, most notably studies on flexibility and reduction in working time.

Finally the Programme proposes the implementation of a **common vocational training** policy and the setting up of a European Vocational Training Centre. There has been fairly large-scale Community funding of vocational training through the European Social Fund and other programmes, but this does not yet amount to a common training policy. The European Centre for the Development of Vocational Training (CEDEFOP) was, however, established in Berlin in 1978.

<u>Community Charter of Fundamental Social Rights</u> - COM(89) 471 final, Office for Official Publications of the EC, 2/10/89 and Social Europe No 1/90, p.45.

The Social Charter confirms the right to freedom of movement and states that this means a right to equal treatment with nationals in the host country in all fields.

In the field of employment and pay the Charter states that an **'equitable wage'**, particularly at the level of the basic wage shall be established either by law or by collective agreement. The Charter also requires rules to be laid down for workers in part-time, temporary and other untypical jobs. Every individual must be able to have access to free employment services.

The Charter lists the areas where improvements and harmonization are necessary to achieve a European labour market: the organization and flexibility of working time, particularly the duration of working time, improvement of conditions for workers in part-time, temporary and other atypical work, in weekend work, shift work, night work and systematic overtime. The Charter lays down a right to annual paid leave and weekly rest periods. There is also a right to a written contract of employment or employment conditions covered by collective agreement.

The Charter states that every citizen shall have a right to adequate social protection, and to adequate levels of social security benefits. It particularly stresses that people who are unemployed and no longer eligible for unemployment benefit must be able to receive a minimum income.

The Charter lays down a right for every employee to belong to a union and the freedom to negotiate and conclude collective agreements. In this context it looks forward to Europe-wide agreements on employment and working conditions and 'social entitlement'. The Charter also lays down a right to take collective action, including the right to strike, save in exceptions specified in existing legislation. A separate chapter deals with the development of information, consultation and participation for workers, particularly when new technology is introduced in a workplace and in the case of restructuring, mergers or bankruptcies.

The Charter includes a commitment to vocational training throughout the working life of employees, including an obligation on public authorities and private enterprise to set up training systems. It reaffirms the Community's commitment to equal opportunities, but contains no new initiatives in this field except the development of amenities enabling parents to reconcile their occupational and family responsibilities more easily.

In the area of health and safety there is a guarantee

of satisfactory health and safety conditions in the working environment and a pointer towards further harmonization.

The Charter sets the minimum employment age for children at fifteen. Young people in employment 'must receive equitable remuneration and, after the end of compulsory education, they must be entitled to receive initial vocational training, which must take place during working hours. Except where permitted by law or collective agreement young workers should be banned from night work and the duration of work must be limited.

The final two sections of the Charter extend beyond the field of employment and assert the right of retired people to a decent standard of living and a right to 'additional concrete measures' aiming at improving the social and professional integration of the disabled.

The fundamental social rights in the Charter are to be implemented by the Member States either through legislation or by encouraging collective agreements.

<u>Communication from the Commission concerning its action programme relating to the implementation of the Community Charter on basic social rights for workers</u> - COM(89) 568 final - Office for Official Publications of the EC, 29/11/89.

The different actions proposed are described in detail under each subject heading in Section I. This document is also useful because it contains a brief account of past development of EC policy in each of the areas covered by the chapters in the Charter. There is also a discussion about subsidiarity. The Commission is limiting its proposals for Directives to those areas where Community-wide legislation seems necessary to achieve the social dimension of the internal market and to contribute to economic and social cohesion. It also promises to leave room in the different legal instruments for agreement to be reached between the social partners on certain types of provisions.

INDUSTRIAL DEMOCRACY/EMPLOYEE INVOLVEMENT

Proposals

Proposal for a Fifth Directive to co-ordinate the safeguards which, for the protection of the interests of members and others, are required by Member States of companies within the meaning of the second paragraph of Article 58 of the EEC Treaty, as regards the structures of societas anonymas and the powers and obligations of their organs - Official Journal of the European Communities, No C131, 13/12/72 or EC Bulletin (Supplement 10/72) Office for Official Publication of the EC.

Amended proposal for a Fifth Directive founded on Article 54 (3) (g) of the EEC Treaty concerning the structure of public limited companies and the powers and obligations of their organs - Official Journal of the European Communities, No C240, 9/9/83.

The amended proposal contains both the text of the original proposal and the amendments, laid out in parallel columns for easy comparison. Both documents will therefore be described under this heading.

This proposal in the series of Directives co-ordinating company law in the member countries deals with the decision-making structures in companies. The original proposal of 1972 required all Member States to introduce the German model of two company boards, one board to manage and one to supervise the management board. It also sought to introduce the German model of employee participation with worker representatives elected by the workforce as members of the supervisory board. The amended proposal introduces the two-tier structure in all countries but permits Member States to offer companies the option of a single board with executive and non-executive members. The draft Directive is divided into two sections with provisions for the two different systems. The

Commission argues that the imposition of a two-tier system throughout the Community is impracticable, but that the two-tier structure should at least be made generally available for public limited companies. The draft Directive is therefore intended to impose certain conditions on one board companies to harmonize their functioning with that of two-tier structures.

The first proposal made employee representatives on the supervisory board obligatory in undertakings with 500 or more employees. The amended proposal increases the minimum size to 1,000 or more persons employed directly or through subsidiaries by the company.

In the amended proposal Member States are permitted three different options for employee participation:

1. employee representatives on the board;
2. employee participation through works councils;
3. systems of employee participation established through collective agreements between the two sides of industry.

In the case of worker representatives on the company board, these board members are to be non-executive members of either the one company board or of the supervisory board in a two-tier company. The draft Directive stipulates that there shall be a minimum of one-third employee non-executive members of the board and a maximum of two-thirds shareholder representatives. However, the company may opt to have up to half of the supervisory board members elected by the workforce. In this case the draft Directive stipulates that the company's voting procedures **'shall ensure that decisions of the non-executive members may ultimately be taken by the members appointed by the general meeting'**, i.e. by the members elected by the shareholders. The Commission does not specify how this shall be achieved, although the chair's casting vote seems to be one obvious method.

Worker representatives are to be elected by all employees by secret ballot in proportional elections ensuring the minorities are protected. Free expression must be guaranteed in the elections.

When worker participation is to take place through a

works council, this body must meet at regular intervals and at least immediately prior to meetings of the company board and shall be given all the documentation and information connected with the company board agenda. The works council has the right to information on the administration and situation of the company including its competitive position, credit situation and investment plans. The works council may request the presence of the Chair, his deputy or an executive board member at its meetings.

In the case of Member States and companies opting for employee participation through collectively agreed systems, whatever system chosen the employee representatives shall have the same position and rights as in employee representatives who are non-executive board members under the Directive.

The Council appointed an ad hoc working party of national government representatives which discussed the technical aspects of the draft between 1976 and 1982. The Economic and Social Committee has issued two Opinions on the original proposal in 1974 and 1978 (Official Journal of the European Communities, No C109, 19/9/74) and the European Parliament debated the proposal first in 1979 and then in May 1982 when a Resolution on the proposal was adopted (Official Journal of the European Communities, No C149, 14/6/92). The Commission gave its response to the Parliament in September 1982. The Commission's revised proposal took account of the Parliament's comments.

<u>Proposal for a Council Directive on procedures for informing and consulting the employees of undertakings with complex structures, in particular transnational undertakings</u> - Official Journal of the European Communities, No C297, 15/11/80.

<u>Amendment to the proposal for a Council Directive on procedures for informing and consulting employees</u> - Official Journal of the European Communities, No C217, 2/8/83.

This draft Directive, commonly called the Vredeling Directive after Commissioner Vredeling, deals with mechanisms for informing and consulting employees in **multinational companies and companies active in one state but with several workplaces or subsidiaries.** Under the draft Directive the management of the dominant undertaking is required to disclose information at least every six months to employee representatives in all subsidiaries employing at least 100 employees. This information shall include: the company's structure and manning, the economic and financial situation, the situation and probable development of the business and of production and sales, the employment situation and probable trends, production and investment programmes, rationalization plans, introduction of new working methods and all other plans liable to have a substantial effect on employees' interests. When the management in the dominant undertaking takes a decision liable to have a substantial effect on its employees, management is required to inform employees of the grounds and consequences of the decision at least forty days before adopting the decision. The employee representatives must be asked for their opinion within a period of not less than thirty days. Where management fails in its duty to consult, the employee representatives are authorized to open consultation. Member States are obliged to provide for appropriate penalties and the right of appeal to tribunals in case of failure to comply with the obligations under the draft Directive. A body representing all employees in the company and its subsidiaries may be created through agreement between management and employee representatives.

Council Conclusions of 21 July 1986 on procedures for informing and consulting the employees of undertakings with complex structures - Official Journal of the European Communities, No C203, 21/7/86.

In this statement the Council concludes that the problem of informing and consulting employees is of great political and economic importance, and that the solution to this problem can contribute towards improving relations between management and employees and thus towards better economic performance. The Council emphasizes the importance of the social area for the completion of the internal market. With reference to its failure to adopt the 5th Company Law Directive on employee involvement, the Council invites the Commission to continue to work in this field and to follow development in Member States. The Council states that it will resume its discussions about this or any other proposal produced by the Commission in this area at the beginning of 1989. However by June 1990 this had not yet happened. The Council invites the two sides of industry to continue their discussions with a view to arriving at agreements in this field.

Proposal for a Regulation on the Statute for a European company submitted by the Commission on 30 June 1975 - Official Journal of the European Communities, Nos C93 and C124, May 1975.

Memorandum from the Commission to Parliament, the Council and the two sides of industry 'Internal market and industrial co-operation, Statute for the European company, Internal market White Paper, point 137' - COM(88) 320 final, Office for Official Publications of the EC, 15/7/88.

Proposed Council Regulation and Directive on the Statute for a European Company - COM(89) 268 final, Office of Official Publication of the EC, 25/8/89.

The Economic and Social Committee published its Opinion on the proposed Statute on 28 March 1990 - Official Journal of the European Communities, No C124, 21/5/90.

For a summary of the clauses relating to employee rights in the Social Charter see the chapter on **European Community Social Policy**.

EQUAL OPPORTUNITIES

Treaties

Article 119

Each Member State shall during the first stage ensure and subsequently maintain the application of the principle that men and women should receive equal pay for equal work.

For the purpose of this Article, 'pay' means the ordinary basic or minimum wage or salary and any other consideration, whether in cash or in kind, which the worker receives, directly or indirectly, in respect of his employment from his employer.

Equal pay without discrimination based on sex means:

a. that pay for the same work at piece rates shall be calculated on the basis of the unit of measurement;

b. that pay for work at time rates shall be for the same job.

Directives

Council Directive of 10 February 1975 on the approximation of the laws of the Member States relating to the application of the principle of equal pay for men and women - 75/117/EEC, Official Journal of the European Communities, No L45, 19/2/75.

The Directive has its legal base in the principle of equal pay laid down in Article 119 of the EEC Treaty. Article 1 of the Directive states that the 'principle of equal pay' means, for the same work or for work to which equal value is attributed, the elimination of all discrimination on grounds of sex with regard to all aspects and conditions of remuneration.

The concept of 'remuneration' has by the European Court of Justice been deemed to include occupational pensions (Case 170/84 **Bilka**). With regard to work of equal value the Directive requires job classification systems to be based on the same criteria for both men and women.

Article 2 requires Member States to introduce measures to enable all employees who consider themselves wronged by a breach of the equal pay principle to pursue their claims by judicial process. Member States are further obliged to abolish all pay discrimination between men and women arising from laws, regulations or administrative provisions

Provisions contrary to the principle of equal pay in collective agreements, wage scales, wage agreements or individual contracts shall be declared null and void or be amended. In addition there must be measures to protect employees against dismissal by the employer as a reaction to a complaint.

Member States are further obliged to see that effective means are available to take care that the equal pay principle is observed and that employees are kept informed about their rights under the Directive.

National legislation had to be implemented by February 1975. Finally Governments were requested to report on the application of the Directive by February 1977

Council Directive of 9 February 1976 on the implementation of the principle of equal treatment for men and women as regards access to employment, vocational training and promotion, and working conditions - 76/207/EEC, Official Journal of the European Communities, No L39, 14/2/76.

This Directive puts into effect the principle of equal treatment of men and women as regards access to employment, including promotion, working conditions, and vocational training. The Directive prohibits both direct and indirect discrimination on grounds of sex in particular by reference to marital or family status. The Directive excludes occupational activities which **'by reason of their nature or the context in which they are carried out, the sex of the worker constitutes a determining factor'**. The Directive also excludes from the equal treatment principle provisions for the protection of women, particularly as regards pregnancy and maternity.

Member States are obliged to ensure that in the areas of employment and of working conditions including dismissal:

a. laws, regulations and administrative provisions contrary to the principle of equal treatment are abolished;
b. any such provisions in collective agreements, individual employment contracts, internal rules of undertakings or in rules governing independent occupations and professions shall either be declared null and void or amended;
c. that protective laws, regulations or administrative provisions, which are contrary to the principle of equal treatment are revised, and that where such provisions are included in collective agreements, labour and management shall be requested to revise them.

The Directive requires Member States to take the same legislative and other action to promote equal treatment in the field of training of all types and levels. This includes an obligation to ensure that private training establishments are accessible without any discrimination on the grounds of sex. As in the Equal Pay Directive the Equal Treatment Directive includes an obligation for Members States to provide means by which complainants can pursue their claims through judicial process. As in the Equal Pay Directive Member States are obliged to introduce provisions to protect complainants from dismissal. Member States are finally committed to bring the measures outlined above to the attention of employees.

The Directive announces the intention to legislate in the field of social security but does not include provisions in this field.

The deadline for implementation of the Directive in the Member States was October 1979 and governments were obliged to report to the Council on the progress of the application of the Directive within two years after this deadline.

Council Directive of 19 December 1978 on the progressive implementation of the principle of equal treatment for men and women in matters of social security - 79/7/EEC, Official Journal of the European Communities, No L6, 10/1/79.

The Directive outlaws discrimination between men and women in social security. It applies to statutory social security systems which provide protection against the risks of sickness, invalidity, old age, accidents at work and occupational disease, unemployment and social assistance which supplement or replace statutory schemes.

There are a number features of social security systems which are specifically excluded from the Directive. The Directive does not apply to survivors benefits and family/child benefits. Member States still have the right to set different pensionable ages for men and women. The Directive also permits Member States to give pension advantages to persons who have brought up children and to grant benefit entitlement to parents who stay at home to take care of children. The Directive further does not outlaw widows' pensions or invalidity benefits by virtue of the derived entitlement of a wife. The granting of increases in long-term invalidity benefits, old-age pensions, accidents at work or occupational disease benefits for a dependent wife is also permitted. Persons who have opted out of social security systems before the adoption of the Directive and who therefore receive less or no benefits are also not covered by these provisions. Finally, the Directive excludes maternity benefits from the principle of non-discrimination.

The Directive outlaws both direct and indirect discrimination by reference to gender, marital or family status with regard to the scope and conditions of social security schemes, the obligation to contribute and the calculation of contributions, the calculation of benefits, including increases due for spouses and dependants and the conditions governing the duration and retention of entitlement to benefits.

The Directive includes the obligation on Member States found in most of the Directives and draft Directives on gender equality to introduce measures to enable complainants to pursue their claims by judicial process.

The period of implementation for national legislation was six years. The deadline was reached in January 1985.

<u>Council Directive of 24 July 1986 on the implementation of the principle of equal treatment for men and women in occupational social security schemes</u> - 86/378/EEC, Official Journal of the European Communities, No L225, 12/8/86.

This Directive applies to occupational schemes which provide protection against sickness, invalidity, old age and early retirement, industrial accidents and occupational diseases and unemployment. The Directive outlaws direct and indirect sex discrimination particularly by reference to marital or family status with regard to the scope of and access to schemes, obligations to contribute and the calculation of contribution, the calculation of benefits, including benefits for spouses or defendants and the conditions governing the duration and retention of entitlement to benefits. Maternity benefits are exempt from the principle of equal treatment.

The Directive outlaws fixing different retirement ages for men and women, but permits different levels of benefit insofar as it may be necessary to take account of actuarial calculation factors which differ according to sex in the case of benefits defined by contributions.

The Directive also stipulates that the acquisition or retention of rights must not be suspended for women on statutory paid maternity leave and parents on parental leave.

Member States shall take the necessary steps to ensure that provisions of occupational schemes contrary to the principle of equal treatment are eliminated by 1 January 1993. However, Member States may defer the application of the principle of equal treatment with regard to the determination of pensionable age for granting of pensions until equal pension ages are achieved in statutory schemes or until another Directive requires implementation. The same applies to survivors' pensions. Legislation necessary to comply with the Directive has to be implemented by the Autumn of 1989.

Council Directive of 11 December 1986 on the application of the principle of equal treatment between men and women engaged in an activity, including agriculture, in a self-employed capacity, and on the protection of self-employed women during pregnancy and motherhood - 86/613/EEC, Official Journal of the European Communities, No L359, 19/12/86.

The purpose of the Directive is to ensure equal treatment between men and women who are self-employed where they are not already covered by other equal treatment Directives. The Directive covers all self-employed persons, including farmers and the liberal professions, and their spouses who help out in the family business without being employees or partners.

Member States are required to ensure the elimination of all provisions relating to self-employed persons which are contrary to the principle of equal treatment as defined in the Equal Treatment Directive (76/207/ EEC). This includes taking steps to ensure that conditions for forming a company between spouses are not more restrictive than for the formation of a company between persons who are not married to one another.

Member States are also obliged to take measures to enable spouses who are not partners or employees and who are not covered by any social security scheme to join a contributory scheme voluntarily.

Unusually in a Directive a number of provisions are recommendations rather than enforceable obligations. Member States are required to examine **'under what conditions recognition'** of the work of spouses **'may be encouraged'**. Member States are also required to examine whether self-employed women and wives in family businesses could have access to social security benefits and services supplying temporary replacements during pregnancy and while taking care of children. These two provisions were introduced by Member States during the Council's deliberations of the draft Directive and represent a considerable weakening of the Commission's original proposal. However the Commission, threatening to withdraw the draft proposal altogether, won a concession. Article 11 contains a commitment by the Council to review the provisions of the Directive on a proposal from the

Commission before July 1993.

The deadline for implementation of legislation under the Directive was the end of 1989, but amendments to legislation on matrimonial rights and obligations do not have to be implemented until the end of 1991.

Proposals

Amended proposal for an EEC Council Directive on parental leave and leave for family reasons - COM(83) 686 final, 22/11/83, Office for Official Publications of the EC. Amended by proposal, 9/11/84.

The draft Directive introduces harmonized provisions for parental leave and leave for family reasons in the Member States. The draft covers all wage-earners including public sector employees and part-timers. The Directive specifically does not interfere with existing provisions in some countries for paternity leave granted on the birth of a child. The Commission proposes that all parents and adoptive parents, step parents and persons acting in place of parents who are ill or dead should have the right to parental leave in connection with the birth of a child following the statutory period of maternity leave. The leave period is proposed to be three months for each parent after each birth or adoption, with longer periods possible for single parents and parents of a disabled child. Originally the Commission proposed that the right to parental leave should not be transferable between parents, but the Council decided in favour of transferability. The leave has to be taken before the child is two years old. Parental leave can be taken either as full-time or part-time leave in which case the leave period is extended proportionally. The provision of social security benefits for the leave period is not obligatory in the draft Directive. There are various regulations about minimum periods of notice on the part of both employee and employer.

The draft Directive also provides for leave for family reasons such as illness of a spouse, a child or child carer, the death of a near relative and the wedding of a child. Originally the Commission proposed that all employees should have a right to a minimum of ten days' leave per annum. The Council instead left the number of days to the Member States. There are also possibilities for governments to extend the minimum number of leave days in the case of parents with three or more children or for employees caring for a disabled person in their own household.

The deadline for implementation of these provisions was intended to be two years from the adoption of the Directive.

Proposal for a Council Directive completing the implementation of the principle of equal treatment for men and women in statutory and occupational social security schemes - COM(87) 494 final, Office of Official Publications of the EC, 23/10/87.

The Commission document includes explanations of the different provisions in the draft Directive as well as the text of the draft.

The draft Directive covers those areas specifically excluded from the Directive on Equal Treatment in Social Security, survivors' benefits and family benefits in statutory and occupational social security schemes. The Directive also applies to social assistance which is intended to supplement or replace these benefits.

The Directive applies to the working population including the self-employed, the unemployed, retired workers, disabled workers, family members, survivors and other defendants of the persons listed above.

The Directive stipulates that for survivors' benefits there must be no discrimination on the grounds of the sex of either the deceased or of the survivor. This means that Member States, if the Directive is adopted, would have either to give widowers the same treatment as widows or replace widows' benefits by a system of individual rights open to all surviving spouses regardless of sex.

With regard to family benefit the draft Directive stipulates that if there are no statutory provisions for parents to share this benefit it shall be paid to one or other of the parents without discrimination. The benefit shall be paid to the mother of two-parent families only if the parents have not specified which of them shall receive the benefit. In the case of benefits for dependent adults there must be no discrimination on the grounds of the gender of either the dependent adult or the carer.

The draft Directive also stipulates that the pensionable age for the granting of old-age and retirement pensions must be the same for both sexes. If this leads to an increase in the pension age for one sex, provisions shall be made for the gradual implementation of the new system and for temporary safeguards for workers who have reached the previous pension age, enabling them to claim their pension at the age previously prescribed. If schemes do not specify a pensionable age they must either leave the choice of age to the beneficiaries between age limits which must be the same for both sexes, or make pension entitlement dependent on completion of a given number of contribution years which must be the same for both sexes. The draft Directive also outlaws sex discrimination in pension benefits granted to people who have brought up children or with regard to benefit entitlement accumulated during child-care breaks.

Old-age, invalidity and other similar benefits granted by virtue of the derived benefits of a spouse shall be authorized solely in the case of those spouses, who when the Directive comes into force have not constituted their own personal entitlement to these benefits.

The Directive would not prevent Member States from replacing a system of wives' derived rights by a system of personal rights for wives.

The proposed period for implementing national legislation is three years.

<u>Proposal from the Commission to the Council for a Directive on the burden of proof in the area of equal pay and equal treatment for women and men</u> - COM(88) 269 final, Office for Official Publications of the EC, 24/5/88.

This Commission proposal is the result of a survey undertaken in all Member States on the implementation of the Community's equality Directives (Comparative Analysis of the Provisions for Legal Redress in Member States of the EEC, V/564/84). This study found that one of the main problems for complainants in equal pay and treatment cases was the burden of proof. The draft Directive therefore seeks to reverse the burden of proof in these cases so that the complainant has to show only that she/he has been less favourably treated and that the person more favourably treated was of the opposite sex. The burden of proof would then shift to the alleged discriminator to show that the reason for the treatment was not the complainant's sex. As was pointed out in the European Parliament report on the draft Directive despite the title of the draft, the proposal aims to establish a shared burden of proof rather than a complete reversal of it. In addition the Directive states that the complainant shall have the benefit of any doubt that remains.

The draft Directive also requires national legislation to ensure that all relevant information which is necessary for either party to present their case is made available to them. It includes the first clear definition of the concept of indirect discrimination: **'indirect discrimination exists where an apparently neutral provision, criterion or practice disproportionately disadvantages the members of one sex, by reference in particular to marital or family status, and is not objectively justified by any necessary reason or condition unrelated to the sex of the person concerned'.**

The proposed deadline for implementation of national legislation is three years from the adoption of the Directive.

<u>European Parliament Report drawn up on behalf of the Committee on Women's Rights on the proposal from the Commission to the Council (COM(88) 269-Doc. C2-83/88) for a Directive on the burden of proof in the area of equal pay and equal treatment for women and men</u> - PE DOC A 2-298/88.

This report contains the Women's Committee's amendments to the wording of certain clauses of the proposed Directive with the Committee's comments. The report of the Legal Committee on the draft Directive is included. The Report also contains excerpts from the Evaluation Report on the Implementation of the Equality Directives (see Section III).

Action Programmes and other Council Resolutions

<u>The Community Action Programme on the Promotion of Equal Opportunities for Women 1982-1985</u> - COM(81) 758 final, 9/12/81.

This document contains a detailed description of the action plan and a plan for the development of positive action in the personnel policy of the Commission. The action plan contains areas of action, including:

- Monitoring of the application of the equality Directives.
- Revision of national and Community protective legislation.
- Preparation of new provisions - including equal treatment in social security and for the self-employed.
- Improvement in living and working conditions - including parental leave, the impact of tax on women's employment.
- Development of positive action.
- Protection of women during pregnancy and motherhood.
- Integration of women into working life particularly with respect to new technologies.
- Analysis of trends in female employment.
- Desegregation of employment.
- Sharing of occupational, family and social responsibilities.
- Application of the principle of equal treatment to women immigrants.
- Development of public attitudes.

<u>Council Resolution of 12 July 1982 concerning the new Community Action Programme on the promotion of equal opportunities for women</u> - Official Journal of the European Communities, No C186, 21/7/82.

This pledged intensified Community action to strengthen the individual rights of working women and the achievement of equal opportunities in practice, in particular through positive action. The Resolution emphasized the need to strengthen or to set up national bodies for the promotion of women's employment and equal opportunities. It confirmed the need to increase public awareness and information measures to support a change in attitude about **'sharing occupational, family and social responsibilities'**. It reaffirms the need to promote more equal representation of women at different levels of responsibility. Finally there is a pledge by member governments to take account of equal opportunities in Community policies and to consider favourably relevant budget measures to provide financial resources for the implementation of the Action Programme.

<u>Council Resolution of 7 June 1984 on action to combat unemployment among women</u> - Official Journal of the European Communities, No C161, 21/6/84.

In the light of the fact that unemployment among women is substantially higher than among men in the Community, the Council re-affirms its commitment to the principle of the equal right of men and women to work to acquire personal income on equal terms and to the development of positive measures to correct <u>de facto</u> inequalities. The Council lays down the following objectives for action within the framework of national policies and practices:

- to ensure that measures aimed at encouraging recruitment of additional labour allow for more balanced representation, particularly in jobs in which women are under-represented and in skilled jobs;
- to focus recruitment premiums on the people at the greatest disadvantage on the labour market;
- to adopt adequate measures to promote increased representation of women in the industries of the future especially the high technology industries;
- to make efforts to promote equal opportunities in the public sector, which can serve as an example;
- to enable women to have equal access to financial and other facilities for the creation of business including co-operatives;
- to promote education, vocational training and guidance

to give women a wider choice of jobs particularly in growth sectors;
- to ensure more appropriate qualifications for women in industries subject to restructuring, for women from less-favoured areas and for women returning to work;
- to promote increased representation of women in training programmes.

Governments are asked to ensure that placement and counselling services are staffed with skilled personnel with expertise in the problems of unemployed women and to improve the information on the situation of women on the labour market in order to combat unemployment, monitor the progress of sexual desegregation in employment and identify female unemployment trends more accurately.

The Commission is requested to report on progress at regular intervals and to organize an annual exchange between Member States on the measures undertaken under the Resolution.

Council Recommendation of 13 December 1984 on the promotion of positive action for women - 84/635/EEC, Official Journal of the European Communities, No L331 19/12/84.

The Council recommends that the Member States adopt a positive action policy to eliminate inequalities affecting women in working life and promote a better balance between the sexes in employment. The Recommendation comprises specific measures to counteract prejudice against women in employment and to encourage women into work where they are currently under-represented.

The Recommendation lists *inter alia* the following aspects which should be targeted by positive action measures:

- increasing the awareness of the public and the world of work of the need to promote equality;
- respect for the dignity of women in the workplace;
- qualitative and quantitative studies of the position of women on the labour market;
- diversification of vocational training;

- skilled counselling services for unemployed women;
- encouraging women into positions of responsibility;
- adjusting the organization of work and working time;
- measures to foster greater sharing of occupational and social responsibilities;
- active participation by women in decision-making bodies.

The Council recommends positive action by governments, particularly in employment in the public sector, by both sides of industry and by equal opportunities organizations.

Resolution of the Council and of Ministers for Education, meeting within the Council, of 3 June 1985 containing an Action Programme on equal opportunities for boys and girls in education - Official Journal of the European Communities, No C166, 5/7/85.

The Council declares that education should contribute to eradicating stereotypes, encourage acceptance of the principles of fair sharing of family and occupational responsibilities and prepare young people adequately for working life. The Council also states that positive action is necessary to bring about equality in practice.

The aim of the Council is to ensure equal opportunities for boys and girls in all types of education and training, to enable boys and girls to make fully informed educational and career choices, to motivate them to make non-traditional choices and to encourage girls to participate as much as boys in new and expanding sectors, such as information technology and biotechnology.

The Action Programme includes the following commitment to promote awareness among all participants in the educational process of the need to achieve equal opportunities for boys and girls by:

- encouraging the eradication of sex stereotyping through co-ordinated action to raise awareness;
- encouraging exchanges of information on innovatory projects in the field;
- publishing the results of experience and practical guidance at the national level.

The Resolution stresses the importance of educational and vocational guidance and counselling and of opening up schools to working life and the outside world. Equal opportunities should be included in teachers' initial and in-service training. Co-educational practices should be re-enforced in mixed-sex schools. The Resolution further stresses the importance of developing balance between men and women holding positions of responsibility in education and of eradicating persistent stereotypes from school textbooks. There is a call for special measures to help the underprivileged, particularly girls and the children of migrant workers.

Member States are requested to take action in the form of annual reports on action taken, training of school advisers, reviews of regulations to eradicate stereotypes and discrimination.

The Commission is asked to promote the principle of equality between boys and girls in all Community action and policies connected with education, training and employment. The Commission extended the programme of study visits in education, to promote equality through the EURYDICE programme and to ensure close co-operation with the European teachers and parents organizations.

Second Council Resolution of 24 July 1986 on the promotion of equal opportunities for women - Official Journal of the European Communities, No C203, 12/8/86.

The Council calls on Member States to ensure effective application of existing equal opportunities legislation, particularly through information and by the development of equal treatment provisions. It also asks them to examine all aspects of the problem relating to the establishment of proof with regard to equal treatment provisions.

The Resolution calls for comprehensive and co-ordinated action on education and training in order to create a better balance between men and women in different types of education institutions and to widen career choices. It calls for measures to increase the number of women in new technology jobs.

The Resolution calls for positive action in all fields

and for the revision of protective legislation which is no longer justified. It calls for a review of social security provisions in the light of the changing place of women in employment. It demands the development of measures to encourage the sharing of family and career responsibilities through awareness raising, the adaptation of working time and the development of child-care facilities. It also calls on Member States to promote actively greater participation by women in decision-making bodies and in posts with responsibility. The Resolution requests a Commission progress report on the implementation of the programme by 1 January 1991.

The European Parliament Opinion on the action programme was delivered on 13 May 1986. The ECOSOC Opinion was delivered on 24 April 1986.

Equal Opportunities for women - medium-term Community programme 1986 - 1990, COM(85) 801 final, 19 December 1985

Also published in Women of Europe, supplement No 23

The aim of the programme is to:

- consolidate the rights already provided by Community law;
- follow up the networks established by the first action programme, which provides the framework for a social dialogue on equal opportunities;
- intensify consciousness-raising efforts;
- develop support for women's employment;
- develop action for the most disadvantaged group;
- examine the situation in the Member States.

The programme also states that education and training are fundamental. Under this heading the Member States are asked to:

- increase the awareness of equal opportunities in the education system;
- take action to integrate education and vocational guidance in the curriculum of all pupils;
- reinforce co-education practices in mixed schools;

- introduce measures to ensure a balanced distribution of posts between men and women at all levels of education;
- eliminate sex-related stereotypes from all educational material;
- organize campaigns to promote diversification of occupational choices;
- adapt curricula to take account of problems specific to women;
- provide facilities to enable women with families to take training courses;
- promote low cost and flexible training arrangements;
- develop adequate expert and advisory facilities on equal opportunities at all levels.

The Commission undertook among other actions to use the PETRA programme to carry out experiments on equal opportunities for boys and girls and to carry out a study to ascertain whether handicapped girls have access to the same opportunities and the same standard of education and training as handicapped boys.

CEDEFOP was asked to set up a network of equal treatment councillors and to promote and evaluate training for self-employed women.

In the field of employment, Member States were asked to adopt comprehensive measures to promote women's employment and desegregation of employment through positive action. The Commission states that public sector employers should set an example. Member States are also asked to improve women's participation in decision-making.

The following specific Member State actions are listed:

- specific measures to deal with the disadvantaged: handicapped women, single parents, migrant women;
- removal of statutory and administrative provisions which are contrary to the principle of equal treatment and to encourage the social partners to make the same review of collective agreements;
- examination of the tax system to arrive at a neutral system which does not act as a disincentive with regard to married women's earnings;
- improvement in the social protection for home-workers.

Special attention is given to new technology. Member States are asked among other actions:

- to develop pilot schemes for training women in the new technologies;
- to introduce all girls and boys to new technologies at the end of primary school;
- and to analyze the impact of new technology on women's health.

Under this heading the Commission undertakes to organize studies on the impact of collective agreements on new technology on women's employment and research on the impact of new technologies on the distribution of leisure time and working time. The Commission also undertook to lay down guidelines for action on telecommuting and women's employment.

Under the heading 'Social Protection and Social Security' the programme asks Member States to reform social security budgets to eliminate discriminatory effects on women and to promote the gradual acquisition by women of individual social security rights to eliminate indirect discrimination.

Under the action programme the Commission undertook the further legislative action on equal treatment in social security summarized and the drawing-up of guidelines for the protection of working women during pregnancy and motherhood elsewhere in this section. The Commission also undertook to 'continue its efforts to abolish indirect discrimination, particularly in the case of a spouse's derived rights'.

The final heading is 'Sharing of Family and Occupational Responsibilities'. Here Member States are asked to take action to change attitudes towards acceptance of a more equal sharing of family, occupational and social responsibilities. The Commission urges the adoption of the draft Directive on Parental Leave which, as reported elsewhere, has not yet been achieved. Member States are also urged to improve childcare facilities and to encourage flexible working hours and systems of leave credits spread over a long period. The Commission announces the setting-up of the childcare network and studies of the infrastructure problems, such as transport and opening hours on women's employment, and of assistance for elderly and handicapped persons to find ways of easing the burden on carers.

The Commission also announces its intention to produce guidelines for EC action for certain categories of women: single parent families and single women, immigrant women, women wishing to return to the labour market after a career break, handicapped women and self-employed women. The action programme also contained the authorization for the Commission to issue memoranda on protective legislation and family taxation, summarized in this chapter.

In an annex the programme contains a draft positive action programme for the Commission's own staff. A very comprehensive internal staff programme was adopted in 1988.

The first draft of the new action programme is due in September 1990.

Council Resolution of 23 May 1990 on the protection of the dignity of women and men at work - Official Journal of the European Communities, No C157, 27/6/90.

In this Resolution the Council defines the concept of sexual harassment as 'Conduct of a sexual nature, or other conduct based on sex affecting the dignity of women and men at work, including conduct of superiors and colleagues', and affirms that such conduct 'constitutes an intolerable violation of the dignity of workers or trainees and is unacceptable if:

a. it is unwanted, unreasonable and offensive to the recipient;

b. a person's rejection of, or submission to such conduct is used as a basis for decisions which affects that person's access to any aspect of employment or training;

c. such conduct creates an intimidating, hostile or humiliating work environment for the recipient'.

Member States are asked to develop information and awareness training campaigns on the problem of sexual harassment. Employers should be reminded that they have a responsibility to seek to ensure that the work environment is free from sexual harassment and that victimization of complainants does not occur. Positive measures should be developed in the public sector which can act as a model to the private sector. Finally the social partners are asked to examine the possibility of including appropriate clauses in collective agreements.

The Commission is asked to draw up a code of conduct on the protection of the dignity of men and women at work in the near future and to inform employers, workers, lawyers, courts and tribunals of the fact that sexual harassment may be contrary to the equal treatment Directive (Articles 3, 4 and 5).

Other Initiatives and Documents

European Parliament Resolution of 17 January 1984 on the situation of women in Europe - Rapporteur Dame Shelagh Roberts - Official Journal of the European Communities, No C46, 1984.

The Parliament's Committee on Women's Rights was set up as an ad hoc committee with the primary purpose to produce a report on the situation of women in Europe.

Memorandum on income taxation and equal treatment for men and women - COM(84) 695 final, Office for Official Publications of the EC, 14/12/84.

This memorandum summarizes a survey of the different systems of personal income tax in Member States and their effect on women's work. It concludes that the system with the most neutral effect, from the point of view of equal treatment of men and women workers, is separate taxation. The following features in tax systems appear to have an adverse effect on married women's tax burden:

- systems which aggregate the income of spouses, but the effect of aggregated tax is alleviated in systems which

split the aggregated income between the spouses and by family quotient systems;
- allowances or tax reductions granted a priori to the husband;
- the lack of an allowance for child-care costs for two earner families;
- the inability to declare own income for tax;
- the responsibility for non-payment of tax by the other spouse;
- limitations on the amount of income that can be paid to an 'assisting wife' in a family firm by a husband by imposing limits for tax exemptions.

Equality is seen to be best served when personal allowances and tax reductions may be equally divided between husband and wife. In the UK the Commission recommended the abolition of the married man's allowance.

The aim of the report is to serve to initiate discussion at the Community level on the impact of income tax systems on equal treatment of men and women on the labour market as requested in the new Community Action Programme on the Promotion of Equal Opportunities.

<u>Commission Communication on possible Community action concerning the protection of working women during pregnancy and motherhood</u> - V/232/86.

The Commission suggests that 'a good case' could be made for harmonization of measures to protect women during pregnancy and motherhood under Article 100. However, a Directive in this area would be pointless if it did not represent a significant improvement on existing international standards in ILO conventions. The Commission therefore suggests that it may be sufficient to bring pressure to bear on Member States through continuous monitoring and reporting on national situations.

The Commission's list of basic standards of maternity protection includes:

- all women in employment and those registered unemployed should be entitled to paid maternity leave;
- there should be two weeks' leave for the father;

- it should be unlawful to refuse jobs to women because they are pregnant and to dismiss employees due to pregnancy or parenthood. Allegedly permissible dismissals should be liable to judicial or administrative review;
- rights accumulated before the leave should be maintained, social security protection and accumulation of pension rights should be maintained during the leave.

The document also contains continued commitment to the principles which were included in the original draft Directive on parental leave, including an entitlement to leave for both parents if both are in employment to look after sick children.

Commission Communication on protective legislation for women in the Member States of the European Community - COM(87) 105 final, Office for Official Publications of the EC, 20/3/87.

This is a comprehensive survey of existing protective legislation for women in Member States. It was set up in accordance with Articles 2(3), 3(2)(c), 5(2)(c) and 9(1) in the Equal Treatment Directive (76/207/EEC) which obliges Member States to review and undertake a first revision of protective legislation by 1980. The Commission lists remaining protective provisions in member countries and recommends action to achieve equal treatment. The list is divided into three parts. The first category is anomalous provisions - which, in the case of the UK, includes special administrative controls on the employment of women in the UK, regulation on the employment of women on board ship and particular provisions for women on hygiene at work. Generally the Commission recommends repeal of this type of legislation.

The second type are humanitarian provisions motivated by family commitments, or designed to protect women in strenuous or arduous work, or banning women from night work or from working in mines. This includes, in the case of the UK, limitations on the length of the working day and limitations on overtime which apply to women only, a ban on Sunday work and public holidays, a ban on nightwork, limitations on work with certain machines, limitations on lifting, a ban on women in work involving digging, excavations and earth shifting and on women working in mines. In the case of these provisions the Commission recommends that the rules should either be generalized to cover both men and women - or in some cases persons with family responsibilities - or should be repealed.

The final section concerns health and safety legislation which in Britain includes a prohibition for women to work with mercury and in some types of demolition work. Here the Commission recommends in a few cases (mercury) that the regulations should be made to cover both sexes. In most other cases the Commission proposes that the barriers to women's employment should be abolished.

<u>European Parliament Committee on Women's Rights Draft Working Document on the effects of completion of the internal market in 1992 on women in Europe - Rapporteur Mrs M. Van Hemeldonck</u> - PE 126.071, 24/8/88.

The report deals with the effects of the single market on women's earnings and employment, on social security benefits, on women in family, local and co-operative enterprises and on the consumer. There is a section on the effects of increased freedom of movement for persons particularly on the wives of migrants and of the impact of the single market on remote and underdeveloped regions. There are a number of recommendations. (A completed report is due to be produced in October 1990).

FREEDOM OF MOVEMENT

Treaties

Article 48

1. Freedom of movement for workers shall be secured within the Community by the end of the transitional period at the latest.

2. Such freedom of movement shall entail the abolition of any discrimination based on nationality between workers of the Member State as regards employment, remuneration and other conditions of work and employment.

3. It shall entail the right, subject to limitations justified on grounds of public policy, public security or public health:

   a. to accept offers of employment actually made;

   b. to move freely within the territory of Member States for this purpose;

   c. to stay in a Member State for the purpose of employment in accordance with the provisions governing the employment of nationals of that State laid down by law, regulation or administrative action;

   d. to remain in the territory of a Member State after having been employed in that State, subject to conditions which shall be embodied in implementing regulations to be drawn up by the Commission.

4. The provisions of this Article shall not apply to employment in the public service.

Employment Policy

Article 49

As soon as this Treaty enters into force, the Council shall, acting by a qualified majority on a proposal from the Commission, in co-operation with the European Parliament and after consulting the Economic and Social Committee, issue directives or make regulations setting out the measures required to bring about, by progressive stages, freedom of movement for workers, as defined in Article 48, in particular:

a. by ensuring close co-operation between national employment services;
b. by systematically and progressively abolishing those administrative procedures and practices and those qualifying periods in respect of eligibility for available employment, whether resulting from national legislation or from agreements previously concluded between Member States, the maintenance of which would form an obstacle to liberalization of the movement of workers;
c. by systematically and progressively abolishing all such qualifying periods and other restrictions provided for either under national legislation or under agreements previously concluded between Member States as imposed on workers of other Member States conditions regarding the free choice of employment other than those imposed on workers of the State concerned;
d. by setting up appropriate machinery to bring offers of employment into touch with applications for employment and to facilitate the achievement of a balance between supply and demand in the employment market in such a way as to avoid serious threats to the standard of living and level of employment in the various regions and industries.

Article 50

Member States shall, within the framework of a joint programme, encourage the exchange of young workers.

Employment Policy

Article 51

The Council shall, acting unanimously on a proposal from the Commission, adopt such measures in the field of social security as are necessary to provide freedom of movement for workers; to this end, it shall make arrangements to secure for migrant workers and their dependants:

a. aggregation, for the purpose of acquiring and retaining the right to benefit and of calculating the amount of benefit, of all periods taken into account under the laws of the several countries;

b. payment of benefits to persons resident in the territories of Member States.

Council Resolutions and Directives

Council Conclusions of 13 June 1985 concerning the implementation of Directive 77/486/EEC on the education of the children of migrant workers - Official Journal of the European Communities, No C165, 4/7/85.

The Council urges Member States to begin bilateral discussions about co-operation on the teaching of the language and culture of origin to migrant workers' children and hopes that these talks will result in early implementation of appropriate arrangements.

Council Resolution of 16 July 1985 on guidelines for a Community policy on migration - Official Journal of the European Communities, No C186, 26/7/85.

The Council makes a number of recommendations to Member States on how to facilitate freedom of movement, including: the issuing of a handbook on freedom of movement and legislation applicable to migration; consideration of the rights and procedures required to aid integration and participation by migrants; simplification of social security procedures. The Council also proposes the adoption of a declaration condemning xenophobia and racism; pilot schemes to brief local administration staff who have dealings with immigrants; improvement of the quality of the administration of justice, housing and education for migrants and in particular language assistance.

Three Council Directives - on the right of residence for students - on the right of residence for employees and self-employed persons who have ceased their occupational activity - on the right of residence - 90/366/EEC, 90/365/EEC and 90/364/EEC, Official Journal of the European Communities, No L180, 13/7/90.

These Directives aim to end the efforts of the last two decades to legislate on entry and residence rights of EC nationals not covered by the right to free movement for the purpose of employment. The new approach is to legislate separately for the three groups currently not covered by the free movement provisions: students, pensioners and other non-active persons. The basic purpose of the legislation is to permit Member States to impose conditions aiming at limiting the risk that migrants belonging to any of these three groups will become the subjects of social assistance in the host country.

Students should be granted the right of residence on the basis of registration with a college or university where they receive vocational training. This residence permit may be limited to the duration of the course. Member States may only require that the applicant presents an identity document and proof of registration for the training in question for the purpose of issuing the residence permit.

These conditions will not be permitted to be applied to foreign students who have right of residence by virtue of being employed in the host country or through being the children or dependents of migrant workers.

Pensioners and recipients of other types of allowance should be granted the right of residence on provision of proof of the existence of the pension or allowance. In the case of other non-active persons the host state should have the right to require evidence that they have adequate means of support. Member States are free to set the levels regarded as adequate in the light of the objective to ensure that such persons do not become a liability on the host country's social security system.

These Directives were adopted by the Council on 28 June 1990.

Qualifications

Legislation

Council Directive of 21 December 1988 on a general system for the recognition of higher education diplomas awarded on completion of professional education and training of at least three years' duration - 89/48/EEC, Official Journal of the European Communities, No L19, 24/1/89.

This Directive applies to professional qualifications which are recognized and regulated by a competent authority in the Member State and which require a minimum of three years' post-secondary training. Member States have to recognize professional qualifications of this type acquired in another Member States as sufficient qualification for entering that profession, whether in an employed or self-employed capacity. However, Member States may also require applicants to provide evidence of professional experience, where the applicants' training is at least one year less than that required in the host country. This period of professional experience must not exceed twice the amount of time by which the applicants' training falls short of that required in the host country with an absolute maximum of four years. The Member States may also require applicants to complete an adaption period not exceeding three years, or to take an aptitude test where the applicants' qualifications differ substantially from those of the host country's or the applicants' profession is not regulated in their country of origin, or if the host country qualification contains regulated professional activities which are not part of the profession in the applicants' home country. In these cases the applicants must be offered a choice between aptitude test and adaption period. If the profession in question requires precise knowledge of national law or involves giving advice on national law, the host country may decide to impose a test or a period of practice.

The Directive also sets up a co-ordinating group with one representative from each Member State under the aegis of the Commission. This committee usually meets four times a year and comments on national developments. The task of the group is to facilitate the implementation of the Directive and to collect information about its application in the Member States. The Commission may consult this group about future changes to the Directive. Member States are obliged to translate these provisions into national law by January 1991.

Council Decision of 28 July 1989 establishing an action programme to promote foreign language competence in the European Community (LINGUA) - 89/489/EEC, Official Journal of the European Communities, No L239, 16/8/89.

The LINGUA programme aims at a quantitative and qualitative improvement in the teaching and learning of foreign languages in the EC, with particular emphasis on vocational training, improved communication skills and educational exchanges and on in-service training and preparation of foreign language teachers and trainers for this purpose. A first phase of five years (1990-4) is provided for, with full-scale operation beginning in 1991-2. The EC will provide support for measures to promote:

1. in-service training for foreign language teachers;
2. the learning of foreign languages in universities;
3. knowledge of foreign languages used in work relations and in economic life;
4. the development of exchanges for young people undergoing professional, vocational and technical education;

as well as complementary measures.

The British government objected strongly to the proposal for LINGUA, based in part on the cost of the programme and in part on the principle of interference in national education policy. In July 1989 the Council approved the LINGUA programme, providing a smaller budget allocation than originally envisaged, for 'young people undergoing professional, vocational and technical education'. Member States were left to define what vocational education meant and whether or not it should be extended to schools. On the subject of vocational training, the LINGUA programme says that it is **'up to each Member State to define this and to narrow the scope or to widen it to, for instance, all those over 16 years of age or all in post-compulsory education'.**

Council Decision of 13 December 1984 establishing a third joint programme to encourage the exchange of young workers within the Community - 84/636/EEC, Official Journal of the European Communities, No L331, 19/12/84 (as amended by Council Decision of 29 May 1990. 90/268/EEC, Official Journal of the European Communities, No L156, 21/6/90).

This programme aims to give young people (18-28 years) an opportunity to live and work in another EC country in order to develop their vocational knowledge and experience, their knowledge of living and working in the host country and their knowledge of the EC. Young workers must be employed or available on the labour market and have received basic vocational training or practical work experience. Up to 4,000 young people are now helped annually on short-term exchanges (three weeks to three months) or long-term exchanges (four to sixteen months), mostly in the service sector. SMEs should note the opportunity offered by this programme and the key role played by the national independent promoting body which should be contacted. The programme has now been extended to 31 December 1991.

HEALTH AND SAFETY

Commission Recommendation on a European schedule of occupational diseases qualifying for compensation - Official Journal of the European Communities, No C30, 20/4/62 (amended by Official Journal of the European Communities, No C147, 9/8/66).

The Commission is currently updating the schedule in order to give Member States an opportunity to harmonize their national lists of occupational diseases qualifying for compensation, which presently vary greatly.

Council Directive of 25 July 1977 on the approximation of the laws, regulations and administrative provisions of the Member States relating to the provision of safety signs at places of work - 77/576/EEC, Official Journal of the European Communities, No L229, 7/9/77.

This Directive harmonizes the design and colour of safety signs in industry. Member States are obliged to take measures to ensure that safety signs conform to the signs agreed by the Council and that no other signs are used. The Directive sets up an unusual procedure for future amendments to the annexes of the Directive which deal with the design of the safety sign and detailed provisions for their use. This procedure is designed to give the Commission powers to take decisions if Member States' representatives fail to agree on proposed amendments. The Directive established a Committee of Representatives of the Member States chaired by a Commission representative and it is this committee which is in charge of amendments to the annexes. The Committee takes its decisions by a majority of forty-one votes, with the representatives of the Member States casting the same number of votes as in the Council of Ministers.

- France, Germany, Italy, and the UK - 10 votes;

- Spain - 8 votes;
- the Netherlands - 6 votes;
- Belgium, Greece and Portugal - 5 votes;
- Denmark and Ireland - 4 votes;
- Luxembourg - 2 votes.

If the Committee disagrees with the Commission's proposals or if it fails to give an opinion the Commission shall submit the proposal to the Council which then acts by a qualified majority. If the Council fails to act the measures shall be adopted by the Commission.

Member States had to adopt necessary legislation under the Directive by 1 January 1979 and measures had to be applied by 1 January 1981. The annexes of the Directive have since been amended by:

Commission Directive of 21 June 1979 amending the Annexes to Council Directive 77/576/EEC on the approximation of the laws, regulations and administrative provisions of the Member States relating to the provision of safety signs at work - 79/640/EEC, Official Journal of the European Communities, No L183, 19/7/79.

Council Directive of 12 June 1989 on the introduction of measures to encourage improvements in the safety and health of workers - 89/391/EEC, Official Journal of the European Communities, No L183, 29/6/89.

This is the health and safety framework Directive which lays down general principles about occupational risks and accident prevention and the elimination of risk factors.

The Directive applies to all sectors of activity, public and private and including educational, cultural and leisure institutions. It does not apply to the police, army or civil protection services such as the fire brigade because the characteristics of these services inevitably conflict with the Directive, i.e. are inevitably dangerous. In such areas safety and health of workers **'must be ensured as far as possible in the light of the objectives of this Directive'.**

The basic principle of the Directive is that the employer has a duty to ensure the health and safety of workers in every aspect related to work. This principle is not affected by the employer's use of outside contractors or by workers' obligations for health and safety. However, the Directive does not stop Member States from legislating to exclude or limit the employer's responsibility for unusual and unforseeable events beyond the employer's control which could not have been avoided despite the exercise of all due care. Health, safety and hygiene measures must not involve workers in financial cost.

The employer's obligations for prevention are:

- to avoid risks;
- to evaluate risks which cannot be avoided;
- to combat risks at source;
- to adapt to technical progress;
- to replace the dangerous by the non-dangerous or the less dangerous;
- to develop a coherent prevention policy which covers all aspects of work from technology to social relationships;
- to give collective preventive measures priority over individual preventive measures.

The employer has an obligation to evaluate health and safety risks.

There must be health and safety representatives appointed from the workforce. The representatives must be given adequate time to fulfil their obligations, they must have the necessary capabilities and means and may not be placed at any disadvantage because of their activities. If there are health and safety tasks which are beyond the competence of the staff external services must be enlisted.

Employers must take the necessary measures to provide first aid, fire-fighting equipment and procedures for the evacuation of workers.

<u>Council Directive of 30 November 1989 concerning the minimum safety and health requirements for the workplace (first individual directive within the meaning of Article</u>

16(1) of Directive 89/391/EEC) - 89/654/EEC, Official Journal of the European Communities, No L393, 30/12/89.

This Directive does not apply to vehicles and other means of transport outside industrial workplaces, temporary or mobile worksites, mines and oil extraction sites, fishing boats, the outdoor work sites of farms and forestry companies.

The deadline by which existing workplaces must comply with the Directive is 1 January 1993. For Portuguese workplaces which are in use by 1 January 1993 the deadline is 1 January 1997. The Directive contains four very general requirements:

- to keep emergency and other exits clear;
- to carry out technical maintenance and rectify faults as fast as possible;
- to keep the workplace and equipment clean; and
- to keep safety equipment maintained and checked.

To fulfil the rules on worker consultation in the framework Directive there is also an obligation to inform the workers or their representatives on health and safety measures.

Council Directive of 30 November 1989 concerning the minimum safety and health requirements for the use of work equipment by workers at work (second individual Directive) - 89/655/EEC, Official Journal of the European Communities, No L393, 30/12/89.

The term 'work equipment' is defined as any machine, apparatus, tool or installation used at work. The Directive sets out the requirements for new equipment provided after 31 December 1992 and provides that existing equipment should meet these requirements within four years of that date. It includes provisions on information and training for workers on the use of the equipment.

Council Directive of 29 May 1990 on minimum safety and health requirements for the use by workers of personal protective equipment at the workplace (third individual

<u>Directive)</u> - 89/656/EEC, Official Journal of the European Communities, No L393, 30/12/89.

This Directive includes provisions setting out employers' obligations particularly regarding assessment of the equipment, rules for use and information for workers. The annexes contain non-exhaustive guide lists of equipment and activities which may require the provision of such equipment. Ordinary working clothes; equipment used by emergency and rescue services, the military, police or for means of road transport; sports and self-defence equipment are excluded. Member States should introduce measures to comply with the Directive by 31 December 1992.

<u>Council Directive of 29 May 1990 on the minimum safety and health requirements for the handling of heavy loads where there is a risk particularly of back injury to workers (fourth individual Directive)</u> - 90/269/EEC, Official Journal of the European Communities, No L156, 21/6/90.

The Directive lays down minimum health and safety standards for those required to handle heavy loads and provides for workers to be informed of the potential dangers of lifting these loads. The compliance date is again 31 December 1992.

<u>Council Directive of 29 May 1990 on minimum safety and health requirements for work with display screen equipment (fifth individual Directive)</u> - 90/270/EEC, Official Journal of the European Communities, No L156, 21/6/90.

This Directive establishes minimum requirements in the following fields:

- equipment, including display screens, keyboards, work desk and chair;
- working environment, including lighting, noise and heat;
- operator/computer interaction.

Special provisions are made for the protection of workers' eyesight. The Member States must introduce measures to comply with the Directive by 31 December 1992.

Council Directive of 28 June 1990 on the protection of workers from the risks related to exposure to carcinogens at work - 90/394/EEC, Official Journal of the European Communities, No L196, 26/7/90.

The aim of this Directive is the protection of workers against risks to their health and safety (including the prevention of the risks) arising from exposure to carcinogens at work. Its provisions cover the assessment of such risks, measures to prevent exposure or, where necessary, to reduce it to a minimum, and procedures in the event of an accidental exposure.

Draft Directives

Proposal for a Council Directive on the protection of workers from the risks related to exposure to biological agents at work - COM(88) 165 final, Office for Official Publications of the EC, 5/4/88.

This would require employers to minimize the risks of contact with biological agents at work for their workers, to keep them fully informed during their work and to provide the competent authorities with records of exposure and details of the implementation of safety measures. The Council reached a common position on the proposal in May 1990.

SOCIAL POLICY

Council Recommendation of 10 December 1982 on the principles of Community policy with regard to retirement age - 82/857/EEC, Official Journal of the European Communities, No L357, 18/12/82.

The Council recommends that Member States shall be guided by the following principles in order to achieve the progressive introduction of flexible retirement:

- to ensure that retirement is voluntary;
- financial incentives to promote early retirement in exceptional economic circumstances may not be regarded as forming part of a flexible retirement system;
- employed workers receiving retirement pensions cannot be excluded from any form of paid employment;
- there should be retirement preparation programmes.

Member States are recommended to undertake an examination of their retirement pension systems and to report the results of these examinations to the Commission by July 1985, so that the Commission can propose measures to make the transition from full-time employment to retirement easier for employed persons.

Resolution of the Council and of the Ministers for Social Affairs meeting within the Council of 29 September 1989 on combating social exclusion - Official Journal of the European Communities, No C277, 31/10/89.

This Resolution marks an awareness that poverty is not only a matter of low income but of exclusion from services and activities enjoyed by other citizens, such as education, training, employment, housing, community services and medical care. The Council accordingly requests Member States **'to implement or promote measures to enable everyone to have access** [to these services]'.

Employment Policy

The Council points to the importance of developing policies in participation with local and national bodies and with the people involved. The Ministers undertake to step up the efforts both at the European and national level and to pool their knowledge of the 'phenomena of exclusion'. The Resolution calls on the Commission to study the measures taken by the Member States to combat exclusion and to report on these measures by 1992.

Conclusions of the Council and of the Ministers responsible for family affairs meeting with the Council of September 1989 regarding family policies - Official Journal of the European Communities, No C277, 31/10/89.

In this Resolution the Commission draws together concern for the demographic situation in the Community, the **'irreversible desire for equality between men and women'**, with the importance of the family as the touchstone for solidarity between generations to propose a number of actions at the Community level. These are: the development of regular information on demography, household structure and birth rates; the inclusion of the family dimension in Community policies; the exchange of information on the impact of other Community policies on the family; measures for equal opportunities and access for women to the labour market; and measures in favour of the family. The Resolution requests regular consultation between the Commission and the working party of senior national officials with responsibility for family affairs, and between the Commission and organizations representing families at the European level. Finally there is a commitment to regular assessment of family policies by the Council.

WORKING CONDITIONS

Treaties

Article 120

Member States shall endeavour to maintain the existing equivalence between paid holiday schemes.

Directives

Council Directive of 17 February 1975 on the approximation of laws of the Member States relating to collective redundancies - 75/129/EEC, Official Journal of the European Communities, No L48, 22/2/75.

This Directive imposes certain obligations on employers who make all or part of their workforce redundant. These obligations are to consult with the employees and to supply all relevant information. The reasons for the redundancies, the dates of the expected redundancies, the numbers to be made redundant and the size of the normal workforce have to be supplied in writing. All written material has to be forwarded to a designated public authority who is charged with the supervision of this field. No redundancies can be made until thirty days after notification. Member States are free to extend this minimum period to sixty days in their domestic legislation.

The obligations occur when at least ten employees or 10 per cent of the workforce (whichever is the higher figure) are made redundant over thirty days. Certain employers are exempt from these obligations: employers in the public sector, employers of seafarers. Employers whose business is terminated due to judicial process are also exempt and so are redundancies of workers on temporary contracts.

Council Directive of 14 February 1977 on the approximation of the laws of the Member States relating to the safeguarding of employee's rights in the event of transfers of undertakings, businesses or parts of businesses - 77/187/EEC, Official Journal of the European Communities, L61, 5/3/77.

The basic principle of this Directive is that the transfer of ownership in itself is no reason for dismissal. However Member States may make exemptions to this rule. If employees leave because the nature of the business or the work itself changes due to the take-over the employer shall be regarded as having terminated the contract.

Further, the new owners of a company in a take-over situation are obliged to respect agreements and commitments to the workforce entered into by the previous owners. They are obliged to respect collective agreements. However, Member States may introduce a time limit for the duration of existing agreements in their domestic legislation. Occupational pensions need not be maintained.

There is also an obligation to inform the workforce in good time before the take-over.

Council Directive of 30 October 1980 on the approximation of the laws of the Member States relating to the protection of employees in the event of insolvency of the employer - 80/987/EEC, Official Journal of the European Communities, No L283, 20/10/80.

Member States are obliged to establish a guarantee institution. This guarantees employees' outstanding claims for pay and other remuneration which result from an employment contract in the case of businesses closing down due to insolvency. Member States may limit their liability. They may also make exceptions from the obligation to legislate if other guarantees exist. The UK exempts crews of fishing vessels, spouses of employers, dockers and crews in the merchant navy from this legislation.

Proposals

Amended Proposal for a Council Directive on voluntary part-time work - Official Journal of the European Communities, No C18, 22/1/83.

The draft Directive was submitted to the Council in 1982 and was amended in 1983. It lays down the basic principle that **'Part-time workers shall receive the same treatment as full-time workers in the same situation, except where the difference in hours of work itself objectively justifies differences in treatment'** (Article 1). The draft Directive goes on to define specific areas where part-time workers must not be treated differently from full-time workers:

- working conditions in terms of arduousness of the work, health and safety protection, the organization and conduct of the work and the working environment, work schedules and payment of remuneration;
- eligibility to vote and stand as a candidate in worker representative bodies;
- access to vocational training;
- access to promotion;
- access to social facilities.

The remuneration, holiday pay, redundancy and retirement pay of part-time workers are to be calculated on the same basis and in the same proportion as those of full-time employees.

According to the draft Directive, part-time workers have to be covered by statutory and occupational social security schemes. Contributions and benefits for part-timers have to be calculated on the same basis as those of full-time employees. However, Member States are free to exclude those part-time workers whose hours and/or income fall below the current threshold of eligibility for the country's statutory social security system.

Part-time employees have the right to request a statement of the hours and nature of their work. According to the draft Directive both full-time workers wanting to change to part-time work and part-time workers wanting to change to full-time work shall have priority over outside candidates for appropriate vacancies at their place of work.

The Directive would permit Member States to adopt legislation more favourable to part-time workers than the provisions included in the Directive. The time limit for implementation of national legislation was proposed to be one year from the date of notification of the adopted Directive.

Amended Proposal for an EEC Council Directive on temporary work (supply of workers by temporary employment businesses and fixed-duration contracts of employment) - Official Journal of the European Communities, No C133, 21/5/84.

The Council first dealt with the issue of protection of workers on temporary contracts in a Council Resolution of 18 December 1979 on the adaptation of working time (Official Journal of the European Communities, No C2, 4/1/80) which stated that **'Community measures in support of action by Member States should be undertaken to ensure that temporary work is supervised and that temporary workers receive social protection'**. The draft Directive was submitted by the Commission in response to this Resolution. It deals with the authorization, registration and supervision of employment agencies supplying temporary labour. Under the Directive it would be unlawful to engage in the supply of temporary labour without such authorization and registration. Unusually the draft also includes a provision whereby Member States can prohibit temporary employment agencies registered in another Member State from business within its territory if the business concerned does not fulfil conditions which the host country imposes on its own nationals. If someone engages an unauthorized employment business, the user would be jointly liable, in the event of default by the employment business, for pay, social security contributions, etc.

The draft Directive imposes strict limits on the use of temporary labour. Labour supply contracts may only be concluded in order to cope with genuinely temporary labour needs. The maximum duration of a contract is limited to three months, renewable once only except in exceptional circumstances. It would not be permissible to employ a succession of temporary workers in the same post. However, Member States are free to authorize labour supply contracts where the temporary employment contract is of indefinite duration or is subject to the rules governing individual and collective dismissal.

Temporary workers would have a right to a written contract of employment with the temporary employment agency. Member States would under the draft Directive be obliged to ensure that temporary workers are not barred from accepting employment by the 'user undertaking' - i.e. the firm which is using staff from the temporary employment agency - after the completion of his or her temporary contract. Temporary workers' pay must be comparable to that received by workers with equivalent skills in the user undertaking unless collective agreements within the temporary sector state otherwise.

The draft Directive also stipulates that temporary workers shall be covered by social security schemes on the same conditions as full-time workers. Temporary workers shall be subject to the same regulations and working conditions including all matters relating to shift work, night work, holidays, health and safety, etc. as the user undertaking's normal workforce. Section III contains special provisions for cross-frontier supply of temporary workers.

The rights of temporary workers employed directly on a fixed duration contract are similar to the rights of workers supplied by agencies. Temporary contracts are only allowed for situations of a genuinely temporary nature, but there are no limits on the duration of such a contract. Member States are also free to authorize fixed duration contracts where such contracts are subject to the same rules governing permanent full-time employment. Like agency workers people employed on individual temporary contracts have a right to the same pay and working conditions as the employer's permanent workforce.

Both types of temporary workers must be included in calculations of the user undertaking's workforce for the purpose of applying provisions in legislation which are based on the size of the workforce.

In addition Member States would under this Directive

be obliged to take steps to prohibit the use of temporary workers to replace permanent workers in the case of strikes or lockouts.

This Directive would not apply to the temporary employment of seamen where shipping companies and seafarers' unions have concluded agreements which provide the workers concerned with protection equivalent to that provided in the draft Directive. The proposed deadline for the implementation period is two years from the adoption of the Directives.

Other Initiatives

Council Recommendation of 22 July 1975 on the principle of the forty-hour week and the principle of four weeks' annual paid holiday - 75/457/EEC, Official Journal of the European Communities, L199, 30/7/75.

The Council urges Member States to take appropriate measures to establish that the normal working week is no longer than forty hours. Member States are free to do this either through legislation or by encouraging the social partners to conclude collective agreements, depending on prevailing national practices. Member States may exempt certain sectors and activities because of their special nature from these provisions. Public servants may also be exempt. The introduction of the forty-hour week must not entail a reduction in earnings.

In the same way Member States should ensure all full-time employees four weeks' paid holiday leave.

The Recommendation finally includes an obligation on Member States to report on its implementation. The deadline both for reports and action under the Recommendation was the end of 1978.

Summary report on the comparative study on rules governing working conditions in the Member States - COM(89) 360 final, Office of Official Publications of the EC, 6/7/89.

This comparative study of the rules governing working conditions - mainly in the private sector - in Member States was requested by the European Council. It covers

Member States' legislation as well as conditions laid down in collective agreements and other labour contracts.

The concept 'working conditions' includes different forms of employment contracts, appointment and dismissal, working time issues, regulations of minimum wages, the regulation of industrial disputes and other aspects of industrial relations, consultation and employee involvement. The study does not cover health and safety, in-service training or social security.

Its purpose is to identify specific areas where national policies need to be harmonized to create a common Community labour market.

<u>Council Recommendation of 10 December 1982 on the principles of Community policy with regard to retirement age</u> - 82/857/EEC, Official Journal of the European Communities, L357, 18/12/82.

<u>Draft Council Recommendation on the reduction and reorganization of working time</u> - Official Journal of the European Communities, No C290, 26/10/83.

The primary purpose of this draft Recommendation was to reduce working hours as a means of reducing unemployment. However, the Commission also envisaged that a reduction in working hours would benefit workers, particularly those in arduous or hazardous work and would promote equality by allowing a greater sharing of family responsibilities.

The Commission recommends governments to adapt labour legislation and practice to facilitate the introduction of innovatory working time arrangements. The Commission also states that the public sector as the biggest employer has a particular responsibility to set an example in the reduction and reorganization of working time. The Recommendation also proposes stricter limitations on systematic overtime. The Commission states that overtime should increasingly be compensated by time off in lieu. It floats the idea that the two sides of industry should negotiate lower ceilings on overtime to come into effect in times of particularly high unemployment. The

Recommendation finally recognizes that measures would be needed to protect the interests of the low paid for whom systematic overtime has become part of normal income.

EMPLOYMENT AND TRAINING ACTION

Treaties

Article 123

In order to improve employment opportunities for workers in the common market and to contribute thereby to raising the standard of living, a European Social Fund is hereby established in accordance with the provisions set out below; it shall have the task of rendering the employment of workers easier and of increasing their geographical and occupational mobility within the Community.

Article 124

The Fund shall be administered by the Commission. The Commission shall be assisted in this task by a Committee presided over by a member of the Commission and composed of representatives of Governments, trade unions and employers' organizations.

Legislation

Council Decision of 2 April 1963 on a common vocational training policy - 63/226/EEC Official Journal of the European Communities, No L63, 20/4/63.

This Decision laid down the general principles for implementing a common vocational training policy for the EC and established the Advisory Committee on Vocational Training, which includes representatives of the social partners. The Council stresses in particular the need to promote basic and advanced vocational training and retraining suitable for the various stages of working life. There is also commitment to special measures for persons with special problems.

Council Decision of 16 December 1988 adopting the second phase of the programme on co-operation between universities and industry regarding training in the field of technology (COMETT II) - 89/27/EEC, Official Journal of the European Communities, No L13, 17/1/89.

COMETT aims to promote a **European dimension** in, and better co-operation between, universities and industry related to **advanced training** for technologies; to adapt the content of training to technological and social change; and to improve training opportunities at local, regional and national levels. Projects will be favoured if they group together SMEs, larger companies and universities, and involve new training initiatives. The first four-year phase covered the period 1986-9 inclusive; the second phase (1990-4) has an estimated budget of ECU 200 million. First priority was given to the establishment of a European network of university/enterprise training partnerships (UETPs) as the infrastructure for the other activities supported, in particular an EC programme of transnational university/industry exchanges and EC-level joint training projects in conjunction with high-technology firms in fields where there is a shortage of trained staff. For guidance contact: COMETT Technical Assistance Unit, Avenue de Cortenberg 71, B-1040 Brussels, tel: (02) 733 97 55, and the national members of the EC's COMETT Committee in the relevant ministry: also the Taskforce for Human Resources, Education, Training and Youth in the Commission.

Council Decision of 1 December 1987 concerning an action programme for the vocational training of young people and their preparation for adult and working life (PETRA) - 87/569/EEC, Official Journal of the European Communities, No L346, 10/12/87.

This programme aims to support and supplement the efforts of Member States to ensure that all young people who so wish receive one year's, or, if possible, two or more years', vocational training after the completion of their full-time compulsory education. The purpose is to raise the standard of vocational training and ensure that it leads to recognized qualifications; to diversify the range of training available; and to assist the adaptation of vocational training to technological, economic and social change.

1. The European Network of Training Initiatives seeks to give a European dimension to training measures at national, regional and local levels by facilitating transnational, co-operative partnerships based on innovative projects. Thus the Commission will circulate a 'catalogue' of project profiles, provide study visit and partnership grants and arrange workshops, for example for the twinning of mini-enterprizes or youth co-operatives aimed at joint production and marketing. New types of training consortia are being encouraged, including co-operation between small firms and (vocational) schools and colleges to create new opportunities for fully-fledged training programmes or apprenticeships. Stress is also being placed on opening up new opportunities for non-traditional training providers like co-operatives and 'self-managed' firms. In addition, mini-enterprizes and youth co-operatives are being encouraged to develop transnational contacts in enterprise education schemes, for example on joint projects, staff exchange and use of new communication technology. Also of interest is the theme of creating new forms of training in new non-agricultural occupations in rural areas: for example tourism, cultural heritage, ecology and environment.
2. Youth Initiative Projects give small grants, for one year, to projects planned, organized and managed by young people themselves, in such areas as training, youth information and the development of employment opportunities, many of them involving disadvantaged young people. These projects are intended to sharpen policy makers' awareness of the needs and aspirations of young people and to provide suggestions for how training can be made more accessible to young people. Youth co-operatives and workshops have been strongly represented. Contact: PETRA Support Unit, IFAPLAN, Square Ambiorix 32, B-1040 Brussels, tel: (02) 230 71 06.

Commission Decision of 4 May 1988 on the guidelines for the management of the European Social Fund in the financial years 1989 to 1991 - 88/319/EEC, Official Journal of the European Communities, No L143, 10/6/88.

The ESF aims to increase employment opportunities in the EC by providing financial assistance (normally providing the same percentage level as public authorities) for training and retraining schemes and the resettlement of workers moving from one occupation or area to another. Finance goes to projects receiving public support but can apply to private as well as public projects provided these create or retain jobs. Under the 1983 Fund Regulation (amended 1985) emphasis was on young people and the long-term unemployed in the EC's absolute priority regions; this emphasis was confirmed in the new Fund Regulation of 1989. Contact: DG V (Employment, Social Affairs), 200 rue de la Loi, B-1049 Brussels, and the relevant national government department.

Council Decision of 29 June 1988 on a Community action in the field of learning technologies - DELTA (Developing European Learning through Technological Advance) - pilot phase - 88/417/EEC, Official Journal of the European Communities, No L206, 30/7/88.

The DELTA programme aims to focus the research and development effort of EC industry, universities and publishers on advanced techniques and infrastructures required to support **distance open learning**. Projects must be pre-competitive, cross-national, involve a commercial enterprise and be concerned with advanced educational and multi-media training through new technologies (for example satellite transmission). There is an important market here for SMEs. The pilot phase was to be followed by a five-year main programme from 1989 to 1990. Contact: DG XIII (Telecommunications, Information Industries and Innovation), 200 rue de la Loi, B-1049 Brussels, tel: (02) 236 03 79.

Council Decision of 17 April 1989 on the implementation at Community level of the main phase of the Strategic

Community Programme for Innovation and Technology Transfer - SPRINT - 89/286/EEC, Official Journal of the European Communities, No L112, 25/4/89.

Following a five-year initial phase (1983 to 1988), this programme was adopted in 1989 with the following aims:

- to strengthen the innovative capacity of European producers;
- to promote rapid penetration by new technologies and the dissemination of innovation;
- to enhance the effectiveness and coherence of existing instruments and policies (regional, national or Community) in the field of innovation and technology transfer.

These are to be achieved by action to consolidate existing transnational innovation networks and establish new ones, as well as by support to specific projects of Community interest to promote transfers of innovations within the Community. The budget for the five-year programme (1989 to 1993) is ECU 90 million.

Council Decision of 18 December 1989 establishing an action programme to promote innovation in the field of vocational training resulting from technological change in the European Community (EUROTECNET II) - 89/657/EEC, Official Journal of the European Communities, No L393, 30/12/89.

This is the second and larger programme on training in technology. There are substantial differences between the Commission proposal and the final decision. The finalized programme is summarized here.

The basic aim of the programme is to promote innovation in the field of basic and continuing vocational training in order to adapt to current and future technological changes and their impact on employment, work and necessary qualifications and skills. The purpose of the programme is to establish a network of national and transnational innovatory projects which are designed to develop and improve vocational training policies and systems for the new technologies in the Member States, and to set up a series of Community measures in support of the national and transnational projects.

Common objectives for all action taken under EUROTECNET II are: analysis of the impact of technological change on qualifications and skills for managers, employees and the unemployed; the development of demonstration projects leading to innovations in the provision of vocational training; the provision of an entry into working life for young people and for the unemployed; equal opportunities for men and women: the development of training and retraining of trainers; the dissemination of relevant information.

The planned Community measures include a network of innovatory projects in the field of training; action to strengthen co-operation on and transfer of methodologies and the development of transnational projects; measures to promote continuing vocational training of trainers; research and analysis of the new qualification requirements created by technological change; development of open and flexible learning methods including self-training. The budget allocation for the first three years of the five-year programme is a relatively modest ECU 7.5 million. The Council Decision also establishes an advisory programme consisting of government representatives and chaired by the Commission, which is given the task of drawing up the guidelines for the programme and of determining the overall balance within the programme of different activities.

<u>Council Decision of 29 May 1990 establishing on action programme for the development of continuing vocational training in the Community (FORCE)</u> - 90/267/EEC, Official Journal of the European Communities, No L156, 21/6/90.

In its proposal (COM(89) 567 final) the Commission stressed the importance of training as method of anticipating and adapting to the acceleration of technical, economic and industrial change caused by the single market. The basic principle as stated in the Social

Charter is that **'Every European Community worker must have access to vocational training and be able to benefit from it throughout his working life'**. The public authorities, companies or the two sides of industry should set up continuing and permanent training systems enabling every individual to undergo retraining, more especially through leave for training purposes, to improve his skills, particularly in the light of technical developments. The actions proposed under the programme particularly stress the development of forecasting, analysis, evaluation and monitoring of training. The objectives of the programme are:

- to encourage greater investment in continuing vocational training in particular by developing innovatory partnerships which are intended to stir authorities and firms into action;
- to encourage continuing vocational training measures by, for example, demonstrating and disseminating examples of good practice to those economic sectors or regions where access to, or investment in, such training is inadequate;
- to encourage innovations in the management of such training;
- to take better account of the consequences of the completion of the internal market, by support in particular for transnational training projects;
- to contribute to greater effectiveness of continuing vocational training by promoting measures in particular to monitor and analyse its development.

The programme consists of a framework of general principles designed to support and complement national training policies and a number of EC transitional measures to support national activities. EC financial support will be granted to:

- an exchange scheme to promote rapid dissemination of innovations;
- preparatory work on the design and development of transnational or cross-frontier continuing vocational training schemes.

The EC will also support sectoral surveys of training plans on subjects such as methods of drawing up training plans at the level of individual firms, cost-effective evaluation of training and access for part-time and temporary workers. The programme will run from 1991 to 1994.

Action Programmes and Council Resolutions

Council Resolution of 2 June 1983 concerning vocational training measures relating to new information technologies - Official Journal of the European Communities, No C166, 25/6/83.

The Resolution requests Member State action to train both workers and managers in information technology and to develop qualifications in electronics and data processing. However, the main point is the establishment of a five-year programme to create a network of demonstration projects designed to encourage the transfer of experience and promising innovations.

Council Resolution of 11 July 1983 concerning vocational training policies in the European Community in the 1980s - Official Journal of the European Communities, No C193, 20/7/83.

This Resolution is focused on training as **'an instrument of an active employment policy'**, as a means of preparing young people for working life and as an instrument for promoting equal opportunities. Member States undertake to improve the quality and scope of vocational training, to ensure that training programmes lead to recognized qualifications, to ensure adequate training facilities in business management, particularly for SMEs, and to improving the quality and scope of instructor training and of vocational guidance counsellors. The Commission is asked to encourage innovation and improvement of training systems. It is also asked to undertake comparative assessment of existing projects in linked work and training, to support pilot projects and the development of training/production workshops and to implement a programme of exchange visits by training specialists.

Council Resolution of 19 December 1984 on action to combat long-term unemployment - Official Journal of the European Communities, No C2, 4/1/85.

'The Council is seriously concerned about the problem of long-term unemployment' and states that special action is required to resolve this serious problem. The Resolution proposes three types of action: training; greater efforts to create new jobs and increase labour market flexibility and analysis; and the development of comparable information on long-term unemployment.

Member States are requested inter alia to take action:

- to ensure that counselling and training is provided in good time in the case of collective redundancies;
- to ensure that employment services are equipped to identify and follow up those who are likely to become long-term unemployed and to identify those who already are in that category;
- to review the functioning of labour markets, including existing practices for recruiting, selecting and laying-off workers, which may aggravate long-term unemployment;
- to overcome obstacles to the introduction of reductions of working hours - a long-standing demand from ETUC;
- to provide specific work programmes for the long-term unemployed;
- to assist people who wish to set up their own business for example by providing continued income support;
- to promote the recruitment of long-term unemployed through the use of government incentive schemes;
- to support voluntary and community job creation efforts.

Action at Community level includes efforts to improve information and statistics on long-term unemployment, financial assistance to projects for this group of unemployed from the European Social Fund, further research through MISEP into existing schemes for the long-term unemployed and a biannual Commission report on the progress made in implementing the Resolution.

Council Resolution of 3 November 1986 on an action programme on small and medium sized enterprises - Official Journal of the European Communities, No C287, 14/11/86.

This programme contains a strong component of training both for SME managers and employees.

Council Resolution of 22 December 1986 on an action programme on employment growth - Official Journal of the European Communities, No C340, 31/12/86.

This is one of the most important EC action programmes on the subject of action against unemployment. The Resolution was partly inspired by a joint initiative of the UK and Irish governments. The programme partly deals with the promotion of small and medium sized businesses, which have been identified as one of the main potential sources of employment growth in Europe. This includes a reduction in administrative constraints on SMEs. The most important points directly concerning unemployment consist of:

- a commitment by the Council to the development of local employment initiatives;

- a request directed to the Member States to develop more effective vocational training programmes providing up to two years' vocational education and training for school leavers leading to recognized vocational qualifications; and to establish links between schools and the world of work including greater involvement by industry and commerce in vocational education and training;

- establishing the aim of the removal of obstacles to the development of part-time and temporary work, fixed-term contracts and jobsharing with due regard for social and employment protection.

Commission Recommendation of 24 November 1987 on vocational training for women - Official Journal of the European Communities, No L342, 4/12/87.

The Commission recommends that Member States adopt a policy designed to encourage the participation of young and adult women in training schemes and should develop measures, particularly as regards training, for occupations where women are under-represented. It calls *inter alia* for measures to encourage the participation of girls in higher education and vocational training systems and the setting up of businesses by women. The Member States are required to report to the Commission on action taken within three years.

Council Resolution of 5 June 1989 on continuing vocational training - Official Journal of the European Communities, No C148, 15/6/89.

This Resolution clearly shows the change of focus in EC training policy from training of the unemployed to continuing training of all workers. The Council stresses that continuing vocational training must form an important role in the strategy for achieving the internal market, including its social dimension, and economic and social cohesion, as a determining factor in economic and social policy. The Council states that all workers should have access to continuing vocational training. There are a number of recommendations on actions to be undertaken by the Member States. The Commission is authorized to produce an action programme on vocational training.

Council Resolution of 7 June 1984 concerning the contribution of local employment initiatives in combating unemployment - Official Journal of the European Communities, No C161, 21/6/84.

This Resolution asks Member States to adopt political guidelines for the promotion of local employment initiatives and calls upon the Commission to implement Community action in the form of aid from the ESF, advisory and information transfer programmes and specific studies. In the earlier Communication from the Commission to the

Council, COM(83) 662 final, Community Action to Combat Unemployment - Contribution of Local Employment Initiatives, LEIs had been defined as: **'those initiatives which have occurred at the local level - often involving co-operation between individuals, action groups, social partners and local and regional authorities - with the specific aim of providing additional, permanent employment opportunities through the creation of new small-scale enterprises'**. It points out that LEIs resemble in many respects other traditional SMEs but tend to be distinguishable from them through the reasons for their creation, the social context of those involved and the sectors in which they are active. The term LEI seems to embrace conventional businesses, co-operatives and community businesses that operate on the basis of small-scale local community involvement, assisted by an 'animateur' or local development agent (whether local authorities, enterprise boards or trusts, co-operative development agencies, churches or trade unions). They represent social as well as economic innovations, dedicated to the objective of 'worthwhile' employment and responding to gaps in the market place, and often are set up by people excluded from the declining traditional sectors - women, young people, immigrant workers, older people or the long-term unemployed.

DG V has focused its attention on developing support activities for local development agencies as follows:

1. The establishment of ELISE, the European Information Exchange Network on Local Employment Initiatives, in 1985. Its aims are: to make information available to all private and public bodies and individuals active in local development; to organize the sharing of experiences amongst regions and countries; and to link a minimum of 300 organizations by the network. At the heart of the documentation and information service of ELISE is a database embracing four areas: local and regional development; enterprise and SMEs; training at local and regional levels; and social integration of disadvantaged groups. The database embraces the organizations and innovative experiences in the four areas, encourages information networking amongst

member organizations and assists the production of a monthly newsletter and the provision of a weekly information service for members only. ELISE's development clarified the EC's role as essentially technical, i.e. database development and encouragement of networking. Over time ELISE has become more distant from DG V, working more closely with other Directorates-General notably DG XVI. It also became more dependent on its members for revenue after 1 January 1989. Contact: ELISE/AEIDL, 34 rue Breydel, B-1040 Brussels, tel: (2) 230 52 34. Note also ELISE's (first) European Directory of Local Development Agencies, 1989, with details of almost 1700 agencies covering all Member States.

2. Since 1986 an annual exchange programme has existed between local development agents in the twelve Member States. Over sixty agents each year, mostly from local authorities, have been involved in seven- to ten-day visits on such subjects as training and marketing strategy and, in 1989, on '1992' issues. The visits are seen as a catalyst for energy and motivation and a means of enhancing the credibility and recognition of such agents and LEIs. As in the case of ELISE, DG V collaborated closely with EGLEI, the European Group for Local Employment Initiatives. See 'Broadening the Horizons of Enterprise', ELISE 1987.

3. In 1986 DG V launched the Research and Action Programme on the Local Development of the Employment Market, a study of twelve exemplary pilot projects in twelve different regions of the EC, organized by Haris Martinos. The study underlined the value of the local approach to expansion of SMEs, technology transfer, training young people and helping the long-term unemployed. It suggested greater technical assistance from the EC and greater responsiveness to local needs in the operation of the EC Structural Funds. Published in 1988 as 'Twelve European Regions under the Microscope' by the European Service Network, Brussels.

Other Initiatives

Commission Communication concerning the contribution of LEIs in combating unemployment. Report on the follow-up to the Council Resolution of 7/6/84 - COM(86) 784 final, Office of Official Publications of the EC, 20/1/87.

The Council Resolution of 1984 encourages the Commission and Member States to support LEIs, notably by removing obstacles to their development and granting easier access to financial instruments.

The Commission reports progress on achievements at the level of Member States and proposes priority actions to improve the environment for LEIs. The French government was the first to introduce a national programme of subsidy to LEIs in 1982. Community business is especially strong in Ireland. In the UK, Business in the Community, an association of major companies, has been particularly involved in the development of local enterprise agencies to support local small and start-up businesses. Large companies like British Steel, British Coal, BAT Industries and Rank-Xerox have supported new local initiatives in areas adversely affected by their commercial decisions. A more general development is new partnerships between large and small companies involving start-up packages, spin-offs and management buy-outs, sub-contracting, workshop provision, favourable finance, and research and development and technology transfer.

Invitation to tender for the management of the scheme of grant aid for the creation by women of small businesses or local employment initiatives - Official Journal of the European Communities, No C75, 23/3/88.

The European Commission's 1986-90 aid programme for women (see **Equal Opportunities** in this section, pp. 226-229) was extended in 1988 to women wishing to set up their own business. Start-up aid is granted for the first year of activity, provided that the business creates jobs for women. Subsidies rise to a maximum of ECU 5,000, taking the form of ECU 1,000 per full-time job created (or the equivalent in part-time jobs). They will be granted as a priority to businesses providing jobs for underprivileged groups of women (migrant women, women going back to work after several years without a job, etc.) or operating in sectors where women are poorly represented. Commission aid can be important in winning credibility for projects at the national level, with aid in 1988 being granted to 128 women's businesses in a range of different sectors. Projects also benefit from the support of the Commission's network of experts on local employment initiatives for women, circulating information in their own countries and advising project promoters on how to obtain access to aid.

Contact: Women's Bureau, DG V/A/4, and read the project profiles 'Women in Business', published by ELISE.

<u>Preparing small and medium sized enterprises for Europe 1992: Experimental training schemes</u> - SEC(88) 1860 final, Commission of the European Communities, 17/1/89.

The aim of this experimental scheme is to test, in conjunction with training and advisory agencies at the sectoral or regional levels, a form of training to help SME managers to develop a strategy for expansion in the single European market. This first dedicated SME training programme was developed principally by the SME taskforce, DG III and DG V, building on a concept of training worked out by CEDEFOP which is also preparing a guide to training for SMEs. It was clear that there were plenty of general management training schemes available; the problem was not supply, but how to stimulate demand. SMEs were reluctant to become involved in such schemes because of issues of distance, scarcity of time and doubts about relevance. At the same time management skills were a key determinant of SME success. Hence the scheme starts with the first key step - the need to convince the heads of SMEs of the importance of training. The lever employed is the need of SMEs to know what the single European market means for them, particularly in the area of new competitive pressures. The demand for concrete information about '1992' is to be used to stimulate an appetite for training.

This scheme builds on existing sectoral and regional training agents with experience of small businesses and has two main dimensions:

Employment Policy

1. After a call for proposals the Commission will select agents who will be provided with a training programme of six modules and supporting documents focusing on the elements of strategic management for '1992'.

2. The Commission is supporting regional or sectoral analyses preparatory to education and information seminars for SMEs on '1992' (see Official Journal No S27 of 9/2/89).

Later measures include: networking of training projects and co-operation between training agencies; training SME managers in co-operation strategies; and promoting the role of large firms and banks in the provision of training for SME managers. Co-ordination with the Business and Innovation Centres (DG XVI) is also under consideration to stress support for 'less-favoured' regions of the EC.

SECTION III
OTHER DOCUMENTS OF RELEVANCE TO EMPLOYMENT POLICY

GENERAL

Reports on Social Developments in the European Community, published annually by the European Commission.

Opinion of the Economic and Social Committee on the social developments in the Community 1988, CES(89) 753.
Opinions published once per year.

Employment in Europe 1989, COM(89) 399 final, 26/7/89.
Report on the employment situation in the Member States by the European Commission published first time 1989, planned to be an annual report.

Venturini, P. (1989) _1992: The European Social Dimension_, European Commission, Cat no CB-PP-88-B05, ISBN 92-825-8703-7.
This is an overview of the whole of the social and employment policies of the EC with a special emphasis on the Social Dialogue.

EQUAL OPPORTUNITIES

Von Prondzynski, F. (1987) Implementation of the Equality Directives, European Commission, ISBN 92-825-7172-6.

Report from the Commission: Provisional conclusions on measures taken by the Member States in order to implement the Resolution on actions to combat unemployment amongst women, COM(81) 758 final, 9/12/81.

Report from the Commission to the Council on the implementation of the new action programme on the promotion of equal opportunities for women 1982-1985, COM(85) 641 final, 29/11/85.

This report contains an account of the implementation in all Member States of actions 1 to 16 in the programme. It also deals with implementation of actions by the Commission and of positive action implemented for the benefit of the Commission's own staff.

Communication from the Commission to the Council on vocational training for women, COM(87) 155 final, 3/4/87.

Making Equal Opportunities Work - European Commission Background Report, ISEC/B5/87, 5/5/87.

This report includes summaries of some of the most important recent Court cases in this area.

Report on the implementation of the Council Recommendation of 13 December 1984 on the promotion of positive action for women, 84/635/EEC, COM(88) 370 final, 30/6/88.

Rubenstein, M. (1988) The Dignity of Women at Work. A Report on the Problem of Sexual Harassment in the Member States of the European Communities Parts I and II, European Commission, ISBN 92-825-8764-9.

This is the report of the Commission's network on sexual harassment and summarizes the situation in the Member States. The annexe is an inventory of countermeasures in Member States.

Alexander, M. (1989) Guidelines for lobbying on sex equality, European Commission.

European Parliament initiatives

European Parliament Committee on Women's Rights: Report on the reintegration of women into working life, PE DOC A 2-127/87, 23/7/87, Rapporteur Mrs J. Larive-Groenendaal.

This report which is a European Parliament own initiative, not a response to a Commission proposal deals with the problem of women who return to work after a period of caring for children. The report contains a fairly comprehensive comparative survey of special measures for women returners in all member countries

European Parliament Resolution on equal opportunities for boys and girls in the field of education and vocational training, PE DOC A 2-68/88, Official Journal of the European Communities, No C235, 12/9/88.

European Parliament Resolution on a Charter on the rights of women in childbirth, PE DOC A 2-38/88, Official Journal of the European Communities, No C235, 12/9/88.

Other reports and documents

Meulders, D. and Plasman, R. (1989) Women in atypical

employment. Final report - Women in the labour force network, European Commission, V/1426/89.

Corcoran and Donnelly, Comparative Analysis of the Provisions for Legal Redress in Member States of the EEC, Internal Document, European Commission, V/564/84.

This report was commissioned by the European Commission and contains a detailed comparative analysis of national procedures in courts and tribunals in the member states for dealing with complaints of breach of the principle of equal treatment between men and women.

Cohen, B. (1988) Caring for Children - Services and policies for childcare and equal opportunities in the United Kingdom. Report for the European Commission's Childcare Network. Reprinted 1989 and published by the Family Policy Studies Unit.

This is the report on the UK in the network mentioned above.

Cohen, B. Caring for Children. Forthcoming report to be published by the Scottish Child and Family Alliance.

Moss, P. (1989) Who cares for Europe's Children? The short Report of the European childcare network, European Commission.

This is the report of the Commission's network on childcare. It contains comparative data on child care facilities in the Member States.

The impact of the completion of the internal market on women in the European Community, European Commission V506/90.

Working document prepared for DG V, Equal Opportunities Unit.

FREEDOM OF MOVEMENT

Legislation

Council Directive of 25 February 1964 on the co-ordination of special measures concerning the movement and residence of foreign nationals which are justified on the grounds of public policy, public security or public health, 64/221/EEC, Official Journal of the European Communities, No L56, 4/4/64.

Council Directive of 15 October 1968 on the abolition of restrictions on movement and residence within the Community for workers of Member States and their families, 68/360/EEC, Official Journal of the European Communities, No L257, 19/10/68.

Council Regulation (EEC) No 1612/68 of 15 October 1968 on freedom of movement for workers within the Community, Official Journal of the European Communities, No L257, 19/10/68.

This is the basic regulation on equality of treatment for EC migrant workers and their families.

Commission Regulation (EEC) No 1251/70 of 29 June 1970 on the right of workers to remain in the territory of a Member State after having been employed in that state, Official Journal of the European Communities, No L142, 30/6/70.

Council Regulation (EEC) No 1408/71 of 14 June 1971 on the application of social security schemes to employed persons and their families moving within the Community as mended by Regulation (EEC) No 1390/81, Official Journal of the European Communities, Nos L149, 5/7/71 and L143, 29/5/81.

Council Directive of 18 May 1972 extending to workers exercising the right to remain in the territory of a Member State after having been employed in that state the scope of the Directive of 25 February 1964 on co-ordination of special measures concerning the movement and residence of foreign nationals, 72/194/EEC, Official Journal of the European Communities, L121, 26/5/72.

Council Directive of 17 December 1974 concerning the right of nationals of a Member State to remain in the territory of another Member State after having pursued therein an activity in a self-employed capacity, 75/34/EEC, Official Journal of the European Communities, No L14, 20/1/75.

Council Regulation (EEC) 312/76 of 9 February 1976 extending equal treatment regarding trade union rights, Official Journal of the European Communities, No L39, 14/2/76.

Council Directive of 25 July 1977 on the education of the children of migrant workers, 77/486/EEC, Official Journal of the European Communities, No L199, 6/8/77.

Decision No 135 of the Administrative Commission of the European Communities on Social Security for Migrant Workers of 1 July 1987 concerning the granting of benefits in kind provided for in Article 17 (7) and Article 60 (6) of Regulation (EEC) No 574/72 and the concepts of urgency within the meaning of Article 20 of Regulation (EEC) No 1408/71 and of extreme urgency within the meaning of Articles 17(7) and 60(6) of Regulation (EEC) No 574/72, Official Journal of the European Communities, No C64, 9/3/88.

Employment Policy

Council Recommendation of 21 December 1988 concerning nationals of Member States who hold a diploma conferred in a third state, 89/49/EEC, Official Journal of the European Communities, No L19, 24/1/89.

This recommends that Member States should give the same privileges to EC citizens who hold the kind of diplomas covered by Council Directive 89/48/EEC acquired in a non-member country as it gives to holders of EC qualifications covered by this Directive.

Exchanges

Council Resolution of 9 February 1976 on an action programme for migrant workers and members of their families, Official Journal of the European Communities, No C34, 14/2/76.

First Report covering the first three years of operation of the third joint programme for exchange of young workers 1985-1987, COM(88) 382 final, 8/7/88.

Draft Directives

Commission Proposal for a Council Regulation (EEC) amending Regulation (EEC) No 1408/71 on the application of social security schemes to employed persons, to self-employed persons and to members of their families moving within the Community and Regulation (EEC) No 574/72 laying down the procedure for implementing Regulation (EEC) No 1408/71, COM(88) 538 final, 10/10/88.

Proposal for a Council Directive amending Directive 68/360/EEC on the abolition of restrictions on movement and residence within the Community for workers of Member States and their families, COM(88) 815 final, 29/3/89.

Proposal for a Council Regulation (EEC) amending

Employment Policy

Regulation (EEC) No 1612/68 on freedom of movement for workers within the Community, COM(88) 815 final, 29/3/89.

Commission Proposal for a Council Regulation (EEC) amending Regulation (EEC) No 1408/71 on the application of social security schemes to employed persons, to self-employed persons and to members of their families moving within the Community and Regulation (EEC) No 574/72 laying down the procedure for implementing Regulation (EEC) No 1408/71, COM(89) 370 final, 20/7/89.

The revisions in this proposal are mainly caused by minor changes in national social security legislation in different countries which necessitate detailed changes in EC Regulations to adapt these changes in national law to the requirements of EC migrant workers resident in relevant countries.

Other Documents

Séché, J.C. (1988) A Guide to working in a Europe without frontiers, European Commission, ISBN 92-825-5067-9.

Commission Communication on guidelines for a Community policy on migration, COM(85) 48 final, 1/3/85.

European Parliament Resolution on discrimination against immigrant women and female migrant workers in legislation and regulations in the Community, Official Journal of the European Communities, No C305, 1987, European Parliament Doc. A 2-133/87.

HEALTH AND SAFETY

Directives

Council Directive of 27 June 1967 on the approximation of laws, regulations and administrative provisions relating to the classification, packaging and labelling of dangerous substances, 67/548/EEC, Official Journal of the European Communities, No L196, 16/8/67.

Council Directive of 18 December 1975 on the approximation of the laws of the Member States concerning electrical equipment for use in potentially explosive atmospheres, 76/117/EEC, Official Journal of the European Communities, No L24, 30/1/76.

Council Directive of 29 June 1978 on the approximation of the laws, regulations and administrative provisions of the Member States on the protection of the health of workers exposed to vinyl chloride monomer, 78/610/EEC, Official Journal of the European Communities, No L197, 22/7/78.

Council Directive of 6 February 1979 on the approximation of the laws of the Member States concerning electrical equipment for use in potentially explosive atmospheres employing certain types of protection, 79/196/EEC, Official Journal of the European Communities, No L43, 20/2/79.

The purpose of this Directive is to harmonize safety standards for this type of equipment in order to eliminate technical barriers to trade in such equipment. The Directive sets up a committee of representatives of the Member States on the adaptation to technical progress of Community provisions in this area. The procedures for this committee closely follow the provisions for amendments laid down in Directive 77/576/EEC on safety signs at work. The second Directive introduces a Community safety mark for this equipment.

<u>Council Directive of 18 September 1979 amending for the sixth time Directive 67/548/EEC on the approximation of laws, regulations and administrative provisions relating to the classification, packaging and labelling of dangerous substances</u>, 79/831/EEC, Official Journal of the European Communities, No L259, 15/10/79.

This is more or less a complete revision of the much amended Directive.

<u>Council Directive of 15 July 1980 amending the Directives laying down the basic safety standards for health protection of the general public and workers against the dangers of ionizing radiation</u>, 80/836/Euratom, Official Journal of the European Communities, No L246, 17/9/80.

<u>Council Directive of 27 November 1980 on the protection of workers from the risks related to exposure to chemical, physical and biological agents at work</u>, 80/1107/EEC, Official Journal of the European Communities, No L327, 3/12/80.

<u>Council Directive of 24 June 1982 on the major-accident hazards of certain industrial activities</u>, 82/501/EEC, Official Journal of the European Communities, No L230, 5/8/82.

<u>Council Directive of 28 July 1982 on the protection of workers from the risks related to exposure to metallic lead and its ionic compounds at work</u>, 82/605/EEC, Official Journal of the European Communities, No L247, 23/8/82.

Employment Policy

Council Directive of 19 September 1983 on the protection of workers from the risks related to exposure to asbestos at work, 83/477/EEC, Official Journal of the European Communities, No L263, 24/9/83.

Council Directive of 12 May 1986 on the protection of workers from the risks related to exposure to noise at work, 86/188/EEC, Official Journal of the European Communities, No L137, 24/5/86.

Council Directive of 9 June 1988 on the protection of workers by the banning of certain specified agents and/or certain work activities, 88/364/EEC, Official Journal of the European Communities, No L179, 9/7/88.

Council Directive of 16 December 1988 amending Directive No 80/1107/EEC on the protection of workers from the risks related to exposure to chemical, physical and biological agents at work, 88/642/EEC, Official Journal of the European Communities, No L356, 24/12/88.
This is called 'the exposure units Directive'.

Draft Directives and Recommendations

Commission Recommendation of 20 July 1962 to the Member States on occupational health services, Official Journal of the European Communities, No 80, 31/8/62.

Proposal for a Council Directive laying down basic standards for the health and the protection of workers and the general public against the dangers of microwave radiation, COM(80) 340 final, 26/6/80.

Proposal for a Council Directive on the protection of workers from the risks related to exposure to benzene at work, COM(85) 669 final. (Amended proposal COM(87) 526 final, 16/11/87).

Action Programmes

Council Resolution of 29 July 1978 on an action programme of the European Communities on safety and health at work, Official Journal of the European Communities, No C165, 11/7/78.

This is the action programme which provided the foundation for all proposals and Directives in the field of health and safety.

Council Resolution of 27 February 1984 on a second action programme of the European Communities in the field of health and safety at the workplace, Official Journal of the European Communities, No C67, 8/3/84.

Council Resoluntion of 21 December 1987 on safety, hygiene and health at work - Official Journal of the European Communities, No C28, 3/2/79.

Reports and other Documents

Gevers, J.K.M. (1987) Health and safety protection in industry: Participation and information of employers and workers, European Commission, Report EUR 11314, ISBN 92-825-8057-1.

Report in the 'Industrial health and safety' series published by the Directorate-General V. This is a survey of the occupational health and safety systems in the EC member countries. It also contains a series of recommendations on future Community action in the field of health and safety. There is in addition a substantial bibliography.

Employment Policy

Safety and health at the workplace in the European Community, Consolidated Report, European Foundation for the Improvement of Living and Working Conditions, Dublin, 1981.

WORKING CONDITIONS

Council Resolution of 18 December 1979 on the adaptation of working time, Official Journal of the European Communities, No C2, 4/1/80.

New Forms of Work: Labour law and social security aspects in the European Community, European Foundation for the Improvement of Living and Working Conditions, 1988.

This report deals with all forms of atypical employment in Member States and the effect of national labour law and social security systems on the development of this type of employment.

SOCIAL POLICY

Legislation

Council Resolution of 27 June 1974 establishing the initial Community action programme for the vocational rehabilitation of handicapped persons, Official Journal of the European Communities, No C80, 9/7/74.

This was the first action programme for disabled persons.

Council Resolution of 21 December 1981 on the social integration of disabled people, Official Journal of the European Communities, No C347, 31/12/81.

Council Decision of 19 December 1984 on specific Community action to combat poverty, 85/8/EEC, Official Journal of the European Communities, No L2, 3/1/85.

This decision launched the second poverty programme.

Council Recommendation of 24 July 1986 on the employment of disabled people in the Community, 86/379/EEC, Official Journal of the European Communities, No L225, 12/8/86.

Conclusions of the Council of 12 June 1989 on the employment of disabled people in the Community, Official Journal of the European Communities, No C173, 8/7/89.

Commission proposals and reports

Problems of Social Security - Areas of common interest.

Employment Policy

Communication from the Commission to the Council, COM(86) 410 final, 1986.

Commission interim report on a specific Community action programme to combat poverty, COM(88) 621 final, 28/11/88.
This report contains a short discussion of the causes of poverty and of the situation of the 30 million people in the European Community who earned less than half the average income in their country. There is a detailed description of the aims and themes of the second poverty programme. The bulk of the report deals with the ninety-one action research programmes financed by the Commission under the poverty programme and a discussion of the evaluation of the projects. Also published in Social Europe 2/1989 under the title 'The fight against poverty'.

Report from the Commission on the application of Council recommendation No 86/379/EEC of 24 July 1986 on the employment of disabled people in the Community, COM(88) 746 final, 15/12/88.

Communication from the Commission on family policies, COM(89)363 final, 8/8/89.

Proposal for a Council decision concerning the further development of the HANDYNET system in the context of the HELIOS programme, COM(89) 450 final, 27/9/89.

European Parliament documents

European Parliament Resolution of 21 January 1988 on the delay in decision-making on the reinforcement of economic and social cohesion within the Community and the connection between this option and the completion of the internal market, Official Journal of the European Communities, No C49, 22/2/88.

Employment Policy

European Parliament Report drawn up on behalf of the Committee on Economic and Monetary Affairs and Industrial Policy on economic and social cohesion in the Community, PE DOC A 2-307/88, 9/12/88.

European Parliament Resolution on economic and social cohesion in the Community, (Doc A 2-307/88), Official Journal of the European Communities, No C47, 27/2/89.

European Parliament Report drawn up on behalf of the Committee on Social Affairs, Employment and the Working Environment on the Community Charter of Fundamental Social Rights - Rapporteur Mrs M. Buron, PE DOC A 3-69/89, 9/11/89.

See under Social Charter in Section II.

EMPLOYMENT AND TRAINING

Legislation

Council Regulation (EEC) No 337/75 of 10 February 1975 establishing a European Centre for the Development of Vocational Training - CEDEFOP, Official Journal of the European Communities, No L39, 13/2/75.

Resolution of the Council and the Ministers of Education, meeting within the Council of 9 February 1976 comprising an action programme in the field of education, Official Journal of the European Communities, No C38, 19/2/76.

This Resolution led to the setting up of the EC Education Committee.

Council Resolution of 18 December 1979 on linked work and training for young persons, Official Journal of the European Communities, No C1, 3/1/80.

This is the first EC Resolution on the need to develop better links between training and the world of work.

Council Resolution on measures relating to the introduction of new information technology in education, Official Journal of the European Communities, No C256, 24/9/83.

Conclusions of the Council on technological change and social adjustment, Official Journal of the European Communities, No C184, 11/7/84.

Council Decision of 16 July 1985 on the comparability of

vocational training qualifications between the Member States of the European Community, 85/368/EEC, Official Journal of the European Communities, No L199, 31/7/85.

This Decision established a programme of surveys of national qualifications for different occupations. This programme is being carried out by CEDEFOP which has published a number of detailed lists of all national qualifications in certain areas, such as electrical installations, hotel and catering and motor vehicle repair. This work continues and more reports will be published.

Council Decision of 24 July 1986 adopting the programme on co-operation between universities and enterprises regarding training in the field of technology (COMETT) - 86/365/EEC, Official Journal of the European Communities, No L222, 8/8/86.

Commission Recommendation of 24 November 1987 on vocational training for women, (IRIS), Official Journal of the European Communities, No L342, 4/12/87.

Commission proposals and reports

Communication by the Commission to the Council on technological change and social adjustments, COM(84) 6 final.

Communication by the Commission to the Council on new information technologies and the school systems in the European Community - work programme for the period 1985-1987, COM(84) 722 final.

Communication from the Commission to the Council on vocational training and new information technologies - work programme for the period 1985-1988, COM(85) 167 final, 18/4/85.

Employment Policy

The COMETT programme: a report of activities in 1987 - COM(88) 36 final, Office for Official Publications of the EC, 12/8/88.

Communication from the Commission. The future of rural society, COM(88) 501 final, 23/9/88.

APPENDIX I

BIBLIOGRAPHY

General

Reports on the Activities of the Council of Europe, published annually and obtainable from the Council of Europe - see address list.

The social policy of the European Community, Social Europe, 1/87, p.51.

The social dimension of the internal market, Social Europe Special Edition, 1988, ISBN 92-825-8256-6.

Cecchini, Paolo, The European Challenge, 1992 - The Benefits of a Single Market, Wildwood House, 1988, £6.95, ISBN 0-7045-0613-0.

The social aspects of the internal market, synthesis of the first three seminars which were held in Brussels in November/December 1987 and January 1988, Volume 1, Social Europe, Supplement No 7, 1988.

The social aspects of the internal market, synthesis of the first six seminars which were held in Brussels in November/December 1987 and January, April, May and June 1988, Volume 2, Social Europe, Supplement No 7, 1989.

Social Europe, 1/90. The whole issue is devoted to the Community Charter of Basic Social Rights for Workers and the Commission's Action Programme.

Statistics

Basic Statistics of the Community, 26th edition, Eurostat,

1989. Comparison with some European countries, Canada, the USA, Japan and the USSR.

Demographic Statistics, Eurostat, annual publication.

Earnings in Agriculture, Eurostat, annual publication.

Earnings in Industry and Services, Eurostat, annual publication.

Employment and Unemployment, Eurostat, annual publication and monthly publication.

Euro-Barometer public opinion surveys have been conducted on behalf of the European Commission each Spring and Autumn since 1973. It is a survey of nearly 12,000 respondents covering all member countries. The survey usually includes sections on 'Satisfaction with life and feelings of happiness', 'Basic attitude to social change' and questions relating to 'A People's Europe'. Periodically the survey includes questions on gender issues and some years there has been a section on attitudes to poverty.

General Government Accounts and Statistics 1970-86, Eurostat, 1989.

Labour Force Sample Surveys, Eurostat, biennial publication.

Long-Term Unemployment. Its wider labour market effects in the countries of the European Community, Eurostat, 1988.

Principal Economic Indicators of the EC, US and Japan 1970-83, Eurostat, 1984.

Rapid Reports on Population and Social Conditions, Eurostat, monthly bulletin.

Appendix 1

Health and Safety

Industrial Health and Safety. A series of reports published by the European Commission.

The Law and Practice Concerning Occupational Health in the Member States of the European Community, report prepared by Environmental Resources Limited, 1982.

Indicators for assessing exposure and biological effects of genotoxic chemicals, Social Europe, 1/88, p.104.

'Great leap forward' for health and safety, Social Europe, 2/88, p.48.

Cardoso, F., Protection of workers against risks related to biological agents: the Commission's approach, Social Europe, 1/89, p.139

Six Directives for the protection of workers, Social Europe, 1/89, p.140.

The role of the Safety and Health Commission for the Mining and Other Extractive Industries (SHCMOE), Social Europe, 1/89, p.146.

Hunter, D., Europe and health - The Commission's programme of work for 1989 in health-related fields, Social Europe, 2/89, p.97.

Morettini, Yves, Advisory Committee on Safety, Hygiene and Health Protection at Work - an increasingly important role, Social Europe, 3/89, p.123.

Measures to Combat Unemployment

Employment growth

Long-term unemployment: recent trends and developments, Social Europe, 1/87, p.9.

Appendix 1

Specific measures taken under the Community policy relating to the employment market - exchanges of officials from the national employment services, Social Europe, 1/87, p.13.

Small and medium sized enterprises and employment creation in the European Community, Social Europe, 2/87, p.41.

Employment in the European electronics industry, Social Europe, 2/87, p.45.

Adaptability in the labour market, Social Europe, 3/87, p.9.

Actions to combat long-term unemployment, Social Europe, 3/87, p.17.

Action programme on local labour market development, Social Europe, 3/87, p.49.

New forms and new areas of employment growth in France, Germany, Italy, the Netherlands and the United Kingdom - a comparative study, Social Europe, 3/87, p.52.

Employment trends and prospects in Europe, Social Europe, 1/88, p.9.

The social policy of the Community and participation of the social partners in decision-making at European level, Social Europe, 1/88, p.13.

Elise, the information available to the Local Employment Initiatives, Social Europe, 1/88, p.69.

The changing nature of employment: new forms, new areas, Social Europe, 1/88, p.75.

Managing change: working for growth and employment, Social Europe, 1/88, p.80.

Research among undertakings regarding innovative practices

in the employment of young people, CEGOS, Social Europe, 1/88, p.87.

Work programme of the European Foundation for the Improvement of Living and Working Conditions, Social Europe, 2/88.

Programme of exchange of local development agents, Social Europe, 2/88, p.3.

The recession in the shipbuilding industry - European response proposed by the Commission to ensure rapid industrial redevelopment and new employment opportunities, Social Europe, 2/88, p.9.

Youth and employment, Social Europe, 2/88, p.72.

Employment creation in small firms - trends and new developments, Social Europe, 3/88, p.47.

Adaptability of employment in medium-sized enterprises in several Community Member States, Social Europe, 3/88, p.55.

Employment in the banking sector today and some prospects for 1992, Social Europe, 3/88, p.62.

Individual adaptation to technological and social change, Social Europe, 3/88, p.83.

Action programme on local labour market development, Social Europe, Supplement No 3, 1988.

Youth and employment, conference report, Marseilles, September 1987, Social Europe, Supplement No 6, 1988.

Local employment development, the contribution of the LEDA programme, and LEDA conference: employment creation through local development, Social Europe, 1/89, p.9 and p.41.

Appendix 1

A survey of European enterprises' employment strategies, Social Europe, 2/89, p.26.

Negotiated flexibility in the enterprise and the industrial district, Social Europe, 2/89, p.28.

Employment and working conditions in producer services firms - a synthesis report, Social Europe, 3/89, p.7.

Social and economic problems of large cities in Europe, Social Europe, 3/89, p.12.

Policy measures for combating long-term unemployment in the European Community since the 1984 Council Resolution - Study by Amin Rajan and Kenneth Walsh, Social Europe, Supplement No 5, 1989.

Education and training

Recent progress made in introducing new information technologies into education, Social Europe, Supplement No 4, 1986.

The training and preparation of young people for adult and working life, Social Europe, 2/87, p.28.

Developments in the introduction of new information technologies in education, Social Europe, Supplement No 2, 1987.

Educational and vocational guidance services for the 14-25 age-group in the European Community, Social Europe, 3/87, p.70.

Activities of the Commission of the European Communities in the field of education and training during 1985 and 1986, Social Europe, Supplement No 3, 1987.

Educational and vocational guidance services for the 14-25 age group in the European Community, Social Europe, Supplement No 4, 1987.

Appendix 1

Transition of young people from education to adult and working life, Social Europe, Supplement No 5, 1987.

Community initiatives on vocational training for women, Social Europe, 1/88, p.27.

Transborder projects: the role of the European Social Fund, Social Europe, 1/88, p.44.

EuroTecNet: past experience and future outlook, Social Europe, 1/88, p.46.

Continuing training: challenge and prospects, Social Europe, 1/88, p.50.

Transition education for the '90s, Social Europe, Supplement No 1, 1988. An overview of pilot schemes supported by the Commission in Member States under the PETRA programme and designed to facilitate the transition for young people from school to the world of work. (See Section II for details of PETRA).

European Social Fund: the pilot project for the use of new information and communications technologies in the vocational preparation and training of disadvantaged young people, Social Europe, 2/88, p.20.

Piehl, Ernst, CEDEFOP: European Centre for the Development of Vocational Training, Social Europe, 2/88, p.26. This is an account of CEDEFOP's activities during 1986-1988 and an introduction to the work programme for 1989-1992.

European conferences to disseminate the results of the transition programme, Social Europe, 2/88, p.75.

School-industry links: progress in the European Community, Social Europe, 3/88, p.32.

The role of education and training in the completion of the internal market, Social Europe, 3/88, p.36.

Appendix 1

Comett - Community programme for education and training for technology, <u>Social Europe</u>, 3/88, p.41.

Outlets and training opportunities for unemployed young people in the fields of urban renewal and the rehabilitation of housing conditions, <u>Social Europe</u>, 3/88, p.58.

Activities of the Commission of the European Communities in the fields of education, training and youth policy during 1987, <u>Social Europe</u>, Supplement No 5, 1988.

Youth initiative projects in the context of vocational training policy, <u>Social Europe</u>, 1/89, p.121.

EuroTecNet action programme in the field of new information technologies and vocational training 1985-88, <u>Social Europe</u>, 1/89, p.124.

The leading edge - a review of the growth of school/ industry partnership in the European Community, <u>Social Europe</u>, Supplement No 1, 1989.

Comett I and Comett II, <u>Social Europe</u>, 3/89, p.103.

Training young people for 1992: new developments in the Petra programme, <u>Social Europe</u>, 3/89, p.106.

Petra programme: research strand, <u>Social Europe</u>, 3/89, p.108.

European value-added in advanced training for technology - a mid-term Comett conference, <u>Social Europe</u>, 3/89, p.117.

Erasmus and Comett in 1988, <u>Social Europe</u>, Supplement No 4, 1989.

Activities of the Commission of the European Communities in the fields of education, training and youth policy during 1987 and 1988, <u>Social Europe</u>, Supplement No 8, 1989.

Appendix 1

Equal Opportunities

Women and Men in Britain, Equal Opportunities Commission. Published annually by Her Majesty's Stationary Office in the UK. This is a comprehensive set of statistics on life for women in Britain including some comparative European statistics in each section.

Summary of the survey report on European women in paid employment - their perception of discrimination at work, Women of Europe, Supplement No 20, 1985.

Networks for contact exchange and action: a new instrument of Community policy to promote equal opportunities, Social Europe, 1/87, p.41.

Equal treatment for men and women in occupational social security schemes, Social Europe, 1/87, p.45.

The specific training needs of migrant women, Social Europe, 2/87, p.57.

Application of Directive 79/7/EEC - equal treatment for men and women in matters of social security, Social Europe, 3/87, p.38.

Report on the dignity of women at work: developments in the Member States - an inventory, EIRR 171 April 1988, March 1988.

Editorial: Commission Communication on protective legislation for women, Social Europe, 1/88, p.5.

The enforcement of Community law on equality at national level, Social Europe, 1/88, p.21.

Applicability of Directive 79/7/EEC (continued), Social Europe, 1/88, p.30.

Proposal for a Council Directive completing the implementation of the principle of equal treatment for men and women in statutory and occupational social security schemes, Social Europe, 1/88, p.37.

Equality of treatment for men and women in social security matters, Social Europe, 2/88, p.42.

Business creation by women - action taken by the Commission of the European Communities, Social Europe, 2/88, p.62.

Seminar: the industrial challenge: the new role of women, positive actions, Social Europe, 2/88, p.65.

Provisional conclusions on measures taken by the Member States in order to implement the resolution on actions to combat unemployment amongst women, Social Europe, 3/88, p.14.

Positive action for women taken by the Member States and the Commission to implement the Council Recommendation of 13 December 1984, Social Europe, 3/88, p.18.

The Commission proposal on the burden of proof and the law of the Member States of the European Community, Social Europe, 3/88, p.23.

Network on the implementation of the Equality Directives, Social Europe, 3/88, p.73.

Women of Europe: 10 years, Women of Europe, Supplement No 27, June 1988. This special issue of Women of Europe contains a survey of equal opportunities legislation and other initiatives in the Member States.

Positive action - Equal opportunities for women in employment, Social Europe, 1/89, p.65.

The proposal for a Council Directive on burden of proof and the law of the Member States of the European Community, Social Europe, 1/89, p.69.

Appendix 1

The institutional conditions necessary for the equal treatment of men and women in the EC, Social Europe, 1/89, p.81.

Childcare and equality of opportunity, Social Europe, 1/89, p.84.

IRIS - the new Community network of demonstration projects on vocational training for women, Social Europe, 2/89, p.49.

The evaluation of Community policy on equal opportunities - Toledo, April 1989, Social Europe, 3/89, p.63.

Women in statistics, Women of Europe, Supplement No 14, 1989. A comprehensive set of comparative statistics on women in Europe covering employment, education, demography and women in politics. (Updated in December 1989, Supplement No 30).

Freedom of Movement

Equivalence of vocational training qualifications between Member States, Social Europe, 1/87, p.27.

Development of teaching materials for migrant workers' children, Social Europe, 1/87, p.28.

Erasmus - an investment in the future of the Community, Social Europe, 3/87, p.34.

Study abroad in the European Community: results of a recent evaluation, Social Europe, 3/87, p.67.

Young Worker Exchange Programme, Social Europe, 2/88, p.31.

Twenty years of freedom of movement for workers within the Community, Social Europe, 1/89, p.93.

The scope of Article 48(4) of the EEC Treaty and the means

of action by the Commission of the European Communities on the basis of the jurisprudence of the Court of Justice, Social Europe, 1/89, p.102.

Launching the 'Youth for Europe' programme, Social Europe, 1/89, p.134.

Proposals for the consolidation of the right of free movement for itinerant workers, Social Europe, 2/89, p.55.

Improvement of national protection in the field of social security in the light of the co-ordination of Community law, Social Europe, 2/89, p.59.

Young worker exchange programme - future options, Social Europe, 2/89, p.87.

Coyne, David, Lingua programme, Social Europe, 3/89, p.98.

Social Policy

Vandammes, Jacques, New Directions in European Social Policy, Croom Helm, 1985.

The social integration of disabled people, Social Europe, Supplement No 7, 1986.

Recent Changes in Family Structures, Report by the Council of Europe 190 0, 21 May 1987, Doc MMF(87)3.

The deaf community in action, Social Europe, 1/87, p.18.

Problems of social security - themes of common interest, Social Europe, 1/87, p.38.

Educating the children of gypsies and travelling people, Social Europe, 3/87, p.73.

The second EC programme to combat poverty - action research projects and the clearing house, ISG Sozialforschung und Gesellschaftspolitik, Köln, 1988.

Appendix 1

Linke, W., Changes in household structures in Europe - Report of the Select Committee of experts on household structure, Strasbourg, May 1988.

New action programme for disabled people, Social Europe, 1/88, p.54.

The European youth card, Social Europe, 1/88, p.63.

A European seniors' concession card, Social Europe, 1/88, p.66.

The employment of migrant women, Social Europe, 2/88, p.57.

Report on the fight against illiteracy, Social Europe, Supplement No 2, 1988.

Roll, Jo, Lone Parent Families in the European Community: Final Report, Family Policy Studies Centre, January 1989, V/545/89.

Community action to combat poverty, Social Europe, 1/89, p.110.

The financing of social protection within the Community: the debates at Toledo, Spain, Social Europe, 1/89, p.117.

Helios: a new step towards integration and independent living for disabled people in the European Community, Social Europe, 2/89, p.62.

Van Loo, Dora, Poverty: a new programme proposed by the European Commission, Social Europe, 2/89, p.66. This is a presentation of the poverty action programme 1990-1994.

The fight against poverty - interim report on a specific Community action programme to combat poverty, Social Europe, Supplement No 2, 1989. This report includes the Commission's proposal for a Council Decision establishing a medium-term Community action programme to foster the economic and social integration of the least privileged groups. (See section II).

A European over-60s card, Social Europe, 3/89, p.69.

The vocational rehabilitation of disabled women in the European Community, Social Europe, 3/89, p.81.

Social Security

Comparative tables of the Social Security Systems of the Non-Member Countries of the European Community, Council of Europe, 1984.

Holloway, John, Social Policy Harmonization in the European Community, Gower, 1981.

Tables of social benefit systems in the Member States of the European Communities, Portugal and Spain (Position at 1 January 1985), International Relations (Social Security), Department of Health and Social Security, 1985.

Compendium of Community Provisions on Social Security, 3rd Edition (31 December 1986), Directorate-General V, 1988.

Social indicators and evaluation of social security in Belgium, Social Europe, 3/87, p.62.

Comparative Tables of the Social Security systems in the Member States of the European Communities. Situation at 1 July 1988 - General scheme (employees in industry and commerce). Published every three years by the European Commission. Latest is the 15th Edition, published in 1989.

Employee Consultation and Participation

Unions: need for permanent co-operation between scientific research bodies and the trade unions, Social Europe, 1/88, p.90.

Appendix 1

Work organization and industrial relations in data-processing departments in the United Kingdom, Denmark and the Netherlands, Social Europe, 3/88, p.65.

Working Conditions

Social Europe. Each issue in the last three years has included an article on changes in 'Employment policy in the Member States' and on 'New technology and social change: overview of recent events in the Community countries'.

New production systems: implications for work and work organization in the factory of the future, Social Europe, 1/87, p.72.

New forms of work and activity initiating a new research programme, Social Europe, 1/87, p.77.

Homeworking in Italy, France and the United Kingdom, Social Europe, 1/88, p.98.

The social situation in maritime transport - priority issues and Community actions, Social Europe, 2/88, p.55.

Four-year rolling programme 1989-92 of the European Foundation for the Improvement of Living and Working Conditions, Social Europe, 3/89, p.72.

Seminar on the social aspects of the Common Agricultural Policy, Brussels, 24 to 26 June 1987, Social Europe, Supplement No 3, 1989.

Periodicals

European Parliament Briefing - published in connection with the Parliament's plenary sessions.

Free from the European Parliament's Directorate General for Information and Public Relations, 2929 Luxembourg, tel. (352) 43001.

Appendix 1

Social Europe - is the vehicle for news and comments on developments in the social sphere by the European Commission's Directorate General V.

Social Europe is a good source for comparative information. It is published three times per year but the Social Europe Supplements, which are devoted to single issues or EC programmes are published more frequently. Obtainable from the Office for Official Publications of the European Community, 2 rue Mercier, L-2985 Luxembourg, tel. (352) 499281. (Annual subscription in 1990 for periodical only ECU 36; including Supplements ECU 87.50).

Women of Europe - magazine published every two months by the European Commission, Directorate General X, Women's Information Service.

The magazine covers developments, both at the national and European level, of social and women's affairs. It also publicizes future events, contact addresses of researchers, voluntary and public sector bodies in the field of women's rights. The magazine can be obtained free of charge from the Women's Information Service, DG X, European Commission, 200 rue de la Loi, 1040 Bruxelles.

INFORMISEP - the quarterly journal of the European Commission's Mutual Information System on Employment Policies (MISEP).

National correspondents report on changes in Member States' national employment policies. INFORMISEP can be obtained free of charge from the MISEP Secretariat, Institute for Policy Research, PO Box 985, 2300 AZ Leiden, Netherlands, tel. (31) 71253737.

Dyson, K., Combating Long-term Unemployment - Local/EC Relations, Routledge, 1989.

Janus - newsletter published by Directorate General V (four issues per year) aimed at promoting the flow of information between Member States on health and safety at work.

Available free from the Janus Secretariat, Instituto Nacional de Seguridad e Higiene en el Trabajo, Centro

Nacional de Condiciones de Trabajo, C/Dulcet, s/n, 08034 Barcelona, Spain, tel. (93) 204 45 00.

CREW-Reports - this is a monthly, modest but very useful publication which covers both EC initiatives in the social sphere and developments in the member countries.

Published by the Centre for Research on European Women, 38 rue Stevin, 1040 Brussels, tel. (02) 230 51 58. (Subscription in 1990: individuals BF 1100; institutions BF 2150).

Equal Opportunities Review - has a strong European angle. Published bimonthly by IRS/Eclipse 18-20, Highbury Place, London, N5 IQP, tel. 071-354 5858. (Annual subscription in 1990, £99).

European Industrial Relations Review - monthly publication which covers EC legislation and initiatives, national legislation in the social sphere and information on collective agreements and other aspects of industrial relations in all countries in Western Europe.

Published by IRS/Eclipse 18-20, Highbury Place, London, N5 IQP, tel. 071-354 5858. (Annual subscription in 1990, £160).

IDS European Report - monthly newsletter covering EC and national news in the social sphere.

Published by Income Data Services, 193 St John Street, London, EC1V 4LS, tel. 071-250 3434. (Subscriptions in 1990, £130-£175 depending on location of subscriber).

APPENDIX II

USEFUL ADDRESSES

European Commission:

200 rue de la Loi
1049 Bruxelles
Belgium

Tel: 010 322 235 1111

Directorate General V - Social Affairs and Education

Directorate A - Employment
Directorate B - Living and Working Conditions and Social Protection
Directorate C - European Social Fund
Directorate D - Safety and Health

Taskforce: Human Resources, Education and Training and Youth

Directorate General X - Information

The European Commission's Statistical Office - EUROSTAT

Batiment Jean Monnet
Rue Alcide De Gasperi
2920 Luxembourg

Tel: (352) 43011
Telex: 3432 or 3446 or 3476 COMEUR LU

Appendix 2

The European Parliament has three addresses:

The Secretariats of the European Parliament's Committees are in Luxembourg:

2929 Luxembourg

Tel: (352) 43001
Telex: 2894 EUPARL LU or 3494 EUPARL LU

(the Chairs are most easily reached at the Brussels address below).

European Parliament's Committee on Social Affairs, Employment and the Working Environment
Chair: Willem van Velzen, MEP (Socialist, Netherlands).

European Parliament's Committee on Women's Rights
Chair: Christine Crawley, MEP (Socialist, UK).

The Political Group Secretariats are in Brussels. This is also where the Parliament's Committees meet and where therefore the Committee Secretariats can be reached when the Committees are in session.

Main address: 97-113 rue Belliard
1040 Brussels
Belgium

Tel: (02) 234 21 11

The Groups are listed in order of size:

The Socialist Group

The Group of the European People's Party (Christian Democrat)

Appendix 2

The Liberal, Democrat and Reformist Group

European Democratic Group (Conservative)

The Green Group in the European Parliament

Group for the European Unitarian Left (Communist, Italian)

Group of the European Democratic Alliance (Gaullist and Fine Fail)

Technical Group of the European Right (Fascist/ultra right)

Left Unity (Communist, mainly French)

Rainbow Group in the European Parliament (Danish anti-EC and various Nationalists)

(Each group has their own telefax facility).

The Plenary Sessions are held at Strasbourg in:

Palais de l'Europe
Strasbourg
France

Tel: (88) 61 49 61

The Council of Ministers

General Secretariat
170 rue de la Loi
1048 Bruxelles
Belgium

Tel: (02) 234 61 11

Appendix 2

The European Court of Justice

Palais de la Cour de Justice
2920 Luxemburg

Tel: (352) 43031
Fax: (352) 433766

Office for Official Publications of the European Commmunities

2 rue Mercier
2985 Luxemburg

Tel: (352) 499281
Fax: (352) 488573
Telex: PUBOF LU 1324b

The European Foundation for the Improvement of Living and Working Conditions:

Loughlinstown House
Shankill
County Dublin
Ireland

Tel: Dublin 826888
Fax: 826456
Telex: 30726 EURF EI

European Centre for the Development of Vocational Training (CEDEFOP)

(Bundesallee 22)
Post Box 3105 29
1000 Berlin 31
West Germany

Tel: (030) 884120
Fax: (030) 88412222
Telex: 184163 EUCEN D

European Community Youth Exchange Bureau (ECYEB)
51 rue de la Concorde
1050 Brussels
Belgium

Tel: (02) 5121733
Fax: (02) 512 1734

Animation and Research for the European Poverty Programme Department

Evaluation Unit - EC Poverty Programme
School for Social Sciences
University of Bath
Claverton Down
Bath
BA2 7AY

Tel: 0225 826090

The Council of Europe

Palais de l'Europe
67006 Strasburg
France

Tel: (88) 614961

Non-governmental Organizations

Union of Industrial and Employers' Confederations of Europe (UNICE)
Bte-4,
40 rue Joseph II,

1040 Brussels
Belgium

Tel: (02) 237 6511

European Trade Union Confederation (ETUC)
37 rue Montagne aux Herbes Potagères
1000 Brussels
Belgium

Tel: (02) 219 1090

European Trade Union Institute (ETUI)
66 boulevard de l'Imperatrice
1000 Brussels
Belgium

Tel: (02) 512 3070

Centre for Research on European Women
38 rue Stevin
1040 Brussels
Belgium

Tel: (02) 2305158
Fax: (02) 2306230

CREW publishes a monthly news bulletin

European Network of Women
Featherstone Street
London

Tel: (071) 720 9382
Contact: Eva Eberhart

<u>or</u>

Appendix 2

Jacqueline de Groote
Avenue de Mercure 11
Bte-4
1180 Brussels
Belgium

Tel: (02) 2179020

Organizations for and with migrants and ethnic minorities

The Churches Committee for Migrants in Europe
174 rue Joseph II
1040 Brussels
Belgium

Tel: (02) 2302011
Director: Mr Jan Niessen
(monthly newsletter)

Confederation de l'association des immigres en europe (CAIE)

44 rue de Geneve
1004
Lausanne
Switzerland

CAIE
46 rue de Montreuil
75011 Paris
France

Migre Europe
115 rue Stevin
1040 Brussels
Belgium

Tel: (02) 2304621

Appendix 2

Euro-Link Age (EPSO Secretariat) (pressure group for the aged)

Wetstraat 121
1040 Brussels
Belgium

European Anti-Poverty Network

Local Development Unit
National Council for Voluntary Organizations
26 Bedford Square
London
WC1B 3HU

Tel: (071) 636 4066
Contact: Diane Burrage